THE RADICAL KINGDOM

THE RADICAL

The Wester

PAULIST PRESS

New York, Paramus, Toronto

KINGDOM

xperience of Messianic Hope

ROSEMARY RADFORD RUETHER

The Radical Kingdom. Copyright © 1970 by Rosemary Radford
Ruether. All rights reserved. Printed in the United States of America.
No part of this book may be used or reproduced in any manner
whatsoever without written permission except in the case of brief quo-
tations embodied in critical articles and reviews. Cover photo by Anne
Macksoud. Cover design by Morris Berman. Published by Paulist Press
by arrangement with Harper & Row Publishers, Inc. **Editorial office:**
1865 Broadway, N.Y., N.Y. **Business office:** Paramus, N.J. 07652. ISBN:
0-8091-1860-2.

LIBRARY OF CONGRESS CATALOG CARD NUMBER: 70-109080

This volume is dedicated to

DANIEL BERRIGAN, S.J.

and those who risk world-transcending action

From the days of John the Baptist until now the
kingdom of heaven has suffered violence, and men of
violence take it by force. . . . and if you are willing to
accept it, he is Elijah who is to come. He who has
ears to hear, let him hear. But to what shall I compare
this generation? It is like children sitting in the market
places and calling to their playmates, "We piped to
you, and you did not dance; we wailed, and you did
not mourn."   Matt. 11:12–17 (RSV).

Contents

PART III: *Contemporary Movements*

CONCLUSION

THE RADICAL KINGDOM

INTRODUCTION

Chapter 1

The Theology of Revolution and Social Change: The Basic Motifs

The Basic Motifs

The title of this book is sufficiently problematical to the average reader to call for some definitions and historical justification of its appropriateness at the outset. In what sense does Christianity have a gospel of revolution, a gospel of radical reform of the human community in history? What is really meant by the suggestion that the gospel is a sociopolitical message? Is this meaningful in terms of theology as traditionally understood or is this a modern anachronism that reaches for some sanctification of its current preoccupations? Is it not true that religion, and especially theology, have for most of their history been very little interested in social reform, appearing to see no relation at all between the gospel and social reform? Is it not true that the orientation of almost all traditional theology and the residue of contemporary preaching are toward the reinforcement of the status quo and the saving of the personal soul for some "pie in the sky by and by," a salvation without any apparent relationship with present or future society? Is it not also true that social radicals, when they arose in a Christian context, stood on the fringes of the church and were regarded by most as out of bounds entirely, and when social reform as a sociological mood and movement arose in the West, its thrust was one of antagonism toward Christianity and the historical church? Thus it would seem that neither the church nor theology has any particularly notable record in this field. The eminent political scientist Hannah Arendt, in *On Revolution,* can quite frankly deny that Christianity has anything to do with a movement toward a new order in history for the simple reason that no such movement for a new order has ever been espoused in the name of Christianity.[1] These are facts that I do not intend to avoid, yet, nevertheless, I hope to demonstrate an identity between Christianity and an élan toward a new order in history that is not only very close but can even explicate this negative data as well.

In postulating a relationship between Christianity and social change, the basic assumption is that social change is never intended to be neutral change. It is never intended to be merely change from one set of conditions to another on the same plane of value; the ideology of change always implies conversion or redemption: a change from an old, bad, fallen, lost, or inauthentic state to a new, good, restored, and redeemed state of existence. Then both the gospel and ideologies of social change center on a doctrine of redemption. In traditional Christian theology, the doctrine of redemption is essentially an anthropology, a description of the human situation in history. The doctrine of redemption ramifies out into the basic credal elements that describe the movement of man from beginning to end. Man as created good in the beginning; as fallen from his original estate; as redeemed through divine intervention; and yet still moving toward and expecting an ultimate and final redemption that will transform and perfect all mankind and the entire cosmos. The theological doctrine, therefore, was never properly understood as simply a doctrine about the individual soul, but about man in his entirety; in his bodily, social, and historical existence. As soon as we see that the doctrine of redemption is about the human community in history, its affinity with ideologies of social reform becomes evident. The church has often avoided this implication by preaching redemption individualistically and in a "disembodied" fashion, but this belies the very words of the creed itself, which say, "We expect the resurrection of the dead and the life of the world to come." Thus it is not simply "I," but "we, the community" that expects this. What we expect is not individual spiritual immortality "above," but bodily resurrection in a future *world*. Thus the sociohistorical dimension of redemption is basic to it.

However, there has been from the early centuries of Christianity several different ways of getting together the complex elements of the credal message that result in very different pictures of the sociohistorical dimensions of redemption. This introductory chapter will sketch several different patterns of redemption found in traditional Christian thought and life to show how these different patterns suggest alternate patterns of relationship between the world—secular society—and the church, and between world history and Heaven or the "Kingdom of God." Within the doctrine of redemption there are some irreconcilable tensions that can be resolved by suppressing its social implications; this is one reason why this side of the doctrine may then be revived in a form antagonistic to this ecclesiastical tradition. To say that this sociohistorical side of the gospel was revived in a *secular* form is actually tautological, since secular simply means sociohistorical, and the use of secular in this antagonistic way itself indicates the way the popular imagination has lost the sense of this sociohistorical context of the gospel.

The following chapters will describe historical movements and ideologies that yearned for the radical renewal and transformation of society. Such movements will be followed as they arose from the Christian context, passed over into an antiecclesiastical form, and were then often "re-Christianized" by liberal churchmen. The commentary of theologians, social scientists, and social philosophers as it reflects upon the struggles for social redemption in Western history since the Reformation—and especially since the French Revolution when the revolutionary drama gradually became worldwide—will also be part of the complex story. The parallels between the theological patterns and their counterparts in secular social theory will become apparent. This is assumed to be true because the structure and dialectic of human existence is the same, and so secular ideologies (i.e., mythologies in socioscientific dress) construct patterns of social redemption that fall into patterns parallel to those of the theological tradition. Often the social ideology will even revert unwittingly to the theological terminology without realizing it or being fully aware of the tradition from which this language comes. This is because the social ideology is also dealing with transcendence; it is dealing with the human community transcending its own conditions and state of existence and leaping beyond itself to a new state in a future world. Even though this drama may be projected in a more "one-worldly," less dualistic fashion than the theological tradition, the themes of an old and a new world and the recreation of man in his historical community are allied, and the theological tradition has the most emotive, inspiration-laden words to express these themes.

As a somewhat simplified way of introducing this problem, we might sketch three basic patterns of redemption that decree different understandings of the world and different imperatives. The first pattern might be called "the apocalyptic crisis"; the second, the "inward journey"; and the third, "the Great Master Plan." These three views are, of course, not mutually exclusive. They are closely allied and can flow from one to another by a slight shift in psychological and theoretical emphasis. Nevertheless each one is a compelling vision with its own special dynamic, and not surprisingly, the most vehement hatred arises between brothers in "the movement" who fall into one or the other of these moods. Modern movements that tend inevitably to fall into antagonistic factions of utopians, evolutionaries, and revolutionaries illustrate this point.

The first pattern, the apocalyptic figure, is the original view in which Christianity itself was born. Yet apocalypticism itself must be seen as a development out of Jewish prophetic futurism, and was found as a flourishing movement in the period from about 200 B.C. to A.D. 100. The extant Jewish apocalypses beginning with the Book of Daniel and ending with works such as III

Baruch and the Christian Book of Revelation span this period, which corresponds to the period from the Seleucid occupation of Palestine and the Maccabean revolt to the Jewish war and destruction of the Temple and the final uprising under the Jewish zealot, Simon Bar Kocheba, in A.D. 132. Thus this period of apocalyptic writing corresponds to the period of Jewish national struggle against foreign occupation ending with the final dispersion of the Jewish people and the birth and separation of Christianity from Judaism.

The prophetic tradition of the Old Testament, from which apocalypticism developed, operated within the two poles of the Abrahamic faith, the poles of covenant and promise. God had made a covenant with his people that He would be their God and they would be his people. God's covenant implied a promise of fulfillment as a people. The covenanted people would be a mighty nation. They would inherit a land flowing in milk and honey. They would possess the land in peace, virtue, and prosperity. These are expressions of the expectation of fulfillment as a people in obedience to God. In the light of the covenant and promise, catastrophes upon the people were interpreted as the infidelity of the people to God and God's wrath in return. So enters the prophetic motif of judgment. The prophet appears as one who proclaims God's judgment and God's wrath. However, God's wrath is never absolute. It does not imply that God has broken his covenant with his people. Indeed, this wrath itself implied that God upheld the covenantal relationship and insisted that the people should be his people. The work of judgment itself assumes a relationship within the covenant and the promise. Through God's wrath, pronounced as judgment by the prophet, God seeks to convert the people and bring them back to fidelity to Him. When that happens, then the long-awaited promise will be fulfilled. The images of godliness, happiness, prosperity, fruitfulness, and peace can then be brought forth as symbols of this expected deliverance. These structures of thought provided a constant key by which the Jewish people interpreted their own history in relation to God.

This expected fulfillment of the promise was not an other-worldly salvation but a future-worldly era that stands as both the ideal and the historical goal of the community. However, as the Jewish people suffered repeated exiles, hardships, and overlord-ship of conquering powers, and as the expectation of fulfillment was continuously postponed and mocked by the tides of events, the concept of the expected goal took on an increasingly radical and dualistic tone. The promised era ceased to be seen as happening in continuity with present world history. Instead there was to be a radical break, a cosmic intervention of God, an overthrow of evil powers. As the view of the expected good age becomes radicalized, so too the view of man's present dilemma and adversaries was radicalized as well. The adversaries are no longer failings of the people and national enemies. These come to be seen as agents for some cosmic evil power. This cosmic evil power is seen as having captured the world, so that this world has escaped from the dominion of God and become alien to Him. It has become the kingdom of the evil one. The cosmos is ruled by alien and hostile forces contrary to God. Redemption can no longer be conceived in continuity with this present framework of nature and history because these have been taken over by evil, so much so that their basic ruling principle has become diabolic. Salvation can come only by a radical overthrow of this present world, this present epoch, and the inauguration of a radically new world and epoch founded on a different principle; on the principle of God's dominion and not that of the demonic powers. There must be a great cosmic showdown between God and the powers and principalities of "this world," an overthrow once and for all and the creation of a new order in which God's justice and righteousness will be vindicated and prevail.

In the apocalyptic perspective, all nuances are eliminated and the human situation is polarized into radical opposites. History is foreshortened. One no longer looks back to a development of good and evil within history; one no longer looks forward to some future process that may, some day, lead to the expected goal. Rather, one looks back to the lost paradise, the original state of perfect goodness that was wiped out by the fall of the world under the dominion of the demons. The original paradise is the point of reference and foundation for the expected restoration of the future. The frequent contrast between the Jewish view as "linear" and the Greek view as "circular" is clearly too simple, for the Jewish view was simultaneously linear and circular. History drives forward to a restoration of its original state. The Kingdom of the future recapitulates the paradise of the past, and the paradise of the past is the foundation of hope and faith in the capacity of "nature" for this Kingdom of the future (i.e., Revelation 22, where the rivers of Paradise and the Tree of Life are restored in the New Jerusalem).

Here and now the cosmos is seen as having fallen into evil hands. God's elect are there, but they are oppressed and powerless under the might of alien powers. But their vindication is imminent. Any moment now the great intervention and world revolution will begin. The reversal is total and without ambiguity. There may be a period of trial and battle, but this is not envisioned as taking place over a long period. It is to be brief and decisive. Then the rule of God and the inauguration of the New Age will begin.

We might mention here the double model of the future age that developed in the late period of apocalypticism (i.e., the apocalypses of the first century B.C. and thereafter). The earlier prophetic view had seen the future goal as simply a future historical era of bliss and virtue, but one that was temporal and mundane and would pass away; those within it would die as well. There was originally no idea of resurrection or immortality in this conception, and when the idea of resurrection was introduced (to satisfy the demands of individual justice), this allowed those of the past to participate in the future promise, but it was assumed that they too would die again. Man was intrinsically mortal and his history temporal. His history moves forward to a final satisfaction of his ideal and fulfillment of the demands of justice, but this still presumes a temporal framework. History does not escape into a timeless absolute. In the development of apocalypticism, this temporal ideal became insufficient. The future age became increasingly transmundane and eternal. But the apocalypticists had to reconcile this new development with the earlier tradition of a temporal, future historical Kingdom. In the apocalypses of the second century we see the prophetic kingdom becoming increasingly transmundane and eternal. Resurrection of the dead is introduced, but still with many "temporal features." Then in the apocalypses of the first century B.C., the old temporal prophetic kingdom is reintroduced as a preamble to this new eternal Kingdom. The old view is put somewhat awkwardly side by side with the later one and the fulfillment is given two stages: an initial overthrow of evil powers and a thousand-year messianic reign of goodness and prosperity on earth, and then a final binding of the demonic powers, judgment and creation of an eternal heaven and earth. These two kingdoms did not really imply an evolutionary view of redemption as a gradual process, however. There is really no process here at all, but two alternate models of the future age stitched together. The two can be merged so that the temporal kingdom takes on eternal characteristics such as resurrection, a very long and seemingly endless life, transfiguration of nature, while still assuming it to be mundane, the resurrected ones to be mortal, and so on. Or the eternal age may still have many mundane features such as eating, harvesting, trees which "yield their fruit each month" (Revelation 22), and the like. The two kingdoms are duplicates, so that some apocalyptists will have two resurrections, two cosmic battles, two judgments; one at the beginning of the temporal kingdom and one at the beginning of the eternal Kingdom. There was considerable confusion about which features go where. The emergence of this double model points to the great contradiction between historical goals however highly conceived and an eternal, timeless absolute, and the gap in thought that is involved in the effort to leap from one to the other.

Within the apocalyptic perspective, however, this thousand-year messianic reign is not seen as an evolutionary process, although it was later interpreted as such. Rather, evil is seen as eliminated once and for all in a sudden intervention that takes place between present history and the beginning of the messianic reign. Thereafter good reigns without ambiguity. This cosmic crisis was always expected very soon by the apocalypticist at whatever point he might be writing; it was always just around the corner. The present world crises testify to its imminence. Indeed, we are already in the time of travail and struggle that is giving birth to the final dénouement and the advent of the messianic age when every tear will be wiped away. The time of travail is seen as already present, and it is to last no longer than the lifetime of the present generation. However, the messianic age itself cannot, from a Jewish perspective, be said to be present until evil is actually eliminated. It would be contradictory to say that "Christ has come" and yet still to have wars, diseases, and injustices abroad in the land. The coming of the Messiah and the coming of the messianic age are identical.

The apocalyptic view of redemption is basically social and outer-directed. One does not look inward to the salvation of some personal essence; one looks outward at history and society, at injustice, oppression, and cruel and irrational destruction. It is this historical realm that is to be grappled with and radically reversed. The apocalyptic view is also one borne of social extremity and despair. One despairs of progress and change within the present system. The present system (world) is totally corrupt. There can be no salvation within it. Salvation can only come when the present situation is totally overthrown and a new order founded on opposite principles of life. Apocalypticism is the social religion of oppressed people, not oppressed into unconsciousness, but conscious of their oppression and without the power to alter their situation under the present circumstances. Because of its radicalism and uncompromising confrontation within the present system, it is the implicit or explicit underpinnings of every revolutionary faith. Every movement that preaches the irreformability of the present system and its total corruption, that believes that the only solution is radical overthrow and reconstitution of the world on an entirely new and different basis is apocalyptic in structure, even if it uses social-scientific rather than religious language.

The second pattern of salvation can be called "the inward journey." This view also sees the world as being in the grip of demonic powers. The world is fallen and antidivine, and this evil nature is associated with social and political structures, particularly with the "material" forces that make this world go: sexuality, power, money. The outward structures of society, even the outward structures of the physical world, its bodily form, are evil. But rather than salvation as a historical overthrow and reconstitution of the world system, salvation is seen as a journey inward to some pure realm beyond the system. Salvation is a metaphysical rather than a historical drama. Salvation is an inward transcending of this present order rather than a historical transcending of this present epoch. This second view is antisocial and antihistorical. The pure land coexists in time with the fallen realm. One does not have to wait for it to come. It is available here and now, but one must move out to find it. It is above or outside of this present system. The evil, fallen world persists basically unaltered by this inward journey. One simply removes oneself from it and finds freedom and peace by negating its power. This is the limitation of the utopian view, but its strength is that it allows one to begin to build and experience the Kingdom of salvation now rather than merely waiting and struggling for a time that has not yet come.

The heart of the "inward journey" is the mystical ascent of the soul to God and the development of systems of life and practice conducive to this mystical journey of "inner space." The eternal world is already present "above" this present one, and the soul, by a gradual process of purification from the attachments of body and mind, can escape from the limitations of the finite and move into an immediate experience of and communion with the eternal. As long as man is still in the finite temporal world this communion probably cannot be sustained for long, but in the fleeting moments when it is achieved it is complete and whole and salvation is achieved. Moreover, one reconstructs one's life so as to keep this commingling of the eternal with the day-to-day life as close as possible.

The inward journey releases several social impulses. Most characteristic is some sort of physical removal of the seeker from the present system. Since this evil world is associated with political and economic structures, one withdraws from involvement in the forum and in the marketplace. One often physically removes from the city as the center of worldly activity and flees to the country as the site of unspoiled nature. Such a removal sometimes carries a romantic assumption that civilization is bad and nature is good, nature being symbolized both by uncultivated physical nature and, by implication, one's own original human nature that can be recovered by removing from society. The retreat to the countryside suggests that one's true and original nature is not so much destroyed as simply overlaid and stifled by the false bondage of civilization. Once one flees from the city to unspoiled creation, one's true human nature will reemerge.

Poverty is a theme indigenous to this view. Poverty stands for many kinds of withdrawal from inauthentic states of existence as "having" to the authentic state of "being." Material possessions and economic pursuits are the most obvious expression of this, standing for a dispersion and loss of the soul amid false consciousness and business. One begins by "selling what one has and giving to the poor," dropping out of the economic system and surrendering economic security. Personal needs are simplified to the elementary level of subsistence. One lives as a beggar or gatherer of wild foods in the woods or returns to subsistence farming. Freed from the pursuit of a "living," one can begin to live in freedom, inward peace, and joy. The Fransciscan mendicants, with only a tunic and cloak as garment by day and a bed by night, walking the dusty roads, without destination, without duties, singing as they go, in intimate communion with sun and wind, flower and beast, serving whomever they meet, sleeping wherever they may be when night falls, begging for their simple frugal meals: this is the classical Christian model for salvation by economic dropout.

In the mendicant ideal there is a strong direction toward service to the poor, yet this impulse has generally carried very little suggestion of a need to alter the conditions that make people poor. This seems to be due to the identification of evil with economic and political power, and a seeking of salvation by their rejection. Poverty was idealized as freedom from this evil world rather than itself an evil to be combated. One goes to the poor, the outcast, the leper, not so much to alter their condition as to identify with those outside the system. Unjust poverty due to social imbalance and exploitation is confused with the elitist poverty of inward freedom. Thus the long tradition of charity in the ascetic tradition did not release an ethic of social reform but operated on a world-negating ethic. Sometimes social reform, amelioration of poverty, and the inclusion within the system of those previously excluded was the result of such charity, but this was more an accidental benefit rather than the main intention.

Nature in its uncivilized state is a symbol of the pure, good world, but also of the demonic world as well. Nature is an ambivalent symbol of Christianity. It can be both the trackless wasteland of desolation and the garden of paradise.[2] In the Desert Fathers of the fourth century, where Christian asceticism originated, uncultivated nature is associated with the realm of the demons. The hermit drops out of society as the snare of the devil, but he goes out into the trackless waste in order to confront the demons in their plain and naked state. The demons howl in the desert wastes and in the tombs of the dead, and the hermit deliberately takes up his residence in these places and engages in hand-to-hand combat with them.[3] In a direct contest of wills, with prayer, fasting and self-denial as his weapons, the hermit gradually conquers the demons, and in so doing converts the trackless waste into a paradise. He redeems the desert and brings it back into the original garden. The themes of the hermit fed by manna in the desert, the springs of water that appear at his feet, the ravens that feed him, the dragons and lions that fawn at his feet symbolize the redemption of the desert and its return to the original paradise.

In the later monastic tradition that replaced hermitism, these more mythological views of the redemption of the wilderness took a more practical turn. The monks leave evil civilization for the trackless forests and deserts, but there they create a paradise. They plant a colony in the wilderness and build up a model community. Under their labor the uncultivated land becomes a fruitful farm, resplendent with fields and orchards. The redemption of man and the wilderness by the route of withdrawal then becomes a utopian movement. The present fallen society is deserted, but in the wilderness an ideal society is formed. Out of the impulse to drop out of the present world, the building of a paradisiacal nature and a higher society is projected where men will begin, here and now, to live in the harmony with nature and his fellow man that God intended. Utopianism is the enduring social reform contribution of the movement to "tune in and drop out," and it has a unique power to project alternatives and new possibilities and, by moving out of the present set of assumptions, to begin to experiment here and now with these alternatives. Nevertheless the world-negating ethic of utopianism means that one does not move directly against the present evils but challenges them only incidentally in one's movement away from them. Utopianism is limited in scope by definition. It assumes a powerlessness to effect universal salvation. It does not expect total renovation; it removes itself from the present and creates an elite, redeemed community where the new age can be glimpsed, but the present world is abandoned to fester. It creates a small sphere of perfection outside the present system but has no message for the city of man which it has abandoned, except perhaps a kind of wistful hope that the elite community may be an earnest example and beachhead of a new world that will become universal at some point of apocalyptic renovation in the future. However this renovation is beyond man's present powers.

Finally, the third pattern of redemption can be called the Great Master Plan. Salvation here is also a historical drama, but not one of sharp conflict and reversal, rather one involving a long evolutionary process. This world historical process leads from an original good state and a fall or reversal of this state at the beginning of history through a long restorational and redemptive process that defines the rest of history to its final conclusion in the Kingdom of God. History is a redemptive process that defines its course from beginning to end. The sharp conflict between good and evil takes place at the beginning when creation, originally good, is attacked by evil powers or falls through its own fault, taking on a reversed state of existence. The gradual reversal of this fallen state begins immediately in God's providential care and leads through a series of stages to the final restoration at the end of history when the original good state is not only recovered but also elevated to a higher level, so that there is both progress and circularity in this view. The evolutionary view is closely related to the apocalyptic drama and yet it has a very different existential mood. Polarization and sharp conflict are excluded as an immediate program because the powers of good and evil are both made immanent within the present order and are working themselves out to a final victory for the righteous by an inevitable process whose outcome is assured. Thus as apocalypticism is the religion of impotence and despair, evolutionary progress is the religion of possession, power, and confidence. In the apocalyptic view, only evil is present and regnant. Good is transcendent, a power that descends from beyond man's present powers. In the evolutionary view, good is present and victorious in principle, although the processes by which this victory is being worked out have not been completed, and the saints are already within that system that is advancing to its glorious conclusion. Evil, though still powerful, is defeated in principle and can be regarded as already "behind us."

Classical Christian theologies operated within this concept of salvation as historical process in contrast to classical Christian spirituality, which has been of the ascetic, world-negating variety. After the first generation or so, the original apocalyptic view of salvation began to fade from the center of the church's thought to its left-wing, heretical fringes, and the church, which had once viewed itself as the beachhead of an apocalyptic revolution, incorporated itself back into the historical process and interpreted itself as the bearer of the new and final stage of salvation history. With the shift from the expected messiah to the Christ who had already come, the mood shifted from revolutionary crisis to victorious advance from the basis of present possession. This possession was read backward into a salvation history that began with the first promise made to Adam and Eve after the expulsion from Paradise and ended in the coming of Christ and the historical mission of the church.

This world historical view has its earliest statement in the "early Catholicism" of the Gospel of Luke, but receives its classical development in Augustine's *City of God*. Augustine's decisive contribution was the reinterpretation of the thousand-year messianic reign as the era of the historical mission of the church. The two cities, the city of God and the city of the devil, are elected from the beginning. The city of God is hidden as a mysterious leaven within history and the two cities mingle in their development and contest with each other, with the city of the elect gradually growing in sanctification as we move from the promises of Adam and Abel to Israel to Christ and to the church, when the city of God finally appears as a visible society. The conflict is between two principles of existence: the principle of selfless love created from above in grace, and the principle of self-enclosed egoism and carnality. Hence there can be no synthesis or salvation of the earthly principle as such but only its final expulsion along with all those elected to its sway. The final culmination is the separation of the heavenly from the worldly city and its elevation to its eternal reward with the corresponding casting of the earthly city into damnation.

Such a view, in practice, tended to bind salvation within the sphere of the historical church as the expression of the final and definitive epoch of salvation. The roots of the absolutization of the church, the infallibility of its insight into truth and the perfection of its possession of grace, clearly lie in this interpretation of the epoch of the church in terms of a realized eschatology of an already present messianic age. There is literally no future history beyond the church because the church has become the fulfillment and goal of world history. Beyond the church there is only a timeless heaven to which the church itself provides the exclusive gateway.

But the Augustinian merger of the messianic age with the era of the church had its challengers from the apocalyptic and pentacostal left wing. The Montanists and, in Augustine's own day, the Donatists, projected the idea of a Third Age of the Spirit that was still to come, thereby challenging the finality of revelation through Christ, at least as this had become monopolized by the institutional church. The development of the doctrine of the Third Age is particularly associated with the twelfth-century monk and visionary, Joachim of Fiore, who mediated this view to the late medieval radicals. More and more among this left-wing fringe of the late medieval church, the official church came to represent, not the definite bearer of the messianic age, but the "Beast" of the Apocalypse, the antichrist. Revelation through the Son was relativized as a provisional revelation of the past, but still to come was the final definitive revelation through the Spirit (typically seen as beginning in the dissident communities themselves) when there would be ushered in the final redeemed state of the universe. The doctrine of the Third Age restored the revolutionary expectation that was lost in the Augustinian domestication of the messianic age into the already accomplished era of the church. This was decisive for the release of the germ of revolutionary expectation within history that has remained latent in the Christian worldview since its domestication into the established church.

From this perspective the following conclusion can be offered: When it is said that the gospel is a revolutionary message or the biblical view is future-oriented, the proper qualifications must be introduced into these statements. Potentially, the elements of the Christian worldview could be formulated in a social revolutionary manner, but, in actuality, this did not occur and could not occur until Christendom itself—that society founded on the idea of the church as the final age of world history—went into dissolution. Strictly speaking, this potential in the Christian worldview could only be released in a post-Christian world, in a world where the monopoly of Christian society upon history had been thrown into question, where the dispensation of the historical church and the society it had founded had been relativized, thus releasing again the idea of a genuinely new event occurring in future history. While the Christian message implicitly carried a social revolutionary idea, in practice, after the absorption of the apocalyptic message of the new age into the age of the church and the projection of the fulfillment of the gospel into an other-worldly heaven unrelated to future history, this potential could only be released through the secularization of the society, the dethroning of the Christian establishment. Therefore it should not surprise us to discover that historical expectation reenters Western history in a social revolutionary form as a movement that sets itself in opposition to the established church and Christian society. Historical expectation reemerged with the movement of the West into a post-Christendom era. As a full-blown movement, it took the form of the secular doctrine of progress and the evolutionary development of mankind that regarded the era of the church as a past era of darkness that was being overcome by the new dawn of enlightenment. Yet this secular doctrine of progress was preceded by bands of religious radicals who, from the fourteenth century on, began to create a reversed mythology of the ecclesiastical establishment and to hold out a reborn hope for an age of the Spirit yet to come. Therefore, when we say that historical expectation was reborn in a secular language after the dissolution of Christendom, we have to define secularization carefully. What is suggested is that some fundamental substance of the gospel was rescued from its domestication in the ecclesiastical institution and reinserted into the stream of historical experience, but the cultural monopoly of the church on the language of the religious tradition, the discrediting of this church and its traditions, dictated a reappearance in nonreligious language and antiecclesiastical form. Messianic expectation reappeared in the language of philosophy and science, which now stood in the popular mind for "truth" in constrast to the "superstition" of religion.

Part I

HISTORICAL MOTIFS:

CHRISTIAN AND SECULAR

Chapter 2

The Radicals of the Reformation
and the Puritan Revolution

Any account of the foundations of modern revolutionary ideology would hardly be complete without some attention to the radicals of the sixteenth and seventeenth century. These figures, so despised and ignored until recently, have enjoyed a great renaissance in recent scholarship and have been attributed with being the forerunners of a great variety of modern social radicalism. Norman Cohn's well-known account of Christian apocalypticism ends with these figures as the founders of modern totalitarian movements, an attribution that he intends to be unflattering.[1] Socialists and Marxists have also embraced these early radicals. Although Marx himself seems to have been unaware of their existence, when scholarship began to revive their story in the late nineteenth century, Marxist theoreticians quickly claimed them as a part of their own lineage.[2] As precursors of many kinds of modern social movements, the radicals of the sixteenth and seventeenth century are extraordinary figures, yet their direct historical influence was relatively small. Rationalism and the Enlightenment intervened between these earlier radicals and those of the nineteenth century, and their memory was buried in the triumphs of established churches and restored monarchies, so that when social radicalism was reborn in a secular form in the nineteenth century, it was usually without knowledge of the earlier movements. Yet this parallel development of similar types of social radicalism, despite the break in historical continuity, testifies to the durability of these themes as expressions of the tensions of historical existence.

The mainstream of the sixteenth-century Reformation was, of course, not a radical Reformation. The Henrician reform in England was no more than a nationalizing of the English Catholic church. In Lutheran lands there was a reform of theology, but the parish structure was retained, only now under the rule of the princes. Calvinist churches also remained established churches as well, characterized only by the new relationship between the Presbyterian council with the magistrates of the town council. In Scotland and in the Puritan revolution in England, this Presbyterian structure could be built up into a national assembly paralleling the Parliament. All of these churches assumed a single territorial church in an established relationship with the state. The dissenter from this territorial church thereby became a social rebel and traitor as well. Thus the Constantinian assumptions of the right of the church to rely on the state to coerce and persecute the dissenter were carried on by Reformation churches.

However, there grew up on the left wing of this Magisterial Reformation a diverse group of dissenters who were lumped together under the category of the "Radical Reformation."[3] These individuals and groups had such a diversity of views that this designation often appears an arbitrary dumping ground, but they did have certain common themes. They were particularly all united in rejecting the established church, rejecting the identification of church and civic society. For this reason they may all be called "sectarians," i.e., they all advocated a view of the church as a distinct and separate community from civic society.

The churches of the Radical Reformation can be distinguished from those of the Magisterial Reformation by both a distinct doctrine of the church and a distinct doctrine of man.[4] Here the Radicals are more the heirs of late medieval mysticism and pietism, and they rejected the nominalist Augustinianism of the

Reformers. The Reformers saw salvation in an extrinsic way. Man has radically fallen out of God's grace, and in his present depraved state he has no capacity for God. The Reformers tended to equate man's "nature" with this present depraved state. This fallen state defined his natural capacities, although it was not his original nature. But this original nature is lost, and so man's historical nature is that of an alienated and self-enclosed creature who cannot get out of his dilemma by his own "works." Consequently, when God elects fallen man, it is as though a hand were laid on him that was completely beyond his present historical nature. Martin Luther's favorite term, "alien righteousness," expresses this theme. The righteousness with which God clothes us is an alien righteousness laid on us like a garment beyond our present natures. It is laid upon us not as something to which we have a right or can make our own, but which we always have as a gift and which we do not so much possess as it possesses us. This is the radical Reformation doctrine of salvation by faith through grace alone.

The left wing of the Reformation rejected this view of man. Man's nature is understood not from his fallen, historical nature, but from his original, created nature. Hence the radicals insisted that man has a natural capacity for God. As God's creation, man has a natural affinity for his Creator. Although he has fallen into sin, he has by no means lost this affinity, which still remains his "true nature." Consequently when God's grace descends on man, it is not as a garment of alien righteousness clothing a wretched being; rather, it speaks to the depths of man's proper self as like to like. Man's will is not in bondage, but is free. He can choose to assent or dissent to God.[5] Salvation is then the direct consequence of personal decision. Consequently baptism, the symbol of spiritual rebirth, should correspond to personal conversion. Baptism is merely an outward sign and witness to this inward decision. Adult or believer's baptism is characteristic of the Radicals.

The Reformers defended infant baptism on the grounds of the priority of God's grace over our response, but infant baptism also had the second aspect of coinciding with the civil view of the church. The visible church coincided with "Christian" society. In baptism one simultaneously joined the established church and became a member of decent, law-abiding society. This coinclusiveness of church and society meant that the church functioned as the religious sanction of the social consensus, and there was no room in such a view for religious opposition to such a consensus.

The Anabaptists (rebaptizers) rejected this view of man and the church. Baptism apart from the personal decision of faith is meaningless. So infant baptism is null and void, and the man who becomes a believer is to be baptized at this time—not baptized again, but baptized for the first time—because his previous baptism was a gesture without substance. By the same token, the church is not an ecclesiological form of a worldly body, but it is a new body that gathers out and over against worldly society. To enter the church is to enter a new community that lives out of an opposite principle of existence and to depart from the worldly city.

The rejection of infant baptism for believer's baptism coincided with the rejection of civil religion. The church is not the religious sanction of civil society but a new creation opposed to the present system of society and the world. To join the church is to separate out from the world and to stand as the avant-garde of a new world that is being founded by God in the midst of the old world that is dying. Believer's baptism is the sign that the Christian has forsaken this dying world and the whole principle of existence on which it is founded, and has entered the new creation and principle of existence that is being built up as the old order dies. This new order subsists within the present era as a hostile and antagonistic beachhead of a new and coming world, which will soon take over completely as the messianic community of the New Heaven and Earth which is to be openly manifest with the return of the victorious Christ.

Anabaptists recovered the primitive apocalyptic view of the church as a transcendental community that leaps ahead of this present world in anticipation of the future age to come. Such a view represents the original dynamic of the messianic understanding of the church, as opposed to the degenerate Augustinian view, which identified absolutist characteristics with the present age and domesticated them within an established church, and so lost the dynamic tension with the future age, which then becomes a timeless other world "above" and without relationship with future history. This apocalyptic view of the church was suppressed by the official church, particularly after the Constantinian settlement, when the church became the religious institution of the Empire, but it was carried along in an underground stream through the Middle Ages. The Anabaptists reinstituted this apocalyptic view, hence rejecting the Constantinian settlement, and characteristically dated the fall of the church from the time of Constantine when, in their view, the church became a part of the world and the true church disappeared from the earth.

For this reason the Radical Reformation believed in "restitution" rather than reform of the church. They believed that it was not possible to reform the existing church because this institution was not the church at all. It had lost the whole principle of existence of the church and was simply an ecclesiasticized expression of the world. It was the church of the antichrist, which mimics the church of Christ, but is, in fact, its opposite. The Reformers believed that the true church still existed but was debased and needed to be pruned back to the essentials. They had a moderate doctrine of the fall of the church, but a radical doctrine of the fall of man. The left wing, by contrast, had an optimistic view of man's present capacities, but a radical doctrine of the fall of the church. They turned from the idea of reform to that of restitution. They believed that the church must be born into the world anew, and this could come about only when the church again separated out of established society and reinstituted itself as God's revolutionary avant-garde that stands over against worldly society and its churches. The Anabaptists regarded Luther and the other magisterial reformers as halfway men, insufficiently radical in their estimation of the dilemma of the church, and they did not hesitate to lump the churches of the Reformation with that of Rome as the churches of the antichrist, which represent the snare of the Devil and have no part in the Kingdom of God.

This separation of the church from established society, including the civil religion, was expressed in various forms. Most fundamentally, the left wing formed free communities that broke with the territorial parish and met as a voluntary community entered through personal conversion and believer's baptism. All ties with the state were broken. The church was to receive no support from the state and to accept no coercion from the state upon its doctrine and membership. In the sixteenth century, this meant that the left wing rejected the traditional view of the right of the state to persecute heretics as dangers to the body politic.[6] Even state requirements for church attendance, tithing, and the like were to be rejected. The only discipline upon church membership that was in conformity with the church of Christ was fraternal spiritual discipline exercised by the community among themselves. Fraternal admonishment, advice, even shunning and banning of a church member from the community could be practiced by way of maintaining the high standards of the community and either reconverting or excluding the backsliding member. But since membership in the Anabaptist church was voluntary, banning carried no special stigma in the civic community. The backsliding member was simply sliding back into the world where he could then operate as the rest of the world did, but the world had no right to coerce him in matters of the church.[7] Spiritual government and discipline was an essential characteristic of Anabaptist churches. Church authority was to rest on congregational loyalty alone. The purpose of internal discipline was not to punish but to win back the erring member and to create a purified community that would shine forth as a paradigm of the community of the New Creation.

The separation of the disciplined, converted community also took the form of certain breaks with the socioeconomic order that varied in scope. In some cases frivolous possessions and gaudy clothes were rejected in favor of the "plain" style of dress, speech, and life. Often marriage with unbelievers was forbidden. Military office and sometimes civil office were rejected. The believer could not be a magistrate and most certainly not a soldier. The Anabaptist churches were characteristically pacifist, rejecting war and all activities that pertained to war, the most essential expression of fallen, worldly society. The more radical Anabaptists moved out of the society, especially as found in towns, and established themselves as rural communities where they could cultivate the redeemed life away from the distractions of the world. Civilization and technology, too much book learning, and traffic in commerce were regarded with suspicion. The best life was the simple life of man and nature in their rustic communion. Man as tiller of the soil was man in his right relation with God.

Along with this primitivism often went a communist ethic. The fall of man coincided with the rise of private property. When man learned to say "mine" and "thine," he lost his original community with God and his fellow man. Restoration of this original community demanded abolition of private property and a style of life in which all goods were held in common. Among the Swiss Brethren the communist idea took the form of a community of consumption, of charity and shared fruits of labor. Among the Hutterites there was a more radical effort to create a total community of production and consumption in which all was held in common. Among the Anabaptists a fusion of paradisiacal and eschatalogical motifs took place. The Anabaptist community was primitivist or restorational in that it restored some presumed paradisiacal state of the beginning. For this "beginning" there were, however, two points of reference: the primitive church, particularly as pictured in the early chapters of the Book of Acts, and the Paradise of Eden. When stress was laid on the restoration of Eden greater social radicalism resulted, since the state of man before the Fall was associated with communism of property, often communism of marriage, and the overthrow of all social hierarchies and conventions. But this restoration of the beginning was also an anticipation of the End, an anticipation of the coming of the Kingdom of God. The Anabaptist community is both a restoration of the unfallen church and unfallen man, and a beachhead of the new order of Heaven and earth that will be inaugurated by the final coming of Christ.[8]

The apocalyptic view of the church also underlies the sectarianism of the Anabaptists. For the mainline Reformers, salvation or election has taken place in the eternal decrees of God that apply the fruits of the cross and resurrection to the chosen. But this election operates by means of the historical church, which travels through history mingled with the city of man. There is a church of the elect, but it is an invisible church, hidden within the historical church and known only to God. The final separation of the wheat from the tares will take place not within history, but only at the end of history. However, for the Anabaptists, this end of history was already taking place. The final process of judgment and sifting of the elect from the damned was already happening. The restituted church was the true church, the church of the elect become a visible community in the believer's churches, which have finally separated out of the fallen, unredeemed society and manifested the new principle of existence of the world to come. In Melchior Hofmann's words, "And now in this final age the true apostolic emissaries of the Lord Jesus Christ will gather the elect flock and call it through the gospel and lead the Bride of the Lord into the spiritual wilderness and betroth and covenant her through baptism to the Lord."[9] The separation out of the believer's church is itself a part of that apocalyptic crisis, and the community exists in a narrow isthmus of time between the "messianic woes" and the speedy return of Christ as apocalyptic judge to bring to an end the worldly kingdoms, including the worldly ecclesiastical Kingdoms, and inaugurate the New Jerusalem.

Taking its self-understanding from this concept of apocalyptic crisis, the Anabaptist church annulled church history and itself expected no church history, but awaited the speedy return of

Christ. The Anabaptists brought back in full force the pilgrim and martyr view of the church. The church was a pilgrim community briefly sojourning in the world, but having its true home in the world to come. As a new community which stood for the overthrow of the current social order, it was antagonistic to and persecuted by that social order. It was a suffering church that was prepared to have no security in this world, to be harried from place to place by the established order, and to die for its faith. Indeed, this was the situation of the Anabaptist communities, persecuted by Protestants and Catholics alike, driven from their homes, seeking refuge in forests and distant lands, many of their numbers suffering torture and death.[10]

Any left-wing view of the church, by its very nature, is inaugurated in a crisis relationship with present history and society. It is born in a movement of rejection of the present order and an anticipatory leap into a radically new age to come. In its original form, such a view is necessarily short-lived. It has no principle of institutionalization and historical perpetuation and can enter the stream of history only by reformulating its original viewpoint. The initial aspect of the Anabaptist churches was that of an apocalyptic, revolutionary movement, although this was acted out only by a minority. Such a sectarian revolutionary view, which identifies the particular moment of historical crisis with the ultimate revolution, is particularly congenial to oppressed and desperate people, the disenfranchised lower class of society that feels it has no stake in this present order. Their effort to rise up and throw off the shackles of oppression is given a transcendent motive power by this fusion of the particular revolution with the final revolution. The little band of insurrectionists, often setting out with a ragged force against great odds with only stones and pitchforks in their hands, become, in their own imaginations, the right arm of God's wrath. The flash of their pitchforks in the moonlight becomes the lightning of the Coming of the Lord. The trampling of their boots is the thunder of the messianic horseman "tramping down the vineyards where the grapes of wrath are stored." Such a fusion of the momentary with the final revolution is both transcendently heroic and transcendently self-deluding. The result of such a projection was often the pathetic slaughter of men whose visions far exceeded their practical capacities, but at the same time, these visions lent them the strength of ten or even a hundred men, and enabled a tiny band to astonish and terrorize those in power. This is why the apocalyptic revolutionary is typically cut down with such vehemence by the possessing classes, who may mobilize an army of tens of thousands to destroy a motley crew of a few hundred. This is because the apocalyptic revolutionary represents the ultimate and uncompromising threat to the status quo.

Examples of this kind of apocalyptic uprising can be found in peasant and proletariat revolts in the late Middle Ages, the Reformation period and extending into the left wing of the Puritan revolution.[11] The Taborites of the Hussite revolution in the early fifteenth century took up milleniarist ideas in such an activist form. The doctrine of the imminent return of Christ, preached by popular preachers and prophets, became the occasion of a general uprising of the peasants against both the church and the merchant and feudal classes. Identifying themselves with the avenging angels, these insurrectionists saw themselves as purging the earth of sinners and minions of the antichrist, i.e., the ecclesiastical and social hierarchy. Once the earth had been wiped clean of these vermin, the Taborite revolutionaries confidently expected the advent of the messianic age of ease and felicity. In Cohn's words,

They were utterly convinced that the earth had only to be cleansed of sinners for Christ to descend from the Heavens in majesty, while they, the Saints, soared through the air to greet him (I Thess. 4:17). Then would come the "messianic banquet" which would take place in the holy mountains of the Taborites; after which Christ would take over the royal office in the place of the unworthy Emperor Sigismund. He would rule over the millenial realm in which the Saints, "living, radiant as the sun, quite without stain," would rejoice for ever in a state of innocence like that of the angels or of Adam and Eve before the Fall. And this millenium was to be at the same time the Third and Last Age of the pseudo-Joachimite prophecies.[12]

Here again we see the union of paradisiacal and eschatological motifs. The Taborites particularly thought themselves to be restoring the condition of political anarchy and communism that were presumed to exist in the lost Paradise and were to be restored in the millenium of the future. In the social radicalism that followed from this view, they began to act out the final drama of apocalyptic vengeance and the overthrow of all political and social hierarchy, political power, rents, dues, or taxes and private property. Such anarchic communism is regularly associated in messianic movements with the "once and future age." Other peasant uprisings in the late Middle Ages as well as the Peasant Wars of the sixteenth century, associated with such radicals as Thomas Müntzer and the Zwickau prophets, were embued with the same ideas.

In the left wing of the Puritan revolution over a century later, a similar radicalism reappeared. The Digger and Leveller movements of the mid-seventeenth century harked back to this medieval radicalism as well as pointed forward to later democratic and socialist reforms. These movements based themselves on the original rights of man in the "state of nature," this state being associated with the rights enjoyed by all Englishmen in the period before the Norman invasion.[13] The Levellers argued on this basis for the natural rights and political equality of all men. The Diggers went further and hoped to restore economic equality as well, and attempted to abolish private property and to set up agrarian communes, restoring the original communism of the state of nature and overthrowing the feudal servitude of the English peasant. The Fifth Monarchy Men gathered up all these hopes for paradisiacal restoration into an expectation of an imminent advent of the victorious Christ, the avenger of the poor, who would right all social, political, and ecclesiastical wrongs and set up the direct reign of God on earth.

First Charles I and then Oliver Cromwell were associated with the "little horn" of the Book of Daniel that heralded the end of the fourth of the worldly monarchies and the advent of the reign of "King Jesus."[14] The Fifth Monarchy Men staged several abortive uprisings toward the end of Cromwell's rule, and although these activists never numbered more than a handful, they caused such terror that they may be said to be largely responsible for the speedy decision to restore the monarchy after Cromwell's death. Far from being democrats, as were the Levellers, the Fifth Monarchy Men looked forward to a rule of the saints, which they associated with the leaders of the "gathered" or independent congregations, but this itself constituted a kind of "party" of the poorer classes, and they seemed particularly to speak for the newly emerging industrial proletariat.[15] They also spoke for the equality of women and expected that the millennial revolution, having once swept England, would go on to other countries and become a world revolution.

Such expectations of imminent apocalypse obviously cannot be sustained at an activist pitch for very long. Although reborn again and again in moments of historical crisis, they can be maintained only for brief and climactic moments. The belief in the coming of the Kingdom, expressed in a direct revolutionary way, leads either to bitter reversal or, even when successful in its immediate aims, to eventual disenchantment and frustration. In order for the belief in the coming Kingdom to become the principle of a more stable community, it must be internalized or spiritualized in some way. One way this takes place is for the revolutionary community to overcome the world not by direct attack, but by separation and the creation of a provisional alternative.

This is essentially what happened to the Anabaptist communities of the sixteenth century after the great debacle of the New Jerusalem at Münster. Migrating to rural areas, the Mennonites and Hutterites set up agrarian utopias. The left-wing community developed what George Williams calls "the provisional paradise."[16] Here and now they have already passed over to the new principle of existence of the Kingdom of God and are living separated from "the world and from the Kingdom of Satan and from all that is of the Old Adam." Their ethical discipline, their quiet harmonious style of life freed from all striving and competition, their sharing of goods in fraternal love all point to their separation from false society and their attempt to live according to the pattern of redemption. However they know that redemption is not complete. They themselves must keep up a constant effort to maintain the new moral style of life. The evil world still persists around them. To be sure, Christ will someday come and hopefully very soon complete the revolution and do away with the lingering imperfection, but meanwhile the redeemed community settles down to a quiet, orderly pattern of living the authentic life, maintaining a mild sort of messianic expectation that can be more or less indefinitely prolonged. "We are already beginning the new paradisaic state of life. Soon Christ will come and abolish the remains of the evil world and complete our salvation. But, meanwhile, we wait and cultivate our garden." This is the theological stance that underlies and supports the Anabaptist agrarian utopia, some examples of which will be examined in more detail later.

A somewhat different way of relating the Kingdom to the present time is found among the Spiritualists, such as Casper Schwenckfeld and Sebastian Franck in the sixteenth century, as well as among the Quakers in the period of the Puritan revolution. The Spiritualists understand the Kingdom of God as a spiritual principle of the "inner light." Communing with the inner light, which is the presence of God within, the spiritualist is translated into salvation. But this does not necessarily take the form of physical separation from present society. The Spiritualist continues to live in the world, but as one who is free from it. Personally delivered from its false conventions, he walks abroad in the fallen kingdom overturning and prophesying against its evil ways. The early Quakers also expected a rapid advent of the messianic kingdom, but here and now they could live out of the inner light which is the "provisional paradise" within each man's soul.

One might also mention in this connection a very small but persistent option that began to appear in the late medieval period and had its followers in the sixteenth and seventeenth century. This option was the perfectionists, who were radical rather than provisional in their view of the spiritual kingdom within the soul. Very likely this option has roots in ancient gnosticism and was passed by an underground stream into the Middle Ages. The radical spiritualizers can be either extreme ascetics, as were the Manichaeans, or libertines. The libertine is in some ways the spiritualist analogue to the apocalyptic revolutionary, in which the effort to make the absolute totally present in the moment results in a kind of boundlessness often expressed in psychological reversal. This kind of expression was found in the Adamic sects of the late Middle Ages, the "libertines" of the sixteenth century, and groups such as the "Ranters" in the Puritan revolution. In effect, the radical spiritualist tries to create a total fusion of the self with the absolute so that no distance or limitation remains between the self and the final completed salvation. The Adamite quite literally declares that he has become one with God, that he *is* Christ or *is* God.[17]

The psychology of such self-absolutization is frequently a kind of demonic reversal that is found in libertinism. The reborn are totally redeemed. They are beyond the ambiguity of human good or evil, therefore everything is legitimate for them. In a culture of sexual asceticism, this frequently took the form of sexual debauchery, community of wives and husbands, a declaration that total salvation was expressed in promiscuous sexual intercourse. This also found expression in a kind of "hippie" and looter ethic. Total freedom was expressed in a boundless reversal and mocking conflation of all things previously kept strictly apart by social convention. The Adamite mixed rags and dirt with jewels and velvet gowns. The child's rhyme, "Hark, hark, the dogs do bark. The beggars are coming to town. Some in rags, and some in tags and some in velvet gowns" may reflect such Adamites in seventeenth-century England. The Adamite throws away all security. He steals what he needs and yet shares everything he has with his brethren and gives everything away. He is both childishly innocent and indulges in any evil that he pleases. Antinomianism and deliberately contrived forms of reversal and mixing up of social conventions and styles associated with the highest and lowest levels of the social hierarchy are the ways the Adamite expresses his freedom and transcendence of all limitation.

Needless to say, the Adamite, like the apocalyptic revolutionary, is a short-lived option. He too burns himself out rapidly. Their boundlessness and rapid extinction in both cases lies in the effort to fuse totally the finite moment or self with the infinite. However there are those who cultivate the provisional paradise, recognizing the limitations of their present powers and the distance that still separates them from the final salvation, creating a partial expression of salvation either in inner experience or communal utopia, yet still recognizing the continuation of evil around them and in themselves, the need for continued struggle and the continued futurity of final salvation; these have been successful in creating enduring and viable radical communities.

Chapter 3

The Enlightenment, Liberalism, and the French Revolution

In the period from the Renaissance to the liberal revolutions of the late eighteenth and nineteenth centuries, we can trace a long period of disintegration and transformation that gradually dissolved the ideological, cultural, social, economic, and political foundations of Christendom, replacing them with those democratic, secular, and scientific foundations that we call "the modern world." The solvents upon this classical Christian view were many. The emergence of the new national monarchies gave the death blow to the medieval universalism of empire and Papacy. Classicism and the new textual criticism promoted the autonomous intellect and gave it an alternative to the Christian synthesis in a revived non-Christian, classical past. Travel and the era of exploration opened up vistas of new worlds and, with them, new cultures untouched by Christian civilization. The myth of the philosophic Chinese or the savage still existing in the unspoiled state of nature acted much like science fiction today in holding up to the imagination an image of an alternative to the present state of Western civilization. Above all, science, taking its first steps in the late medieval and Renaissance periods and then advancing by giant leaps in the seventeenth century, raised up a whole new set of possibilities and, for the first time, suggested to European man that his own age might surpass that of classical antiquity, which up to them had been the standard of human achievement.

This prodigious growth of natural science in the seventeenth century, culminating in Newtonian physics, was creating a new method of thought and a new concept of the universe and man's place in that universe. The combination of empirical observation and mathematical systemization that formed the scientific method was such as to set aside all arguments from tradition and authority and to proceed on reasoned inference from observation alone. Until the advent of science, men had relied on the past and the authority of tradition for the norms of thought. Even when they criticized existing conditions and sought to introduce change, it was justified in terms of reformation or renaissance, a bringing back of the true tradition of the original foundation as against a corruption of that tradition. But science taught men to rely solely on their own minds and their contact with direct experience.

The successes of this method gradually dissolved the habit of turning to the past as a golden age. It was in European scientific circles that the doctrine of progress was first tentatively announced, when men ventured to think of their own age as a new thing that was coming into existence, transcending not only the medieval period but even the golden age of antiquity itself. Renaissance man had freed himself from his immediate past by reference to this alternate and, in his eyes, more glorious past, but science suggested a complete reorientation from this sense of guilt toward one's own times, a cutting loose from the past entirely, and a facing around toward the present and future age which was then coming to birth. In a similar way, Cartesian rationalism, modeled on the mathematical method of science, dissolved the sense of debt to tradition, giving man a method of thought that abolished history in order to start *ab integro* from "pure principles."

Science, exhibiting its fruits in Newtonian physics, raised up a vision of an orderly, self-sufficient universe running by its own immanent laws that could be deduced from rational investiga-

tion. The arbitrary caprice of "providence" was abolished in favor of invariable "natural law," and this contemplation of nature
supplanted as the ultimate source of "truth" the Reformation
reliance on Scripture and revelation.

Calvin had seen the Scriptures as the "spectacles" by which we
were enabled to read the book of nature obscured through sin.[1]
The influence of science gradually reversed this relationship of
nature and Scripture, so that, for the seventeenth-century ration-
alists, it was the book of nature that was the light by which
Scripture was read, and only those things in Scripture that could
be reconciled with the book of nature were to be accepted. Matthew Tindal, in his tract "Christianity as Old as Creation" (1730),
put this relationship as succinctly as possible:

> There is a religion of nature and reason written in the hearts of every
> one of us from the first creation by which all mankind must judge the
> truth of any instituted religion whatsoever, and if it (instituted religion)
> varies from the religion of nature and reason in any one particular, that
> alone is an argument which makes all things else that can be said for its
> support totally ineffectual.[2]

God's self-revelation was seen more convincingly in the order
and design of nature. Scriptural proofs shifted to second place,
and the primary way of proving the existence of God came to be
the argument from "design," from the order of nature. God was
no longer seen primarily as the God of Abraham, the God who is
the Father of Jesus Christ, but the Supreme Being who is the
architect of the universe, the God of order and rationality who is
the presupposition of the rationality of the universe and who can
be proven by reference to this order and rationality, a circular
argument that was rather effectively punctured in David Hume's
skeptical *Dialogues on Natural Religion* (written about 1751, but
published posthumously in 1779). In the late seventeenth and
eighteenth centuries this "natural religion" became the normal
assumption of the learned man, and any special position for a
supernaturally revealed Scripture, doctrine, or religious institution came under fire more and more.

The earliest school of rationalism arose in England after the

Restoration when, wearied of religious controversies, she tried to pull herself together around her traditional religious and national institutions. The mood was summed up by the term "latitudinarian"; a mood not so much of toleration as of narrowly rationalistic prejudices about what was, in fact, "tolerable." What was intolerable was the enthusiasm and fanaticism, the bickering over points of religious doctrine, the apocalyptic messianism that had characterized the period of the Puritan revolution. What was cultivated was a pedestrian sort of Christianity in which the watchmaker God, who was the architect of the Newtonian universe, served as sanction for the decent law-abiding morality of the English possessing classes. In fact, the traditional Christian distinction between reason and revelation was commonly interpreted in this period as a class distinction. It was said that the content of Scripture and revelation was essentially identical with that of reason and natural religion, but, for the sake of the ignorant masses, God had revealed this religion of nature in a simple colorful form complete with miracles to impress their imaginations, whereas the enlightened classes did not stand in need of this revelation, being able to attain this knowledge by their own intellects. In effect, the Christian doctrine of the Fall and the debasement of man's reason had here become a doctrine applicable only to the lower classes.

Such a latitudinarianism, far from being revolutionary, was in a sense counterrevolutionary, and was not infrequently espoused by the most impeccable of English high-churchmen. Yet, when the restored Stuart monarchs began to break the national balance by sliding back too far toward Rome, thus threatening to repeat all manner of religious disputation, this same ethos engineered one of the quietest revolutions in history by which the Protestant monarch, William of Orange, replaced the Romanizing James II.[3] In the hands of these latitudinarians, rationalism did not so much challenge as it sought to bulwark traditional religious and political institutions, and its energies were expended in proving the full and complete harmony of traditional revealed religion with reason and natural religion. Tindal's book cited earlier as well as John Toland's *Christianity Not Mysterious* (1696) and Locke's *The Reasonableness of Christianity* (1695) are examples of the genre.

However, when this rationalist thought began to penetrate France in the early eighteenth century it encountered a very different situation, and in the hands of the French *philosophes* reason and natural religion became the encampment from which they began to launch a full-scale attack on all the traditional institutions of church and state. For Voltaire and the writers and pamphleteers that contributed to Diderot's *Encyclopédie,* the history of Christendom could be summed up in one word, "superstition." The *philosophes* were not so much philosophers (as that term has been influenced by the tradition of German scholarship) as they were "sophists", literary and social critics and educated men who applied their minds to any and all subjects. Their turn of mind was rational in a critical sense, but deeply opposed to metaphysical theorizing. They were empirical and utilitarian in their bent of mind, and, although French was their lingua franca, Locke and Newton were their patron saints.

For them, Christian civilization was, in Voltaire's words, a "catalogue of crimes." Institutional religion was "priestcraft," a snare set by the possessing classes to control the unsuspecting masses. Behind this dark age of Christendom they sought out the Enlightenment of Greece and Rome as a point of reference for their own spirit, but this classicism served essentially as an alternative to Christianity and as a pipeline into secular modernity, which they confidently believed was being ushered in by science and the new dawn of critical thinking.[4] They used history as their medium, yet history for them was not a detached neutral science but a polemical tool by which they systematically demythologized traditional religious and political institutions, seeking to dissolve the divine sanctions that underlay these institutions and to bring them under the control of natural reason. Their program can be seen as a concerted effort to "disenchant" nature and society and to naturalize all human life; this was nothing less than a thoroughgoing construction of a new worldview.

The invective of the *philosophes* was, of course, predicated on the assumption that there was indeed a new alternative at hand. Man's nature, symbolized by the hypothetical "state of nature" and the myth of the noble savage, was essentially good. It was irrationality, incarnated in repressive social and religious institutions, that had been responsible for his demoralization. Starting again with man's basically upright rational nature and cultivating it properly through empirical science, it should be possible to organize a new society harmoniously structured for the benefit of all.

Such thoughts of a new and better age began only fitfully in the early eighteenth century but grew in breath of conception and optimism as the century went on. The seventeenth-century scientists had boldly suggested that, in their field at least, the modern world was beginning to surpass the ancient. Around the turn of the century there raged a rather tedious discussion about the relative merits of the ancients and the moderns in the realm of literature. Much of the argument in favor of the superiority of modern literature to ancient was rather jejune, but it symbolized the widening of the battle against authority in that very area that the Renaissance had held up as the unsurpassable pinnacle of human achievement. In the "Digression Sur les Anciens et les Modernes" (1688), Fontenelle argued from the invariability of natural powers that man could build on the heritage of the past to create an infinite progress in the arts and sciences. Toward the middle of the eighteenth century this hope for a new age that would surpass even the achievements of antiquity began to move from the purely intellectual realm of the arts and sciences to the possibility of progress within social institutions as well. The idea of modern progress in knowledge gradually became transformed into a hope for the general progress of mankind.

This new expectation was exemplified by a figure such as the Abbé de St. Pierre, who was perhaps the first of the modern "do-gooders." The Abbé spent his life, which spanned the eighteenth century until the French Revolution, in a continual series of projects aimed at the general betterment of mankind. This included everything from projects for the improvement of French roads and tracts, to proposals to the Pope for the abolition of clerical celibacy, to elaborate plans for the perfection of government and the development of a federated states of Europe that would abolish war and insure perpetual peace.[5] The Abbé's numerous reform projects, and the naive confidence with which he assumed that society could be readily transformed into the "best of all possible worlds" if only everyone would adopt his easy-to-follow plans, may appear ludicrous, and yet he exhibited a turn of mind that was generally unknown before his time and has become taken for granted today, namely, the possibility of social change through reorganization of man's institutions and environment.

In effect, what gradually emerged in the eighteenth century was a new secular version of the doctrine of the millenium that was to be brought about within history and on this earth by the immanent workings of the forces of history. The preliminary condition for this emergence of secular reformism was the rebirth of the sense of the future as the realm of the ideal. The concept of the historical future as the realm of promise was, as we have seen, very much a part of the Old Testament prophetic tradition, but it had been eliminated in Christianity through the domestication of the millenium in the already fulfilled epoch of the church and the abstraction of the hope of fulfillment into a transhistorical Heaven that had lost its connection with future history. The sectarians had, to an extent, recovered some of the dynamic sense of history, and believed that their own community was the beginning of the promised millenium, but they still did so in the perspective of awaiting some cosmic intervention from beyond that would bring in the new perfect age in a way unconnected with this present world. But in the new secular tradition of the Enlightenment we can find the birth of a future hope that aimed at the ultimate perfection of mankind on earth.

It has often been said that the difference between the Christian concept of the Kingdom of God and the liberal doctrine of progress is that the latter is this-worldly rather than other-worldly and is brought in through immanent forces working within history rather than through divine grace. But this contrast is too pat and is, in fact, misleading. In the prophetic as well as the patristic view, salvation is world-historical. It is a salvation *of* history, not just a salvation *from* history. Theologically it is possible to view grace not just as a confrontation and repudiation of nature, but as a power immanent in history through Incarnation or even through creation restored through Incarnation; as a power working in history to bring all men and all reality into their final perfection. Its source is transcendental but its workings are immanent.

The chief difference between the secular and the Augustinian view, paradoxically, may really be that the secular view restores the doctrine of transcendence in its dynamic relationship to history; it views transcendence as a future possibility rather than as an eternity unrelated to history. The secular view restored that catholicity of salvation that had been lost through a narrowing interpretation of the saved community as solely historical Christendom and finally only the ecclesiastical community. It restored the patristic concept of salvation that we find in Origen and Irenaeus, where it is seen as truly universal and world-historical. It also opened up the sense of the future as a place of transcendence vis-à-vis the present and the realm of new possibilities, a sense which had been lost through the domestication of future historical hope in the church. It said, in effect, that the last age of the world has not yet come. The church was not God's final word, at least if we mean by the church that kind of religious society that has become the established religion of Christendom. A new age, a new dispensation, a new world was still possible. Such a view could only arise initially in a hostile relationship with that established religious society whose pretensions to be the last age of the world had to be dethroned before a new future hope could be born.

This faith in the dawning of a new age in the modern world finds its characteristic expression in the little treatise by the

Marquis de Condorcet entitled *Equisse d'un Tableau historique des Progrès de l'Esprit Humain* (1793), which he wrote in hiding during the terrorist period of the French revolution. Condorcet's hope for a continuous infinite progress was based on his faith in the power of reason that would effect a gradual enlightenment of the whole human race. Wedded to this faith in reason was a corresponding faith in science, the tool through which the development of this world was moved forward, effecting both an enlightenment of the mind through its discipline and an amelioration of the whole human condition. Condorcet envisioned this enlightenment as gradually leveling all unjust distinctions: between social classes, between the affluent and the less privileged nations of the world, and between men and women.

Of all the revolutionary thinkers, Condorcet was the most unstinting enthusiast for the new doctrine of equality. Religious institutions which stood for inequality, superstition, and prejudice would fade away before the noontide of reason. Prejudice based on sex, nationality, or social class would be abolished. Equal rights for men and women, universal education giving all persons in the society equal opportunity, a system of social security that would ameliorate economic distinctions in accumulated wealth, both for the young man starting out in life and the old man retiring from work; these would be the ways of overcoming inherited inequalities. There would still be natural inequities of ability and achievement, to be sure, as the inherent reward of personal capacities, but these would no longer be augmented or retarded by false social status and inherited privilege.

Condorcet looked forward to a perfection of the physical capacities of mankind as well through science. There would be an elimination not only of want, but of disease and other physical imperfections, and the emergence of a new race of supermen whose health of body might be indefinitely prolonged. Along with others of his time, Condorcet expected the elimination of war, as essential to progress, and the establishment of an international federation of nations that would insure perpetual peace. His ultimate vision was one of limitless progress, going on from "glory to glory" toward the ever greater perfection of the human race. We see in Condorcet not only many social, economic, and political programs that continue to underlie modern liberal reform movements, but that kind of boundless optimism, that vision of the "Great Society" that stands like the new "golden Jerusalem" or "promised land" on the future horizon of all programs for social betterment.

Before discussing the French Revolution, which served as the breaking point with this movement and plunged Europe into a new adventure that did not entirely follow the lines predicted by the eighteenth century, although it continued to be informed by its doctrines, we should pick up the threads of the development of liberalism. Liberalism had variegated meanings that were not always easy to reconcile with each other. First of all it meant free thought, the right to freely form, express, and discuss one's opinions on all important questions of life: religion, politics, science, and the like. In this form liberalism fought for free communication and free press, battling the oppressive powers of church and state to restrict and censure free thought and to punish the heretic or the dissenter.

In politics liberalism meant political freedom and equality, equal representation, equal franchise, a government that would be elected by and express the will of the people. As political liberalism was enunciated by John Locke, it rested on a doctrine of equality and individualism that would strictly limit government to its indispensable caretaker functions of maintaining law and order and protecting property, but would leave a large sphere for the exercise of private liberties. In such a view, government was seen as a dangerous power, ever tending toward tyrannical self-expansion, which therefore had to be carefully curbed and restricted. Such a view was likely to regard with suspicion the suggestion that the government itself should take a direct hand in social change or intrude into areas of education, values, and religion that belonged to the individual.

Along with this kind of political liberalism went economic liberalism, the liberalism of the free market, which found its classical exposition in Adam Smith's *Wealth of Nations* (1776). Smith traced the history of the economic progress of mankind through the augmentation of wealth and believed that this would continue indefinitely to the ever-increasing well-being of mankind. He believed that the free commercial trade between all peoples in the world, unfettered by governmental policies, would lead to the greatest advantage of each by a kind of providential economic solidarity through which each man's private self-seeking would lead to the benefit of all.

Liberalism, particularly in the political sphere, has deep roots in the European past, going back into Germanic society, medieval parliamentarianism, and feudal doctrines of contract. In this tradition, freedom resides in the people, who barter a limited portion of their liberty for the protection of the Lord, but who also retain communal representative institutions to check and advise the Lord. Over against this Germanic contractual view of government stands the doctrine of absolute indivisible sovereignty derived from God, which came down through a double stream of Roman law and Christian messianism and was fused in its first representative in the papacy. In the sixteenth and seventeenth centuries, the national sovereigns of Europe shoved aside the Papacy, only to transfer this same concept of sovereignty to themselves. The doctrine of the absolute sovereign was systematized by French royalist lawyers in the seventeenth century in collaboration with Gallican cardinals steeped in this ecclesiastical tradition.[6]

The struggle between these two traditions can be found in the medieval struggle between the papacy and conciliarism, and it was renewed in the revolutionary Puritanism of the sixteenth and seventeenth centuries that struggled against the Papacy and rising absolute monarchs. It was from these Puritan thinkers of Holland that Locke drew his own political thinking in the English struggle between Parliament and absolute monarch. Finally, in the Glorious Revolution, these parliamentary principles of constitutional monarchy were vindicated, and England became a kind of model for political liberty in Europe, particularly in France. When the ineptitude of the French royalty finally brought on the explosion of the French Revolution, its theoretical principles were the pure milk of liberalism, drawn from the English tradition and finding a practical vindication in the new American republic across the seas. The French "Declaration of the Rights of Man" is a veritable catalogue of liberal principles. But the French Revolution quickly began to exhibit another spirit very different from both liberalism and the empirical, utilitarian principles of the Enlightenment, a new spirit that soon engulfed the liberal constitutional reformers and unleashed the Terror and the drive for ideological world conquest that was an entirely new phenomenon in modern history. It was this totalitarian, expansionist drive of the French Revolution that struck such deep repugnance into other European nations, particularly England, who had supported the Revolution in its liberal, constitutional phase.

The transformation can be seen most strikingly in Robespierre, who began his career in the revolution as a liberal democrat, calling for universal suffrage and the transfer of government to a popularly elected legislature. No one struggled more devotedly for the cause of popular sovereignty and more earnestly attempted to find structures that would truly express the "will of the People" as the governing principle of the new democratic state. As a student of Rousseau, Robespierre was aware of the distinction that emerges in the *Social Contract* between the "General Will" and the "will of all." The General Will represents the true will of the People, but this cannot be found simply by counting noses because the People are often unaware of their true will. Rousseau himself imagined that the General Will could be preserved by eliminating factions and subsidiary groups, establishing the principle of "one man, one vote," and by opening communication on public issues. But such primary representation is conceivable only in the town assembly of a city-state.

Robespierre, struggling to bridge the gap between representation and the "General Will," became increasingly aware of the gap between popular sovereignty and the representative assembly, as well as the gap between inchoate popular sentiments and the virtuous self-knowledge presupposed by Rousseau's concept of sovereignty. He became convinced that it was up to the conscious sector of the popular leadership (for practical purposes identified with the Robespierrist Jacobins), who were in tune with this true collective soul and proper self-interest of the people, to be their spokesmen and representatives. Finally Robespierre himself was the only one left who was in touch with the true "will of the people" and who could proclaim unblushingly "Le Peuple—c'est moi." Legal representation was replaced by self-appointed charism as the way of determining the popular will, and Robespierre the Democrat became Robespierre the Autocrat.[7]

Alfred Cobban believes that the secret of this transformation does not lie in the doctrines of the Enlightenment and the liberal doctrines of popular government espoused by Locke but rather in the tradition of absolute sovereignty derived from the papal and monarchial traditions that they opposed. The doctrine of absolute sovereignty embodied in a single national monarch was so inbred in European political thought that, at the time of the Revolution, it was simply transferred to a mystical collectivity called "the People" and whatever party leaders won the right to speak for this mystical collectivity. From the absolutism hidden in this doctrine of popular sovereignty there sprang a kind of boundless will to perfection, initiating purges and indoctrinations within the state and limitless expansionism towards the rest of the world. This hidden seed of totalitarianism that was born in democratic revolutionary states Cobban sees as the root of expansionist nationalism and the democratic totalitarianism that infects not only "Socialist People's Republics" but their American opponents as well, who have steadly deserted the Lockean principles of limited government for a similar totalitarianism.[8]

The absolutistic doctrine of sovereignty may indeed be one

source of totalitarian democracy, but one might also suggest other sources as well, in particular the absolutism implied by the doctrine of Progress and infinite perfectibility. The idea of the continual perfection of mankind through education, science, and technological improvement left hanging the question of who would direct this progress. Liberal theory had envisioned no such role for government, which they would restrict to its negative functions, and liberal economic theory assumed that free enterprise could produce this progress by its own unplanned instincts. But, inevitably, the need for overall planning arose, and government, as the only power available for such a role, began to absorb more and more of the functions of coordinating social change.

A survey of European thought on the morrow of the Revolution reveals a new tradition being formed in Germany that also makes the doctrine of Progress central, but that is very different in spirit from the empirical utilitarianism of the Enlightenment. In the German Enlightenment and its successors, the doctrine of Progress becomes ideological and is elevated to the status of a metaphysical principle that encompasses the very structure of "Being" itself. One has the feeling that with the Revolution European thought had taken a kind of quantum leap to a new level of consciousness, and progress, which was only a kind of hopeful projection from empirical data with the eighteenth century, becomes the very stuff of existence. Essence is plunged into the stream of Becoming so that no reality remains that is self-identical; all reality becomes developmental and historical. It is like the difference between a man quietly contemplating a moving scene from a static prominence and that same man who has now been transformed into that changing scene itself. Progress takes on an ontological quality that it did not have in the eighteenth century, and there is no longer any place of permanence where one can stand aside from history and contemplate its principles.

Some roots of this view may be found in Kant's doctrine of the church as the inner Kingdom of ethical Humanity in its development toward perfect self-realization.[9] This vision is carried forward in the German idealists, who view history as a cosmic drama of Progress toward the self-realization of Humanity. Humanity and Progress now are regularly treated with that veneration usually accorded the deity, as if they were metaphysical realities.[10] In contrast to the French Enlightenment with its polemical view of Christian doctrine and the church, the German idealists regularly claimed to be the vindicators of the authentic essence of Christianity. The historic church was left behind as an outmoded shell of a great idea, but this great idea was absorbed into the new metaphysics, and the ancient doctrines of Christ, the church, and the Incarnation made their new and grander debut in the dress of German idealism.

This demythologization and appropriation of Christianity into evolutionary metaphysics reached its final form in Hegel's doctrine of the dialectic of the Idea in history. Humanity is seen as the objectification of Deity or Absolute Selfhood, which is alienated as phenomenal reality in order that the Deity might bring itself to objective self-consciousness. History is the progress of this absolute self toward full self-consciousness. Mankind is literally God or the Absolute realizing Himself through History. Before this heady vision of absolute Humanity and his Destiny, poor empirical humanity fades away like so many insignificant centipedes upon whose vile miseries, broken hearts, and bowed backs the Absolute strides forward to its final self-realization. The realization of the Absolute Idea Hegel locates in the National State, particularly exemplified in Prussia—an idea which, however demonic, is not so illogical as some have supposed, given the hidden absolutism contained in the new doctrine of national sovereignty.

In the ensuing years of the nineteenth century the doctrine of historical change became more and more firmly fixed in the popular mind as the very texture of life and indispensable fabric of thought, yet with increasing doubt as to the actual direction of this historical change. It was, of course, the wonders of scientific technology that transformed the doctrine of Progress from an elite to a popular doctrine and widely held article of faith by the end of the nineteenth century. Everywhere the application of science produced a steady transformation of man's environment, so much so that modern man is almost as far removed from his ancestors who lived in an environment primarily conditioned by raw nature as from another species of being. Today everything he sees, touches, and does, the whole medium in which he moves is thoroughly conditioned by the new and ever-evolving technological environment that he is creating on earth. Utopia is no longer in a golden past or in some remote island, but is a projection of the progress of scientific technology, a scientific wonderland of a not-too-distant future.

In addition to this, the discovery and vindication of the doctrine of organic evolution gave to the idea of Progress a kind of scientific inevitability that it had not had before. Now the vision was extended into the very bowels of the earth itself, and modern man appeared as the pinnacle of an evolution of species that began when the crust of the earth first began to cool and the first organic cells began to float in the primal sea. Change, development, progress, constant limitless movement has become the inescapable fabric of life, reaching into the very fabric of organic nature itself. Yet, as modern man is carried forward on this accelerating rollercoaster, a cold sliver of doubt has been inserted into his heart. A question that was inconceivable to the eighteenth century has more and more intruded itself. Is the authentic happiness of mankind really found by progressing along the same path carved out by natural and scientific evolution? Is progress really compatible with humanity, or are they, in some mysterious way, at odds with each other? The question can be rephrased in the manner of Camus: Is man at home in this universe, now seen as a progressive evolutionary universe, or is he an alien to it? The scientific utopia toward which man is heading takes on more and more of the aspects of a nightmare in twentieth-century literature, and, far from solving the problem of man, progress simply poses the question all over again.

Even in the 1870s T.H. Huxley recognized the conflict and decided that human social progress could only be made by constantly checking and resisting the forces of natural progress. "Social progress means the checking of the cosmic process at every step and the substitution for it of another which may be called ethical progress."[11]

Chapter 4

Utopianism: Christian and Socialist

The commune or the cooperative community in its many forms has been a persistent motif of social reform, especially in the United States, which has a continuous history of communal experimentation from the earliest days of colonialization up to the present time. Utopian experimentation in America has come in every shape and hue: religious and secular, ascetic and libertine, transcendentalist and socialist. Communalism has waxed and waned but never entirely died out, and new movements of social reform, up to and including the present black liberation and "hippie" movements, have brought new waves of experimentation in communal living.

Utopianism in Western thought can be traced back through a double stream: philosophical utopianism from Plato to Thomas More, Thomas Campanella, and François Fénelon in the sixteenth and seventeenth century; and Judeo-Christian communalism from the Essenes to early Christians to monasticism, up to the left-wing radicals of the Reformation and the Puritan revolution. The first tradition is speculative, seldom tried, and more seldom successful in practice. The second tradition is the active tradition, and has been by far the more successful in practice, with the socialist utopians forced not only to borrow practical tactics from the religious but often to envy them their far greater material success. This chapter cannot expect to detail more than a representative sample of this history.

In America, religious utopianism comes down through various streams of the left-wing Protestant Reformation: Hutterites, Mennonites and Amish, German sectarian movements of the seventeenth-century pietist revival, and English radical sects such as the Quakers and the Diggers. From these have also spun off American sects such as the Shakers as well as uniquely American religions such as the Mormons. Some of the European sectarian groups were not originally communal, but developed communitarian features during the emigration experience. There was indeed something of a utopian fervor in many of the emigrating groups, particularly in those that came under a common religious inspiration, and the dissenting Congregationalists of Massachusetts Bay colony were not alone in seeing the New World as a biblical Promised Land, a new Zion being founded in the wilderness as a foretaste of the Age to Come. To those who came out of the radical Christian tradition, such hopes quite naturally came to mind as they journeyed to this new country to fulfill cherished dreams of religious reform that had been denied to them at home. The "old world" was being left behind and before them lay a horizon of limitless possibilities.

Some of the earliest fully communitarian groups mingled mystical and eschatological doctrines and adopted the practice of celibacy. The earliest successful community was Bohemia Manor on the Chesapeake Bay of Maryland, founded in 1683 by followers of the French pietist leader, Jean Labadie. About a decade later a sectarian group from Wurtemberg, which combined Rosicrucian doctrines and Christian mysticism derived from Jacob Boehme, founded the celibate community of "The Woman in the Wilderness." The name was derived from the image of the believing community driven into the wilderness to await the final destruction of the Dragon (in Rev. 12:6). The community lasted from 1694 to 1708 and had several offshoots, such as the community of "Irenia" or "The True Church of Brotherly Love" founded near Plymouth.

Even more monastic in character was the Ephrata community of Pennsylvania, founded in 1732 by Johann Conrad Beissel, who was similarly inspired by German mysticism and pietism. Remaining relatively static, Ephrata nevertheless continued in existence until 1920. A celibate brotherhood of men and women, wearing rough monastic habits, and living lives of great austerity, they did not, however, reject intellectual and musical culture. Ephrata is perhaps popularly remembered for the startling architecture of their buildings, particularly the doors, which were only twenty inches wide, showing the literal application of the scriptural phrase "narrow the door that leads to life." These early ascetic mystical communities also cherished millennial hopes, although they believed that they had come to the wilderness to await the coming of the Kingdom of God rather than to realize its founding. "The Woman in the Wilderness" community even kept telescopes on the roof, maintaining a constant evening watch for the first signs of the announcing angels of the apocalyptic cataclysm.[1]

Far more ambitious in their missionary endeavors were the Moravian Brethren, a sect which came down from the Hussite Brethren of the fifteenth century, but gathered together and renewed by the Lutheran pietist leader Count von Zinzendorf. The Moravians, who founded Bethlehem, in Pennsylvania, and then spread to a number of daughter colonies, formed a communism of consumption called General Economy. Each member contributed time and labor to the community and from it got food, clothing, and shelter for themselves and their children. No wages were paid, and the land, buildings, and industries were all held by the church.

In the early 1800s there was a quickening of communitarianism partly under the influence of the revivalist preaching of the Great Awakening. This stimulated the rapid westward spread of the Shakers, who were the first English-speaking utopian movement and the first to make widespread American converts. The Shakers, or the United Society of Believers in Christ's Second Appearing, were a mystical millenial offshoot of the English

Quakers. They were led by a visionary woman named Mother Ann, whom the Shakers believed to be the new Incarnation of Jesus in female form (which completed the first Incarnation in male form). Driven from England in the 1780s, Mother Ann's group was joined by the New Light Baptists of the Great Awakening. The Shakers espoused a form of realized eschatology, believing that Christ's second appearance had already taken place and the fulfilled millennium was already available as a spiritual Kingdom experienced in mystical ecstacy. The Shakers believed that the Day of Judgment had already occurred in the founding of their church, and they were already living in the new resurrection order. Consequently they believed all marriage and giving in marriage was to be superceded by the virginal life of the resurrection. The Shakers lived a highly disciplined life of work with very little cultural or social relaxation, and their central outlet was the ecstatic worship of the community, which took the form of Pentecostal dancing and singing. This dancing assembly was the core of the self-understanding of the community, the place where its emotions were sublimated and the belief that the millennial Kingdom was already present and dwelling in their midst was realized in group ecstasy. The Shakers lasted for some one hundred and fifty years, the last members dying out in the 1920s. At their height they constituted a chain of some twenty-two communities with about 5,000 members. Their craftsmanship as well as their folk music continues to be admired.[2]

The nineteenth century also saw the flourishing of new groups of German separatists, such as the Rappites and the somewhat grimmer Zoarite communities. The Rappites, named for their leader, Father Rapp, were quietist separatists from Lutheranism who arrived in 1804, and the Zoarites under Johan Bimeler arrived in 1817. Although the Rappites emigrated in family groupings, they gave up marriage for celibacy soon after their landing in America. They spread over several settlements under the direction of the Harmony Society. Father Rapp, who was a kind of benevolent autocrat, and his son, who was an excellent administrator, guided the communities into great economic prosperity which lasted for seventy years. The Rappite communities began to decline in the 1870s after Father Rapp's death, although remnants remained into the twentieth century. The Rappites were mild milleniarists who had separated out of "the world" in expectation of the imminent Second Coming of Christ. But instead of filling the intervening time with prayer and fasting, they settled down to cultivate their gardens, awaiting the Second Coming in a provisional paradise surrounded by plump flocks, lush fields, and sweetly smelling flower gardens. The Zoarite communities also enjoyed growing economic prosperity, although cultivating a more somber and puritan style of life than their comfortable burgher cousins.

This by no means ends the roster of such German communities in the United States. One could also mention the Amana community, which descended from similar pietist origins. Its founders were "inspirationalists," who believed in a descent of the "spirit" through a succession of individuals who are chosen by God as the vehicles of divine will. In the 1840s the inspired leaders of that generation, who happened to be a tailor, a stocking weaver, a carpenter, and a serving maid (God obviously being no respecter of social class), decided to migrate to the United States. Settling first in New York and then in Iowa, the Amana community thrived under a system of communal property in an unaltered form until 1932. Then the communal system was converted into a cooperative, but the spirit was largely unchanged, and in this form they continue until the present time. The Amish of Pennsylvania and Ohio do not practice community of property, but their communist cousins, the Hutterites, after suffering repeated persecutions and wanderings that led them from Moravia to Hungary, Romania, Russia, and finally to America, settled in the northwestern United States and then Canada in the 1880s, and are still today a growing movement with one-hundred-fifty successful communities. The Hutterites live under essentially the same communal rules established by Jacob Hutter for the refuge Anabaptist communities in Moravia in the 1530s. The members traditionally live in apartments around a courtyard, sharing a common kitchen and dining room, and contributing all the fruits of their labor to the common storehouse. In the traditional Hutterite polity, children were also raised in common, being sent to the communal nursery and school at the age of two, where they were looked after by women and a schoolmaster appointed by the group. This school inculcated the mores of the Hutterites into the rising generation, teaching them to put aside individualism and self-will for the common intent of the *Brüderhof*.[3]

In the nineteenth century the religious communism derived from Christian radical sectarianism met and mingled with secular utopianism of humanist or socialist origins. Although socialists and communist thinkers of the 1880s were to belatedly discover these earlier forebears, it was only in America that such radical sects actually survived in a flourishing form into the nineteenth century, when they could enter into a direct interplay with secular utopianism. New communitarian movements frequently visited older establishments, both to receive advice and assistance and out of a feeling of brotherhood in a common endeavor. Individuals often passed back and forth between religious and secular communes. The religious communities themselves often adopted a more secular tone in the nineteenth century and studied the new socialist thinking, while the socialists found quite a few practical hints from the successful practices of the religious communities. Indeed, it was precisely the success of these communities that emboldened many European theoreticians to try to translate their schemes into practice. The continuity between the old and new movements is perhaps symbolically illustrated by the transfer of the successful Rappite community of Harmony, Indiana, to Robert Owen for the site of his socialist experiment. The secular utopians, moreover, often came to think of themselves as the proponents of a "new religion" or perhaps a new, purified form of Christianity, and thus brought the cycle of secularization of the religious community full circle.

The 1830s and 1840s was a period of great interest in utopian communities in the United States. Renewed interest was taken in communities founded on a religious basis, and numerous experimental communities were undertaken on the basis of secular ideologies. The New England Transcendentalists were responsible for several communities, such as Brook Farm and the even more short-lived Fruitlands. The Transcendentalist combined an ideal of cultural and spiritual cultivation with naturalism of a somewhat idyllic sort. By simplifying their needs to the most basic level and by communal separation in manual labor, they hoped to combine simple healthful communion with nature with a continual round of cultural activities and high-minded conversation. Neither community lasted very long, chiefly because the Transcendentalists did not prove to be very skillful farmers. Brook Farm, however, lasted considerably longer than Fruitlands, chiefly because it was carried along by the excellent school that it created. Indeed, much of the community-building fervor of this period flowed ultimately into new concepts of schools as an "educational" community. Robert Owen's New Harmony, while a failure as a socialist community, had a similar impact on educational theory and experimentation.[4]

Perhaps one of the most unusual and "sensational" of the radical communities was Oneida, founded in 1847 by J. H. Noyes, who later wrote *A History of American Socialisms* (1870). The Oneida community combined religious perfectionism with the most advanced ideas of the day. Like the Shakers, Noyes espoused a doctrine of fulfillment eschatology. He declared that the Second Coming of Christ had already occurred, that the sinless had already been divided from the sinful, and that the saved here and now should begin to live in the state of regeneration. This belief Noyes interpreted, however, not in terms of celibacy but in terms of communal marriage. Perfectionism can, in fact, take either course of an ascetic or a libertine expression. The ascetic expression has historically been more common since it is more conducive to control and discipline. The self-absolutizing drive inherent in the notion of fulfilled salvation can be kept within bounds by routing it through a repressive environment that perhaps finds momentary outlets in ecstatic experience. In this way a state of life can be created that still tacitly handles the continued existence of finitude and limitations. Very few radicals have really been willing to move in the other direction, to declare that salvation is fully present, and therefore that all finite restraint can be abandoned. The Adamite movements have been the chief expression of this libertine direction, and have always been regarded with great horror by the rest of the Christian churches, including radical communities of an ascetic stripe.

The Oneida community did not go to the extremes of the Adamites and thus avoided the demonic reversal that regularly overcomes such movements. They interpreted the presence of salvation as the abandoning of egoism for full communal existence, which they understood as both communal life and property as well as communal marriage. All "mine" and "thine" was to be given up for a sharing of all things. However, they worked out a kind of systematization of such free liaisons within the total ethos of the community that was successful and did not degenerate into jealousy or friction. The ideology of the community also held "liberal" notions of the equality of women and permissive education. Women, it was believed, should be free to separate their love relationships from procreation and should bear children only when they chose. The children, after they were weaned, were raised in a communal nursery where they grew up together in a children's wing of the community. Oneida maintained a very high educational and cultural ethos and, like the Transcendentalists, enjoyed a continual round of plays, concerts, picnics, and stimulating conversation about all the "most advanced" thinking of that time. The Oneida community was highly successful for the first generation of believers but broke up in 1879 chiefly because the children of the community, who had gone on to the best schools and universities, became embarrassed by their unconventional parents![5]

During this same period a number of socialist communities were founded, most of which floundered after a short time; even during their period of life they seemed to be ridden with ideologi-

cal friction and financial chaos. Robert Owen, the English socialist industrialist, Charles Fourier, a French Utopian theoretician,
and Etienne Cabet were the chief ideological sources for these
communities. Fourierist propaganda in the United States was
disseminated primarily by Albert Brisbane, a disciple of Fourier,
through his book, *Social Destiny of Man* (1840), which laid out
the most useful aspects of the Fourierist doctrine in a simple
attractive form, as well as through his regular column in the
New York Tribune. Several journals and newspapers also became organs of Fourierist thought. Some forty communities
were launched, only six lasting longer than fifteen months and
only three longer than two years. The three most successful were
North America, in New Jersey, which lasted for twelve years, the
Wisconsin Farm, which lasted six years, and Brook Farm, which
converted to a Fourierist phalanx for the last two years of its
existence. The Icarian community, founded by the French con-
spiratorial revolutionary Etienne Cabet, enjoyed some brief periods of prosperity, but mostly led a wandering faction-ridden
existence. Robert Owen's experiment at the site of the former
Rappite community of Harmony, Indiana, followed a similar
course of financial disaster and ideological dissension.

   Strange as it may seem, these socialist communities that were
founded on an explicit ideology of economic theory and materialist prosperity seem to have been the least prosperous and the
most mismanaged economically of all the utopian communities.
The utopian socialists seemed to assume that some simple application of pet economic theories, such as labor notes or "attractive industry," would work a kind of magic, dispelling all further
problems of management. Owen's community of New Harmony
was mismanaged from the very beginning, floundering without
leadership while Owen himself gave speeches on his theories to
admiring audiences in New York and Washington.[6] Once the
socialist communities began to show signs of financial hardship,
the members had nothing further in common in the form of
religious faith or common ethnic identity and group experience,
such as held the earlier religious and ethnic-religious communi-

ties together during times of trial. Consequently they rapidly fell apart into warring factions. Yet although the socialist utopias created no outstanding record of economic success, they all seem to have conducted a lively intellectual and cultural life. Like the Transcendentalists, they created a round of stimulating social events, plays, concerts, dances, intellectual seminars, and open forums that left their former members with nostalgic memories of deep and valuable human interchange within an atmosphere of genuine "free thought" such as is rarely found in any human gathering, and many members of utopian communities found themselves unable to live anywhere else. When one community failed they moved on to find another one to join. Thus, paradoxically, the socialist communities, while they were economic failures, were "spiritual" successes, perhaps more so than the often narrow and repressive religious utopias.[7]

The period from the French Revolution to the revolutions of 1848 constitute the first phase of the development of socialism, often called the era of "utopian socialism" to contrast it with Marxism, which claimed that it had replaced these earlier dreamers by putting their speculations on a sound, scientific basis.[8] The results of the French Revolution were to install the new propertied classes in firm political control, toppling the last remnants of feudal privilege. The right to private property was a liberal article of faith for the French as well as the American Revolution.[9] But this shift in the balance of political power to the middle class only served to raise the further question of the working class: their political enfranchisement, and social and economic inequality. Working class movements began earliest in Britain, where the problem of the inhuman living conditions created by the industrial revolution came to a head earliest. The term "socialism" first appeared in Robert Owen's *Cooperative Magazine* to designate the followers of his own doctrines.[10] In this early context it meant those who criticized individualism and the competitive principle in society and wished to supercede it with communal interdependence. Far from carrying the idea of state ownership and direction of the economy, the utopian socialists generally were antagonistic to "the state" and the political principle, and wished political rule to be superceded by direct self-government in the worker's cooperatives. The Marxian dream that full socialization would bring about a "withering away of the state" is here fully an heir of the utopian socialists. The political principle generally was associated with alien rule by a "parasite" nonproductive class (the feudal class; later, in Marx, the "capitalists"). This political principle was to be replaced by the socioeconomic principle of society, i.e., self-management by organizations that directly expressed the productive forces of society.

Unlike his French counterparts, Robert Owen arrived at socialism through practical experience. A successful manufacturer, he had made a fortune in his cottonmills of New Lanark. Owen was horrified by the oppressive conditions of the factories and set about to make his own mills a model of good working conditions. Fair wages, pleasant working conditions, and educational facilities were provided for the children instead of the long hours of factory labor that was their usual lot in this period. A shortened work day, curbing of child labor, factory-provided schools, nurseries, and educational and cultural opportunities for the adults were among Owen's original reforms. Owen proved through his own practices that not only could factories be cleaned up and made reasonably humane places in which to work, but also such humane factories would be even more profitable than the brutalizing exploitation that prevailed. Owen's ideas soon advanced to more radical possibilities for economic reorganization that made him more explicitly a socialist rather than just an exponent of the welfare factory that provided social and educational services for its workers, radical as this idea was at that time. He postulated that capital should not receive the whole profit above minimum wages, but that it should get only a share of the profits, the rest being ploughed back into the development of industry and the welfare of the workers. He began to conceive of a cooperative factory run on a system of profit-sharing between labor and capital.

Owen was a pragmatic man, capable of producing a few ideas that he clung to with tenacious devotion. His chief hobbyhorse and the basis of his theories of social reform was "environmentalism." Man, Owen believed, was essentially good and was made bad only through a bad environment. He accurately perceived that the drunkenness and vice that characterized the English industrial cities were a direct consequence of the inhuman squalor and bare subsistence wages with which they were forced to live. Clean up the factory and homes of the workers, plant grass, trees, and flowers, provide decent wages, social functions, and good working conditions, raise the cultural level through education, and a new and different man can be created.[11] Such a view was very new in Owen's time and more than a little heretical, since the prevailing Puritanism firmly attributed all the evils of the working class to their personal sinfulness and laziness, and saw it as evidence of their lack of regeneration. The doctrines of original sin and election tended to ratify these evils and almost to forbid the idea that the elect should take some responsibility for overcoming them. Owen's environmentalist psychology was doubtless mechanistic and unsubtle. He tended to view human character as an automatic result of good or bad environment, but in terms of the exploitive conditions of his day, his panacea was sound enough, if not quite as all-inclusive as he believed.

At first Owen became the darling of English social reformers and a visit to the New Lanark mills became *de rigueur* for those making the grand tour of England. His popularity began to fade, however, when he became involved in the fledgling labor movement, and a good part of his fortune was lost in his ventures in community building in America. Owen, however, was undaunted by this failure and went back to England where he became involved in the trade union and cooperative movements of the 1830s. Up until this time Owen had conceived of social reform in a paternalistic fashion as something set up from above by benevolent government and industrial leaders. In the trade-unionist phase, Owenism meshed with the popular labor move-

ment where the leadership and initiative rested with the working classes themselves. The ideas set forth at the Cooperative
Congress of 1833 were nothing less than an effort to overthrow
the whole capitalist system by a united union of all workers in
a national trade union. Through cooperative effort, labor was to
set up its own factories based on joint investment and profit-
sharing and gradually muscle out of business the factories run on
a capitalist basis. This ambitious plan collapsed in a few years
through violent countermeasures from employers and government, but the idea of profit-sharing, consumer cooperatives, and
ultimately producer cooperatives became a central idea for socialist reformers.

Owen thought of himself as antireligious, or more specifically
anti-Christian, but there was more than a streak of the old English milleniarist radicalism in his personality. His opposition to
the Christian church stemmed primarily from its association
with the social structures of the landed classes. He particularly
repudiated the doctrine of original sin and the depravity of man,
which he interpreted as a doctrine that robbed men of initiative
and faith in their own ability to improve society, decreeing a
fatalism toward conditions of this world. Owen understood evil
as environmental, not intrinsic to man. It resided in social conditions, not in an irremediably depraved self. These defects of human character could be changed by changing the social
conditions and raising children in a healthful atmosphere. Salvation came from human initiative; it did not wait on divine grace.

However, not unlike other socialists, Owen began to think of
his own doctrines as a religion, a new secular religion of
humanity that he called "rational religion," and in his later years
this religious element among his followers gave birth to a central
organization called "The Society of Rational Religionists." For
Owen, and for the utopian socialist generally, the founding of
communities and cooperatives was not a method of withdrawal
but a beachhead of a new world, a nucleus and example of a new
form of society that they hoped would gradually spread and take
over the whole. In a sense this was true of the religious utopians

as well, for they also saw their communities as a similar beach-head, but they believed that the completion of this new world could only come through apocalyptic intervention from Heaven, while the utopian socialists believed that it would spread from their own beginnings through human initiative.

Owen's counterpart in France as the founder of utopian social-ism, Charles Fourier, had quite a different career. Where Owen started from successful practical experience, Fourier was a pure theoretician, drawing up elaborate blueprints for imaginary so-cieties, placing ads in the paper and sitting hopefully at his table in the café waiting for the rich industrialist (who never came) to put his schemes into practice. Fourier was also a man of one pet theory. This was the idea of "attractive industry." Fourier hit upon the central fact of the alienation of the industrial worker from his work that was to be taken up in a much enlarged form by Marx. Industrial labor was essentially dehumanizing because it was not an expression and fulfillment of the worker. Unlike the artisan of an earlier era, the worker found no pride or per-sonal satisfaction in his work. He was a part of an assembly line, a cog in a machine. However, far from despairing of this condi-tion as an inevitable human loss necessary to industrial effi-ciency, Fourier supposed that it could be corrected by improved social management. Fourier's scheme rested on an implicit faith in the fundamental harmony of nature. Man and nature were so interconnected that there could be no fundamental disharmony between them, and therefore for every kind of work there must be a human personality naturally suited to it. This view, of course, assumes that industrialization itself is not a fundamen-tal departure from nature, and thus can be fitted into the its harmonies. All one had to do, then, was to devise a social system in which each person could gravitate to the work that naturally suited him, and then the whole system could work harmoniously and without alienation or coercion, driven by the motor of hu-man spontaneity.

To fulfill this vision, Fourier imagined small agricultural com-munes that would be economically self-sufficient. Their ideal size would be sixteen to eighteen hundred people cultivating five thousand acres of land. The community would live together in a common building that looked, in Fourier's plan, like a stripped-down version of the Versailles palace set in the midst of farm-land. The community building would be fully equipped with all the necessary services, kitchens, workshops, and nurseries. There was not to be absolute equality in the style of life within the phalansteres, as they were called, but there would be a certain natural differentiation of size and luxury of the apartments, according to personal taste. Work would be variegated. A person would not be programmed into any particular line of employment, but could move around among different tasks, even during the same day. Children, Fourier reasoned, were naturally attracted to playing in dirt, so they could be assigned in little teams to do the dirty work, such as carrying out trash. However, in Fourier's system the more onerous and menial tasks would pay the most, whereas those that carried their own reward, such as artistic and scientific endeavors, would give less material rewards. Fourier worked out an elaborate system of distribution of profits that allowed some private income but with a steep system of graduated income taxes that would redistribute the income of the wealthier members among the whole community and prevent any member from becoming disproportionately wealthy or poor.

Fourier's view of the new communal society particularly emphasized the liberation of women. He went so far as to say that the liberation of women is the index of the liberation of society in general. Since marriage as it then existed was fundamentally inimicable to the liberation of the personhood of women, he believed that it must wither away as an institution in the new socialist society, to be replaced by a free choice of partner(s) and self-development through a variety of cultural and social contacts. Fourier, then, was a radical feminist, an advocate of complete equality between the sexes, and was ahead of his time in his views of the freedom and respect due to the individuality of children as well. In a view that was to be taken up by the Marxists, he believed that the subjugation of women to the chattel relationship in marriage came into existence at the same time as private property and should be abolished with it.[12] This connection between marriage and private property must be said to be implied if not explicitly stated in the practices of most communalists, and some form of modification of the private marriage relationship, either by abolishing it or by communalizing it in some way, is found in both religious and secular utopias.

Fourier placed this vision of the ideal society within a mythology of world epochs. In a scheme reminiscent of ancient Stoicism, Fourier speculated that the world moved through a series of epochs in a cyclical fashion, and the founding of his own ideal communities would be the beachhead of the final renovation of the world in the eighth epoch that was about to come. In this age, his ideal society would triumph over the whole world. This social renovation would be accompanied by a complete cosmic renovation as well. The beasts would become tame and the sea would turn to lemonade, and all the world of man and nature would enter the final epoch of Harmony.

Fourier himself never saw any of his schemes put into practice, but after his death several disciples took up the more practical suggestions in his work, such as his theories on profit-sharing, the communal education of children, the overcoming of alienated labor through "attractive industry," and the general plans for the creation of a cooperative industrial-agricultural community, and attempted a number of experiments along these lines, particularly in America. His more fanciful speculations about the future paradisiacal state of the cosmos were quietly put aside, but other aspects of his thought were developed in a number of books and hotly discussed in many journals of opinion. Marx himself, despite the supposedly "scientific" nature of his analysis of the development and overthrow of present capitalist society, had a touch of the Fourierist dream in his vision of the ultimate communist society where alienation and division of labor would be overcome and a system could be devised that would work on human spontaneity alone. In one of his few speculative passages on the nature of the final classless society, he says,

The division of labor implies the contradiction between the interest of the separate individuals or the individual family and the communal interest of all individuals who have intercourse with one another. . . . For as soon as labor is distributed, each man has a particular, exclusive sphere of activity, which is forced on him and from which he cannot escape. . . . While in Communist society where nobody has one exclusive sphere of activity but each can become accomplished in any branch he wishes, society regulates the general production and thus makes it possible for me to do one thing today and another tomorrow, to hunt in the morning, fish in the afternoon, rear cattle in the evening, criticize after dinner, just as I have a mind, without ever becoming hunter, fisherman, shepherd or critic.[13]

The third member of the traditional triumvirate of utopian socialists is Saint-Simon, in whom there is a prophetic foretaste of the "managerial revolution." Saint-Simon envisioned replacing the political class—the feudal and bureaucratic leaders of the traditional state—with the leaders of the producing class—the bankers, scientists, and captains of industry who would organize the whole society along the lines of a welfare economy. The utopians did not recognize a class struggle between capitalists and workers, although the idea of class struggle had been put forth by earlier radicals, such as the left-wing Jacobin Babeuf in the time of the French Revolution. Rather, Saint-Simon assumed a common interest among the industrial class as opposed to the power structure of the *ancien regime:* the nobles and ecclesiastics.

Saint-Simon also placed his new vision of society within a theory of historical epochs. He believed in alternating cycles of social integration and social dissolution. The period from the Protestant Reformation to the French Revolution was the period of the dissolution of the old integration of Christian society, and this was to be replaced by a new integrated society organized around scientific and technological lines. He soon came to think of his own theories as the new religion of this scientific society, led by the scientists and financiers who would be the clergy of the new social religion and would bring about a new social cohesion around a common vision, just as the Catholic church had been the integrating centre of medieval society. In the new Catholicism, the spiritualism of Christianity would be completed by the addition of the "fleshly" female, or material element, wherein man would emerge in the wholeness that he had not achieved under the previous dispensation.

These speculations, which Saint-Simon embodied in his last book, *The New Christianity* (1825), took a rather strange cultic form among his followers, complete with clergy, sacraments, and the anticipation of the revelation of the material female counterpart of the Messiah, which the Saint-Simonists called "La Mere." These esoteric elements notwithstanding, Saint-Simon's basic vision of a collectivist technological state, with industrial managers and technologists as the clergy and the exaltation of the cult of materialism as the reigning ideology that would replace the Christianity of the past and play a similar role as the ruling orthodoxy, is strangely prophetic of that very totalitarian society that has emerged suddenly both in Communist lands and gradually in so-called capitalist lands. Such totalitarian ideology is quite different from the communalism of the other utopians as well as from that vision of freedom and spontaneity suggested in Marx's own ultimate hopes.

Saint-Simon's ideology thus seems to lead in quite a different direction than the worker's self-government envisioned by the cooperative movement or the autonomy of the Fourierist communes. Again in socialism as in the earlier liberalism there is a tension between democratic humanistic socialism and totalitarian socialism. In Saint-Simon, socialism moves toward the large industrialized collectivist state, where the personal rule of the old feudal society is replaced by a faceless technological elite who cannot even be confronted because they are a corporate personality. In the other utopians, however, we see a different impulse, a suspicion of the state, of the political principle, even a suspicion of largeness in social organization as such and perhaps even a certain primitivism. This is certainly true of Fourier, whose phalanxes were basically agricultural, industry being limited to the simpler arts and crafts. In this utopian socialism there was more than a little desire to curb the burgeoning of large-scale industry and technological expansion in favor of the human principle of dignified and satisfying work. The producer community would be scaled down to human proportions where the worker could be part owner and manager and have a voice in the government of his affairs by direct self-representation in the village forum. Participatory democracy would have been an idea congenial to this branch of the socialist movement.

Perhaps the real heirs to this branch of socialism would be a figure like Pierre Proudhon and the anarcho-syndicalist communism that descends from him.[14] For Proudhon the state was the chief enemy, which must be abolished. Society should be decentralized into cooperative associations on the level of the basic units of the village and the industrial cooperative. These self-ruling associations would federate together in a common coordinating institution, one that would represent their direct association. Power would remain on the local level with self-governing communities.

The key to utopian socialist thought is the effort to humanize industrial production and to curb the rationality of industrial efficiency in favor of wholeness of human life. The human principle, politically expressed in communal autonomy and self-government and economically expressed in personal fulfillment in work, was to restrain and reshape the impersonal demands of technological processes. Technological efficiency was to be scaled down and kept at human proportions where, in Marx's words, a man could still hunt in the morning, fish in the afternoon and criticize after dinner. The utopian, and later anarchist, traditions are thus reactions to industrialization. They seek to surmount the conditions of life being brought about through the new forms of productions by projecting a new communal world that would recapture in ideal form the artisan and agricultural community of the feudal past that was passing away. This also explains a certain affinity for the religious utopians of the radical tradition, since they also preserved in an idealized form that earlier communal society. This primitivist trait soon made the utopians seem hopelessly outdated and "unscientific" by contrast to Marxism, which concealed a certain anarchism in its own ultimate hopes, but which hoped to bring them about through a dialectical appropriation of industrialism.[15] Yet the humanizing element, which made these earlier socialists seem so alien to the impersonal collectivist leviathans that have since developed in the name of the socialist tradition, has also caused a recent revival of them among the New Left, who seek to recover a "humanist socialism" and look for an alternative to the totalitarian rule of the "party."

Chapter 5

Christian Socialism and
the Social Gospel

In his critical study of Christianity, *Religion Within the Limits of Reason Alone* (1793), Kant wrote,

We have good reason to say that "the Kingdom of God is come unto us" once the principle of the gradual transition of ecclesiastical faith to the universal religion of reason, and so to a (divine) ethical state on earth, has become general and has gained somewhere a *public* foothold, even though the actual establishment of this state is still infinitely removed from us. For since this principle contains the basis for a continual approach toward such a consummation, there lies in it (invisibly) as a seed which is self-developing and in due time self-fertilizing, the whole which one day is to illuminate and to rule the world. But truth and goodness ... do not fail to communicate themselves far and wide once they have become public, thanks to their natural affinity with the moral predisposition of rational beings generally. The obstacles, arising from political and civil causes, which may from time to time hinder their spread serve rather to make all the closer the union of men's spirits with the good (which never leaves their thoughts once they have cast their eyes upon it). Such, therefore, is the activity of the good principle, unnoted by human eyes but ever continuing—erecting for itself in the human race, regarded as a commonwealth under laws of virtue, a power and a kingdom which sustains the victory over evil and, under its own dominion, assures the world of an eternal peace.[1]

This passage may be taken as setting the tone for the Christian Socialist and Social Gospel tradition. The Kingdom of God is demythologized and brought back to earth. It is also freed from its ecclesiastical encasement and revealed as the moral Kingdom of the brotherhood of mankind, which is unfolding upon earth through a progressive victory of good over evil, reason over ignorance. Kant thus set the basis by which nineteenth-century progressive churchmen could reincorporate Christianity into modern social movements on the other side of that secularization of the doctrine of salvation that was accomplished by the Enlightenment.

In the neo-Kantian theology of Albert Ritschl, this interpretation of the Kingdom of God as a this-worldly moral kingdom of the brotherhood of man, which was advancing to an inevitable victory through the progressive forces of history, established itself in the heart of the new liberal orthodoxy itself. It was taken for granted by the disciples of Ritschl up to the First World War, most of whom entertained Christian Socialist leanings. Thus the theoretical basis of Christian socialism sprang essentially from the liberal doctrine of progress, and was generally couched in terms of mild bourgeois moral optimism that eschewed the radical fringe of socialism with its doctrines of class struggle and violent revolution. Christian socialism thus flows into that version of democratic evolutionary socialism that was to become the practice of the Socialist parties of Western Europe, promoted by such groups as the Fabian Society and Marxist revisionists such as Eduard Bernstein.[2]

Yet for liberal theology on the continent, this doctrine of the Kingdom of God mostly expressed a comfortable optimism about the present course of society and carried little imperative to engage in active struggle to bring this transformation about. Where social action was undertaken by the churches, it was often done on a paternalistic basis in an effort to keep the working classes in the orbit of Christian faith. Social Catholicism in France, particularly, often had a somewhat reactionary ring to it, an effort to align the workers' movements with older social forms, such as the guilds, over against the liberal secular doctrines of the Revolution.[3] Thus only here and there in Europe was there a proponent of social Christianity in the nineteenth century who really stood with the working classes in an active and forthright way.

Perhaps one of the earliest of these was the leader of Catholic liberalism, Robert de Lamennais, who began his career as an opponent of absolute monarchy and the Erastian state church. Lamennais saw the church as the victim rather than the beneficiary of the tradition of establishment by the state, and hoped to convince the Pope and the bishops that true Christianity lay with the liberal order and not with the *ancien regime.* In 1832 the papal encyclical *Mirari Vos* dashed his hopes for a liberalized papacy. Expelled from the church, Lamennais moved more and more into the radical camp of socialism as an advocate of the rights of the working class. In *L'Esclavage moderne* (1839), he compares the modern worker with the ancient slave, no less exploited by the capitalist than the slave was by the absolute power of his master. Lamennais' description of wage slavery and the antagonism between capitalist and proletariat is scarcely less strong than that of the *Communist Manifesto.* Nevertheless Lamennais did not advocate violent revolution or class warfare. He believed that universal suffrage and freedom of association, whereby workers could form trade unions to bargain with employers, would bring the working class into its own in time. Lamennais found the basis for a reformed society in the doctrine of creation, the fatherhood of God and the brotherhood of man. Like Condorcet, Lamennais had great faith in the efficacy of ideas. He was confident that, as men came to accept the ideas of equality and brotherhood, injustice would fade away before the dawn of a new day. He was one of the first to state the contours of this new day in terms of a struggle between capitalists and laborers, but for Lamennais it was not the materialist forces of history but the guiding power of God over history that would ultimately bring forth a new society.

A counterpart to Lamennais' Christian socialism can be found in England between 1848 and 1854, led by J. M. Ludlow and such eminent Anglican divines as Charles Kingsley and F. D. Maurice. Ludlow had imbibed some of Lamennais' influence during his youth in France, while Maurice was influenced by German evolutionary philosophy which was mediated to him through Coleridge. English Christian socialism was stimulated by the conditions of the industrial revolution. The apathy of the churches toward the new industrial cities was leaving Christianity more and more identified with the possessing classes, while a new working class emerged, unevangelized and alienated from the church. In this situation the Christian Socialist movement sought not only to re-Christianize the working class but to exercise a positive critique of laissez-faire capitalism. They opposed the reigning economic liberalism that had identified free trade with the workings of divine Providence, and argued that socialist doctrines were much closer to the Christian understanding of society. Competition and rugged individualism were the attributes of fallen, sinful man. Sin created egoism and pride, the ruthless drive for self-enhancement at the expense of the other man; this was the root of the competitive spirit. The redemption of man was an overcoming of this selfish competitive individualism and the restoration of man to brotherhood and community.

This indeed is the true meaning of the church, for the church does not refer primarily to the ecclesiastical institution, and certainly not simply the ecclesiastical institution of the possessing classes. The true meaning of the church is brotherhood, community, that loving shared life with one's fellow man into which mankind is being led through the regeneration founded by Christ.[4] Thus Maurice attacked laissez-faire capitalism on theological grounds and put forth a doctrine of the universal Catholic church as the universal brotherhood of mankind on earth. This brotherhood was indeed the inner essence of that just communist order toward which the socialists were striving, and thus socialism itself could be seen as the vindication of the principles of the church or the Kingdom of God on earth.

The English Christian Socialists did not adopt any particular economic theories, but in a generalized way they put themselves on the side of the workingman, resting their case on the doctrines of cooperation and brotherhood as the true meaning of that regenerated mankind symbolized by the church and destined to triumph as the ultimate social order of God's Kingdom. They wrote tracts and edited journals to propagate these views, and were involved in the cooperative and trade-union movements. For a period they even attempted some cooperative ventures of their own along Owenite lines of profit-sharing and joint ownership of the means of production. Later Maurice directed his energies toward the promotion of workingmen's education and became the principal of the London Workingman's College. For Anglican social activists, Maurice remains a progenitor and patron saint.

This kind of social Christianity in England died out in the 1850s but was revived again toward the end of the century. It was in America, however, that social Christianity acquired its greatest influence. A social activist Christianity, based on the doctrines of the Kingdom of God and messianic hope, found a ready soil in America, for the American experiment from its very foundations had a certain millennial drive. The period of the Second Great Awakening stirred not only various forms of sectarian experimentation but also waves of revivalism through the mainline denominations that spilled over into expectations of general social regeneration. The central thrust of evangelistic preaching was that of personal conversion and regeneration. The revivalists sought the individual experience of conversion, yet they assumed that the expression of this conversion would be a moral regeneration of one's life. Often this ethical direction of revivalism pointed toward social ethics as well. Temperance and the curbing of the liquor traffic was an early and continued theme of American social Christianity from the Great Awakenings up to its denouement in Prohibition.

But the most important social issue of the pre–Civil War revivalism was slavery. In the early 1850s a score of religious newspapers became heralds of the antislavery campaign. In the Boston

Methodist *Zion's Herald,* its new editor, Daniel Wise, began to ring out the antislavery theme. In his maiden editorial he declared,

We are for peace, purity, liberty and temperance. Toward slavery especially we cannot show aught but undisguised abhorrence. Our only business with it shall be to seek its extirpation by all judicious and prudent means, especially from the church of Christ.[5]

Around such papers a reformist revivalism arose that canonized the thesis that regeneration must show its fruits in a regenerated life, and the prime expression of this is moral action in a social context. A few weeks later Wise declared in his editorial on "The Christian as a Citizen," "political action is moral action because the Lord expects our every act to be holy. To withdraw from politics is to encourage the growth of evil in the world."[6] The core of this doctrine is still personal regeneration and an individual ethic, but this is directed toward ethical implications in society as well.

The 1840s also saw a tendency to combine revivalism and perfectionist ethics with the doctrine of the imminent Second Coming of Christ. In a declaration in 1835, Edward Beecher wrote that the churches in America were aroused as never before to the belief that the glorious advent of the Kingdom of God was at hand. Christians were coming to see their task

not merely to preach the gospel to every creature, but to reorganize human society in accordance with the law of God—to abolish all corruptions in religion and all abuses in the social system and, so far as it has been erected on false principles, to take it down and erect it anew.[7]

This combination of perfectionist ethics with millenniarism proved a potent combination for turning American Christianity to social reform. The agitation against intemperance, poverty, ignorance, vice, and, above all, slavery was seen in the light of those upheavals and conversions of the world order that signal the end of the evil age and the preparation of the world for the coming of the reign of Christ. During the Civil War and Reconstruction, these ideas went into a temporary eclipse, and many churches, especially in the South, recoiled from a gospel of social agitation that had played a role in fomenting the Civil War. They retreated to the old doctrine of individual regeneration strictly separated from social and political questions. Nevertheless pre–Civil War revivalism spelled out the basic theological themes that were to be picked up later by the Social Gospel.

Social Christianity began to revive again in the 1880s, primarily as a response to industrialization and the trade-union movement. Here again the starting point was revivalism, with its doctrine of personal conversion and ethical regeneration, but in the hands of such thinkers as Horace Bushnell and especially Walter Rauschenbusch, American revivalist Christianity again was led outward from individualism toward a social ethic. The context of this new period of social Christianity was the dislocation of American society created by rapid industrialization. Between 1860 and 1890 the national wealth increased 600 per cent, but over half of this wealth was held by .03 per cent of the population. The national picture was one of extremes of wealth and poverty: on the one hand, the vast percentage of the working masses were held at minimal exploitative wages without any of the social security benefits that the modern union worker takes for granted, and on the other hand, fabulous wealth was held in the hands of a few great families founded by the captains of industry who directed this great period of expansion.

America changed from a rural to an urban nation, and the beginnings of the modern megalopolis began to form. The more affluent began their exodus from the center cities, leaving the urban core to squalid slum housing. Many of the new immigrants that inhabited these urban complexes were Irish or Italian Catholics, and so Protestantism found itself losing contact with the urban masses. When the wealthy classes fled the city their churches characteristically fled with them, and Protestantism found itself becoming the religion of the towns and suburbs. At this period when the wealthy were becoming wealthier, the industrial classes actually became poorer. At a time when the national wealth increased 600 per cent, the average wage of the workingman decreased by 25 per cent. The laboring classes, therefore, turned to unionization. Agitation, strikes, and an aggressive socialist doctrine captured the minds of its leaders. This new struggle between capital and labor came to a head in the great General Strike of 1877.

Somewhat belatedly, Protestant churchmen began to respond to this new crisis. Many were influenced by the writings of socialists or liberal critics, such as Robert Ingersoll and Henry George, whose book *Progress and Poverty* (1879) exposed the enormous disparity between capitalistic wealth and the impoverishment of the working class. Protestantism was challenged to rethink the individualistic concepts of ethics and salvation that had been its dominate ethos. Important Protestant leaders such as Washington Gladden began to criticize the ethical aspects of capitalism and to speak up for a more socialized concept of Christian moral responsibility. Unitarians, with their liberal humanist tradition, easily shifted to a social focus. The liberal Congregationalism of Horace Bushnell found points of adaptation from the old Puritan ethic of individual salvation. The Episcopalians found support in Christian Socialists such as D. F. Maurice.

The critique leveled by the American churchmen followed the same lines as their Continental predecessors. Laissez-faire economics was attacked as both inhumane and unjust. The analogy between ruthless competition and self-interest and the Christian doctrine of sin as selfishness was drawn. In contrast, democratization and socialization of industry, profit-sharing, and economic cooperation were associated with the Christian ideas of love, community, and brotherhood. The socialist hope for a new cooperative society in the future was readily equated with the Christian hope for the Kingdom of God. This did not mean that the churchmen thought socialism itself sufficient for salvation, but they apprehended a harmony between socialist goals and Christian ideals that, while larger and deeper than those of socialism, nevertheless included them. When socialism inveighed against the exploitation of the worker, it was in line with the prophetic attack on the exploitation of the poor by the rich. Socialist hopes for a cooperative economic order were in keeping with Christian doctrines of fellowship and community. The future hopes of a new socialist order were in the same direction as the Christian expectation of the Kingdom of ultimate reconciliation, justice, and peace, except that the Christian hope demanded a deeper and more throughgoing regeneration of man.

The Social Gospel thus moved toward what today is called "secular theology." The old distinctions of sacred and secular, church and world were dissolved, and the Holy Spirit was seen at work not simply or even primarily in ecclesiastical institutions but in the struggle for humanity in society at large. The point of reference for understanding the Kingdom of God, and even the church itself, was the community of mankind in history. This was the "body" that was being shaped by the Spirit, criticized by the prophets, and led toward ultimate salvation in the Kingdom. The Kingdom is not to be found by turning from the world to the religious community; rather, the Kingdom is the goal and completion of the worldly community of man. The American Social Gospel was the child of the liberal progressive philosophy of the Continent. God was understood as an immanent Spirit at work in history and guiding it toward its final goal.

This immanent working of God's Spirit was readily equated with evolution, the leading scientific idea of the day. The progress of mankind under the impelling Spirit of God could thereby be tied in with the innate workings of nature as well in a grand organic vision of man, God, nature, and history. Such a view presupposed a solidarity of all men's destinies. None can be fully saved as long as some are still perishing. Hell is those interlocking forces of selfishness and injustice that retard the progress of the Kingdom. Original sin is not so much an aetiological "event" as a symbol of the universality of this involvement of mankind in evil and the need for all mankind to advance in mutual solidarity to overcome it. To be on the side of human progress in any of its many forms is to be on the side of Christ, because Christ is the head and crown of humanity itself that finds its final realization in the messianic Kingdom of the future. These were the kind of thoughts to which liberal Christians responded as a part of the natural and inevitable *Weltanschauung* of that era.

The man who perhaps most fully summed up this thinking was Walter Rauschenbusch. His own theological training imbued him with the revivalistic doctrine of personal regeneration, but his experience in New York's "Hell's Kitchen," where he served a poor working-class congregation for eleven years as pastor of the Second German Baptist Church of West 45th Street, turned him to social Christianity. In 1907 he became the general spokesman for the movement with his book *Christianity and the Social Crisis.* These were followed by *Christianizing the Social Order* (1912), *The Social Principles of Jesus* (1916), and the final summary of his theology in *The Theology for the Social Gospel* (1917). In this mature statement of his social faith, Rauschenbusch defines the Kingdom of God as the doctrine that lies at the center of the Social Gospel. This Kingdom defines the progressive struggle of mankind from beginning to end. It is a Kingdom that comes not by peaceful development only, but by continuous conflict with the kingdom of evil. This conflict is nothing else but those messianic woes and battles depicted in the apocalypse. It is a Kingdom that knows no final consummation within history. It can never be perfect but it is always on the way, ever struggling toward new vistas, and yet it is tasted as a truly present victory in the concrete achievements of every generation. Those who accused Rauschenbusch of a ready identification of contemporary finite achievements with the absolute victory of the Kingdom did not read him carefully. Rauschenbusch's vision is not one of finalizing any finite achievement, but rather one of continuous growth and aspiration, never perfected in history yet communing with that ultimate Kingdom in each momentary and partial victory. "We are on the march toward the Kingdom of God, getting our reward by every fractional realization of it which makes us hungry for more."[8]

The Kingdom of God means a social order that, at every stage of human development, "will best guarantee to all personalities their freest and highest development." It involves "redemption of social life from the cramping influence of religious bigotry, from the repression of self-assertion in the relation of upper and lower classes, and from all forms of slavery in which human beings are treated as mere means to serve the ends of others." It strives for the replacement of force and legal coercion with love as the regulator of the social order, "the redemption of society from political autocracies and economic oligarchies; the substitution of redemptive for vindictive penology; the abolition of constraint through hunger as part of the industrial system, and the abolition of war as the supreme expression of hate and the completest cessation of freedom"; the voluntary surrender of exploitive relations between man and "the redemption of society from private property in the natural resources of the earth and from any condition in industry which makes monopoly profits possible". Finally the Kingdom tends to the progressive unification of mankind without the surrender of individual and group identity.[9]

Rauschenbusch always saw a close correlation between redemption and freedom. Freedom was, for him, most specifically expressed in the democratic organization of mankind, which he saw as having been vindicated in the political realm and now needed to be extended to the economic realm. Fellowship between men was only possible between equals. Therefore that restoration to community signified by the doctrine of the church could only be fulfilled by the extension of democratic participation to all spheres of life. When workers and capitalists became joint owners and managers, with all having a voice in the direction of the factory, then alienation and exploitation would be replaced by community, based on a recognition of the solidarity of mankind. It is doubtful that Rauschenbusch ever investigated very deeply the economic side of these doctrines. For example, he rejoiced somewhat prematurely at the growing trend toward industrial combinations in the assumption that this signified a growing sense of human solidarity. But in any case his trust was first and foremost in a democratic socialism.

Although Rauschenbusch believed in the immanent workings

of the Spirit of God in history bringing in the Kingdom of God progressively realized on earth, it is a mistake to speak of this conception as purely immanentist or propelled solely by human good works. Rauschenbusch was too well trained in traditional Protestant theology to fall into such a simple one-sidedness. Rather, his was an immanentism that was itself based on transcendence; a doctrine of man's initiative that was based on divine grace. The Kingdom was both a gift and a task, progressively realized yet always still ahead of us. Its source and consummation were transcendent but its workings were immanent.

The Kingdom of God is always both present and future.... It is the energy of God realizing itself in human life. It invites and justifies prophecy, but all prophecy is fallible; it is valuable in so far as it grows out of action for the Kingdom and impels action. No theories about the future of the Kingdom of God are likely to be valuable or true which paralyze or postpone redemptive action on our part.... It is for us to see the Kingdom of God as always coming, always pressing in on the present, always big with possibility, and always inviting immediate action. We walk by faith. Every human life is so placed that it can share with God in the creation of the Kingdom or it can resist or retard its progress. The Kingdom of God is for each of us the supreme task and the supreme gift of God. By laboring for it we enter into the joy and peace of the Kingdom as our divine fatherland and habitation.[10]

For Rauschenbusch, the doctrine of the Kingdom was a dynamic relationship of God's grace and man's work, transcendence and immanence.

But when Rauschenbusch wrote these words toward the end of the First World War he was not just indulging in high-minded platitudes; he could look back on an era of significant practical struggle for social justice within an important segment of the Protestant churches. In this the American Social Gospel differed significantly from similar sentiments that might be quoted from European liberal theologians in that it was based upon and shaped by practice. It was the growth of its practical involvement that impelled the emergence of its theory. This was true of Rauschenbusch himself, whose initially individualistic theology was reshaped through his own practical involvement with his working-class congregation. The detail of some aspects of this period of social involvement by the churches might be useful here.

The decade of the 1890s saw a tremendous outpouring of educational and communications literature on the problems of the church's social tasks. One medium for publicizing the problems of the worker to a popular audience was the novel.[11] Such a novel generally focused on giving a dramatic description of the plight of the urban poor, their desperate living conditions, their lack of health and educational facilities, and their exploitive wages and conditions in the factory. Many such Social Gospel novels were written by clergy and widely read. The novels brought the whole economic structure of capitalism under fire as a system based on exploitation and unbridled self-interest. While the description of the crisis was graphic and realistic, the projected solutions tended to be paternalistic and sentimental, thus revealing the limitations of the imagination of many Social Gospel churchmen. The solution tended to consist of the conversion of some wealthy people, especially wealthy ladies, to the plight of the poor, whereby they would spend the rest of their lives and resources on charitable efforts. Clearly it was one thing to see the crisis and another to project social goals and techniques commensurate with it.

Newspapers and journals also spread the word. *The Dawn,* the voice of the Society of Christian Socialism, was one such paper. It was succeeded by *The Kingdom* as the Christian Socialist organ. Numerous forums sponsored lectures on the subject, and important spokesmen such as Rauschenbusch spent much time on the lecture circuit. Organizations devoted themselves to gathering and disseminating information about urban conditions. As a result of this activity a great deal of sociological data was collected on the actual extent of urban poverty, the extent of the disaffiliation of the working class from the churches, and their income levels and tenement conditions. Sentimental laments began to be replaced by hard facts as a more solid basis for projecting changes. Sunday school materials, such as the widely used curriculum, *The Gospel of the Kingdom,* were compiled to educate Christian students in social problems. Out of this kind of information-gathering an interest in sociology began to develop as the new "handmaiden" of Christian pastoral theology. Departments of Sociology began to spring up in seminaries, and seminary curricula were reformed to stress preparation for the social ministry. The role of the ministry itself was being redefined by the Social Gospel; the minister was no longer primarily priest or preacher, but prophet and midwife of social transformation. A new education and new tools were needed to fit the minister for this new role.[12]

The churches also created organizations for social action. The Church Association for the Advancement of the Interests of Labor (CAIL) continued to be the most effective agency for many decades. It agitated through the press and the courts against tenement conditions and substandard wages, and even dabbled in efforts to expose corrupt city government, such as Tammany Hall in New York. It pioneered the idea of using the economic power of the churches themselves as a direct form of pressure against exploitive employment practices. For example, at one point they convinced the Diocese of New York to give all its printing work only to print shops that paid decent wages. Other similar societies were the Brotherhood of the Kingdom, the Christian Socialist Fellowship and the Episcopal-sponsored Church Socialist League. Most of all, the churchmen did what churchmen do best: they talked and they wrote. Speeches and tracts poured forth in a voluminous stream to alert the public to the needs.

The churches devised new institutions on the local level, such as settlement houses and what were called "institutional churches." The institutional church was one that transformed an inner-city parish from a building used primarily for Sunday worship to a facility for week-long social service. This meant that the parish saw its mission directed not only at its own congregational and denominational members but at all those who lived in its neighborhood. The church's mission itself was redefined in secular terms that reached out to all men in their total human situation rather than to only the church members in terms of "worship." Services such as gymnasia for the youth, day nurseries for working mothers, kindergartens, girls' and boys' clubs, youth sports programs, libraries, medical dispensaries, study classes, lectures on current problems, sewing and cooking classes, advice on legal matters, housing and employment services, banks and loans geared to the needs of the poor, soup kitchens—these kinds of services began to appear in the churches.

Some of them would be taken over by welfare agencies eventually. Others continue to be found in churches, and those that have been given over to welfare agencies could still be usefully supplemented by non-governmental agencies as well. The fact that it no longer appears extraordinary for the churches to engage in such activities is the measure of the transformation effected by the Social Gospel in the conception of the church's mission. The church socialist organizations entered into political agitation as well, supporting or criticizing governmental policies or endorsing presidential candidates. Some of the churchmen even advocated socialism in its revolutionary Marxian form, although the Christian Socialists were mostly mild liberal democratic socialists who believed in reform within present political institutions.

By the first decade of the twentieth century social Christianity was widely enough accepted by several mainstream Protestant churches to become official. It was endorsed through social creeds and platforms adopted by several churches and was put into practice by the establishment of social action agencies in the national boards. The fledgling ecumenical organ of the church, the Federated Council of Churches, created a joint agency called the Commission on Church and Social Service. The social creed adopted by the Methodist Church at the Baltimore General Conference of 1908 was later to be taken as the social platform of the Council of Churches as well. Its articles are a fair summary of what the churches took to be the social imperatives of the gospel after two decades of discussion and experimentation on the subject.

The Methodist Episcopal Church stands:
For equal rights and complete justice for all men in all stations of life.
For the principle of conciliation and arbitration in industrial dissensions.
For the protection of the worker from dangerous machinery, occupational diseases, injuries and mortality.
For the abolition of child labor.
For such regulation of the conditions of labor for women as shall safeguard the physical and moral health of the community.
For the suppression of the "sweating system."
For the gradual and reasonable reduction of the hours of labor to the lowest practical point, with work for all, and for that degree of leisure for all which is the condition of the highest human life.
For a release from employment one week in seven.
For a living wage in every industry.
For the highest wage that each industry can afford, and for the most equitable division of the products of industry that can ultimately be devised.
For the recognition of the Golden Rule and the mind of Christ as the supreme law of society and the sure remedy for all social ills.[13]

It is significant to realize that the most basic and feasible of these demands such as arbitration, shortened work weeks, and abolition of child labor were not to become national law until the Roosevelt Administration of the 1930s, and others still sound so far out of reach that few churches would have the temerity to put forth such demands today in so direct and uncompromising a form.

With the First World War and the Marxist revolution in Russia, as well as the attacks on liberal theology by neoorthodoxy in the thirties, this social Christianity went into a temporary eclipse, but its roots remained firmly planted in American Christianity, to be revived again in the civil rights struggles of the 1960s. It is easy to see the naiveté and cultural parochialism of the Social Gospel today, but it is important to recognize that the Social

Gospel established a whole new working assumption about Christianity: namely, that the nature of the gospel is a transforming mission to all mankind in all aspects of their life, and it is the proper role of the church to be a propagandist and agent of social transformation.

Chapter 6

Marx: The Secular Apocalypse

The writings of Karl Marx are the primary scriptures for revolutionary movements around the globe. Therefore any approach to a critical evaluation of Marxism finds itself in a labyrinth of interlocking theory and historical activity, and an ongoing theoretical interpretation of this activity that has taken on a life of its own. Yet this ongoing involvement of Marx's theory in activity and the ensuing theory springing from this activity is itself not foreign to but rooted in Marx's thought, for he himself was the one who insisted on the "unity of theory and practice." Thought had to cease to be a method for mere contemplation of the world and become a tool for changing the world.[1]

In Marx virtually all the strains of philosophical and social thought current in the mid-nineteenth century were gathered up into a complex synthesis: German philosophical criticism, French social theory, and English political economy are woven together in a vast effort both to grasp the whole situation of man in history, particularly in the era of industrialization and liberal revolution, and to effect a kind of incarnational transformation of the "word" into the "deed," so that theoretical man becomes revolutionary man plunged into the stream of history as the motive power for its dynamic movement toward the point of final renovation of the universe.

The interpretation of Marx has itself gone through a major revolution in the last decade, and this is again closely connected with the struggles for new self-understanding and new policies within now-established Marxist states. In the Eastern European satellites, in the emergence of new forms of communism in the Third World, and in the stirrings of new radicalism in Western Europe (which simultaneously wants to recover the revolutionary hope inherent in Marxism but to repudiate the totalitarianism of Soviet-directed Leninist ideology), such reinterpretation of Marx has direct practical significance. In line with Party Marxists such as Karl Kautsky and Lenin, the interpretation of Marx up to the thirties focused on his theory of historical materialism, viewing Marx as a thinker who had eschewed philosophical or ethical categories for purely empirical socioeconomic analysis.[2]

The new view, based on the recent recovery and study of the writings of the early Marx, particularly his *Economic and Philosophical Manuscripts of 1844,* focuses on a humanist Marxism. Marx's empirical analyses are seen as themselves vehicles of deep ethical and religious passion. Marx presents the paradox of a man who immersed himself in economics out of a deep moral hatred of economic life. He studied the dynamics of economic life as an antagonist studies the tactics of the enemy, in order to grasp and overthrow him and bring to birth a new mode of human living. Thanks to brilliant studies such as Herbert Marcuse's *Reason and Revolution,* the modern student must be much more sensitive to the philosophical pedigree of Marx's thought. The formation of Marx's thought can now scarcely be understood without reference to its origins in Hegelian categories, and his critical transvaluation of these categories by way of Feuerbach. This chapter will briefly summarize the development of the early Marxian humanism and its relation to the mature system of the *Capital.* In the light of this picture, we will then assess the relationship of Marx to the ideological structure of the Communist parties, which act as the "ruling class" of the Communist states.

Hegel's system is a throughgoing effort to carry out an understanding of history from the vantage point of God or the Absolute Spirit. As such it suggests the extraordinary conclusion that Hegel's own consciousness, embodied in his system, becomes the place where the absolute Spirit comes to its final self-realization or self-consciousness, a conclusion from which Hegel himself did not shrink.[3] God alienates himself into history, into the phenomenal objective being of the world, in order to realize himself by grasping himself again in the act of consciousness. The world then is the alienation or objectification of God and the means of his self-realization. Among the left Hegelians, of whom Marx was himself a member, and particularly in the thought of Feuerbach, Hegel's view of history was declared to be "upside down." Hegel, it was said, had stood the world on its head by understanding material reality as dependent and contingent upon ideas, whereas, in fact, primary reality is things, not ideas. Ideas are abstractions of things; things are not projections of ideas. Therefore it was necessary to reverse Hegel's method in order to stand the world back on its feet again.

Feuerbach's reversal of Hegel particularly focused on a critique of religion. Religion is the supreme example of the self-alienation of man by his projection of his own inner substance into the heavens. Man understands himself as a creature of God, whereas, in fact, God is really a creation of man. Alienated man projects his own inner substance into an ideal expression and thereby falls down and worships this alienated projection. Man sees himself as infinitely depraved and impoverished, miserable and completely dependent on the power of God, by having first impoverished himself in this projection of himself as God. Man must recognize God for what he is; namely, his own self-reflection, and by reappropriating his own alienated self-image, he regains all his own wealth, not merely as an individual self, but as a concretization of the whole species-self of mankind. Man's alienation of himself as God and subsequent reappropriation is thereby a progressive self-realization, since man, in pouring all his inner riches into the making of God, now reappropriates a self infinitely enriched by its social expression in the total riches of all mankind. By reappropriating this communal image, man realizes himself as a total communal being.

This anthropological restatement of the Hegelian dialectic was brought another step back to earth by Moses Hess, who interpreted this self-projection of man as the creator of God as itself a mystification of man's economic powers. It was in labor or creative activity that man particularly had his existence as the maker or the creator, and this creative activity was then projected into an alienated expression in the form of money. Money, as Marx himself was to say (quoting from Shakespeare), is the visible god. Money is the alienated expression of man's productivity and the empirical expression of what exists in a mystified form as the creator God of religion. This fundamental economic form of alienation is the basis from which all further alienations in society and religion arise.[4]

It was from the vantage point of this critical transvaluation of Hegel that Marx began to immerse himself in economic theory in 1842–43, making the first tentative statement of his system in the Manuscripts of 1844. The basic alienation and impoverishment of the human substance of man occurs in the process by which man projects his own creativity into objective form as "objects of labor," or commodities. Man is most specifically man, most specifically human, as creator, as maker. This activity is his human self-expression; it is what distinguishes the species-being of man from animals. When man projected an image of a creator God, who creates out of no external necessity or compulsion but in pure grace as free self-expression, he projected an image of the true nobility of his own human substance. Man is most specifically himself, he achieves his full and authentic humanity as the free creator, whose creativity rests on no external compulsion or need but is intrinsically self-rewarding in its very activity. By alienating his productive activity in the form of commodities, and thus making his creativity not self-rewarding, but merely a means to the product, man reifies his own inner creative substance. This is the fall of man and the root of his self-alienation. The product, which arises simply as the objectification of man's creativity, now takes on a life of its own. It now stands as an object over against man, and man falls into servitude to the created object. Instead of recognizing the product simply as his own self-expression, the product becomes the master, and man's creativity now stands in a servile relationship to the object.

Marx speaks of this servility of the creative process to the product as fetishism,[5] for he conceives of it as the empirical expression and basis of what man does in a mystified form in religion when man projects himself into the gods and then falls down and worships them as his creators. Religion, then, is simply the ideological expression of what goes on in the alienation of labor. The empirical counterpart of God (the ideological absolute) is money. Money is the worldly god, the empirical expression of this reification of man's self-alienation of his own creativity, while religion merely expresses this same process in an abstract, ideological way. Marx then turned from Feuerbach's critique of religion to his own critique of political economy essentially as a turning from the ideological expression of man's self-alienation to its real empirical basis in the alienation of man's labor and its objectification in commodities and ultimately in money. Money, as the worldly, visible god, finds its rationalization in the bourgeois science of political economy, and Marx's critique of capital is then a critique of the theology of the worldly god. Money is the root expression of the golden calf on which all theoretical golden calves, in the form of legal, social, and religious systems, are based.

This alienation of man's labor and its objectification in commodities effects a reversal of the authentic relationship of man and nature. The outer world of products, instead of being freely created, joyful expressions of man's creativity, now becomes lord of his creativity. All man's riches flow into the making of the product, while man himself becomes increasingly impoverished.

Marx amplifies with considerable vehemence on the antimonies of this enrichment of the commodity world and the attendant impoverishment of man's inner being.

Marx seems to fuse dynamically two levels of man's impoverishment: the inner impoverishment of his subjective being and the external impoverishment of his physical life. His external impoverishment has its roots in his subjective impoverishment and thus cannot be cured simply by amelioration of the physical condition of the worker by higher wages, since the essential servitude of the relationship would remain. It is necessary to overcome the impoverishment of the worker at its roots by overthrowing the basic conditions of the servitude of labor. Here lies the distinction between Marx's view of the "emancipation of labor" and that of the labor movement. The labor movement, or what Lenin was to call "trade union consciousness," is interested only in improving the wages and physical conditions of labor while leaving the subjective servitude inherent in the productive relationship unchanged; Marx, while he didn't ignore the amelioration of the worker's physical condition, saw this as secondary and dependent on the primary revolution, which was the emancipation of the "soul" of the worker, i.e., his subjective humanity.

The servitude of man's creativity to the product of labor sets up an antithetical relationship between the two. "The worker becomes poorer the more wealth he produces. ... The worker becomes an ever cheaper commodity the more goods he creates. The devaluation of the human world increases in direct relationship to the increase in value of the world of things."[7] The very physical existence of the worker is finally reduced to a marginal fraction of the costs of production. The worker does not work as an expression of life; he is barely kept alive in the most minimal conditions only so he can work. He lives in hovels and dark cellars without the most elementary conditions of light and air and decent food at the same time that his work goes into the constant enrichment of the world of commodities. The worker becomes a blasted and dehumanized adjunct to the labor process, misshappen in mind and body the more the work manifests increasing opulence, beauty, and intelligence. Marx, of course, based these sharp antitheses on the conditions of the worker in the early cities of the industrial revolution. Yet even the material improvements that were eventually to come to the worker, through the labor movement and the advance of technology itself, only partly invalidated Marx's argument, since the real crux of it lies not merely in the physical but in the spiritual or human impoverishment of the subjective essence of man by the servitude of the person to the thing.

This alienation of the product is rooted in the alienation of the processes of labor whereby the activity of work, instead of being an intrinsically satisfying expression of human meaning, becomes insignificant and dehumanizing rote labor. The division of labor inherent in the technological process is responsible for so robbing the activity of any intrinsic satisfaction as a human activity. This alienation finally touches the whole external world: nature, man's communal humanity (what Marx calls his "species being"), and finally, his relationship with his fellow man. Man as free creator makes the world his cosmic body and, in union with all other men, thereby expresses his social humanity. But under alienated labor, the world becomes the bloated stockpile of commodities that allows man only bare existence in order continually to enrich itself.

This self-alienation of the product of labor finds its concrete social expression in the relation between the worker and the capitalist. Alienated labor takes the form of private property, which stands as master over the existence of the worker, sucking him dry of all his human substance; this expresses itself in the social relation of the capitalist as owner of private property. The capitalist is the other half of the alienated selfhood of the worker, the nonworker who produces nothing but merely possesses the reified expression of the work of the worker. Antagonism and alienation in the self is thus translated into class warfare, a social struggle between the warring halves of man's soul: the all-productive impoverished worker, and the owner who does nothing and has everything. The capitalist is equally impoverished by the relationship although he is unaware of it, since he only possesses the externalized soul of the worker, but he has no soul himself.

The relationship that Marx is trying to describe can be translated into analogous situations. In the educational process, learning should be man's direct self-creation, his becoming as man; instead this self-creation is alienated from him in the form of rewards or "grades." The grades then become an alienated expression of his learning activity that achieve a dictatorial power over him, so finally the grades themselves become the chief reason for learning. One learns only to get grades, which means that gradually the real substance of learning as a self-activity dries up, disappearing altogether, to be replaced by the externalized substitute of grades. Finally, the alienated expression of learning takes a social relationship in the power of the administration as master of the grades over the life of the student. The grades become the point through which the administration can threaten and control the life of the student. The administration itself learns nothing. The student does all the learning, but the administration "possesses" the grades as an alien power over the student upon which his very life now depends.

Another analogy might be taken from the sphere of religion. The communal forms of worship, such as the Eucharist, are the self-expression of the life of the community itself. It is the self-expression and celebration of their own renewed life. Yet this celebration, instead of simply manifesting the re-creation of the life of the community, takes on a reified form as the sacrament, which now becomes an objectified "source of life" alienated and beyond the powers of the community upon which the life of the community itself now depends. This subservience to the objectified sacrament then takes on an alienated social modality in the form of the priestly caste. The priest now becomes the master of the sacrament, the one who "possesses" the sacrament upon which the life of the community depends. Marx himself used this same analogy with religious alienation when he spoke of Adam

Smith as the Luther of political economy, who revealed that private property was only the objectification of labor. Thus Smith annulled the hypostatization of private property as a thing in its own right and revealed that the subjective essence of private property is labor, just as Luther annulled hypostatized religion in the form of sacramentalism and sacerdotalism and transferred religion back to the subjective essence of every man.[8] Thus man's self-alienation on every level appears in its practical enforcement as the alienation of producing man to nonproducing possessor.

Man's creation is alienated as the private property of a possessor who himself is impotent, yet who stands as the means of life for the producer. This is Marx's correlation between alienated labor (life) and private property. This correlation then takes social form in class conflict. The worker (the student, the laymen) becomes dependent for his life on the nonproducing possessor of the reified expression of his life. Hence the instinctive hatred of the worker (student, layman) by the capitalist (administrator, priest) and the inherent fear and suspicion of the possessing class for the exploited. This discovery that alienated self-relationship empirically took the form of alienated social relationship is the turning point between the early philosophical manuscripts of Marx and his later writings. Thereafter Marx spoke no more of the problem of the alienation of the self as such, but only in its social form as class conflict between the proletariat and the capitalist. But this supercession of the problem of alienation by the problem of class conflict does not negate the former problem but merely transfers it to another level, namely, to the arena of its social manifestation.[9]

The analysis of alienated labor in the form of capital and alienated self-relationship in the form of class conflict is directed at one purpose: the demonstration of how this alienation finally leads to its own nemesis where it is overthrown and transcended by communism. Marx wrote very little about communism itself. He evidently felt it was not something about which he could project economic and social forms, because it constituted a real transformation and regeneration of man beyond the present conditions of historical existence. Communist man would be so much a "new creation" beyond present historical man that one could speak of all of world history up to the final revolution as only the prehistory of man, while only at the revolution does the real history—i.e., the authentic life—of man begin.[10]

This transcendence of alienated labor in communism could only take place as the culmination of industrial development itself. Industrialization, pushed to its fullest expression, would both create such impoverishment of the worker and concentrate wealth in the hands of fewer and fewer capitalists that, as a social system, it would finally collapse under its own weight and lead to the uprising and expropriation by the workers. But capitalism, at the same time that it was creating the social conditions that would lead to its final overthrow, was also creating the material conditions of abundance and technological proficiency that would make possible the higher stage of human existence in communism. Both sides of this historical work of capitalism are equally important if we are to understand Marx's own thought as well as the continuity and discontinuity between Marxist and Communist party ideology.

The advent of communism in its true form is not to be confused with the mere communalizing of property. Such a crude notion of communism Marx speaks of with particular severity. The mere conversion of the property relation into public property owned by all does nothing to change the servitude inherent in the property relationship itself. It merely turns the state into an abstract generalized capitalist and generalizes the servitude of all men relative to this public capitalist. Such a view of communism as the leveling of all things and the transfer of the property relation from private to public hands is simply the uprising of general greed and envy. Like the community of women, the transfer of property to the public simply reveals in a generalized form the bastardization of man to things. Man's basic root problem of subservience to commodities is left unchanged, but simply transferred from private prostitution to the public prostitution of all.[11]

Rather, Marx insists that the emergence of true communism must go beyond mere socializing of property to the overcoming of the property relationship altogether, i.e., the self-alienation on which the property relation is based. Thus communism supposes a regeneration of man that abolishes all subservience of the world of things over the world of persons. We might express Marx's thought at this point in the language of Martin Buber by saying that the world of I–It relationships are overcome, and henceforth man and man and man and the world live in a direct communion of I–Thou relationships. This is not a Hegelian self-absolutization in which the domineering ego appropriates the whole world and thereby achieves its freedom because it alone now exists. Rather Marx supposes a return to finitude, to humanity, in which all egotistical, domineering relationships disappear. Man lives with man and with all the being of nature in a face-to-face relationship that demands only the relationship of being and overcomes all relationships of getting and having. Man's productivity, his creativity is no longer a means to anything but is simply a self-expression of his being, which is complemented by the self-expression of all other being. In effect the relationship of love replaces the relationship of competition, possession, and use. In lyrical terms Marx describes the birth of authentic communism:

Communism is the positive abolition of private property, of human self-alienation, and thus the real appropriation of human nature through and for man. It is, therefore, the return of man to himself as a social, i.e. really human, being, a complete and conscious return which assimilates all the wealth of previous development. Communism as a fully developed naturalism is humanism and as a fully-developed humanism is naturalism. It is the definitive resolution of the antagonism between man and nature, and between man and man. It is the true solution of the conflict between existence and essence, between objectification and self-affirmation, between freedom and necessity, between individual and species. It is the solution of the riddle of history. . . .[12]

Feuerbach's annulling of alienated divinity for the enrichment of humanity was only an abstract, theoretical philanthropy, while communism is the real and action-oriented philanthropy.

We have seen how, on the assumption that private property has been positively superceded, man produces man, himself and then other men; how the object which is the direct activity of his personality is at the same time his existence for other men and their existence for him. . . . The human significance of nature only exists for social man, because only in this case is nature a bond with other men, the basis of his existence for others and their existence for him. Only then is nature the basis of his own human experience and a vital element of human reality. The natural existence of man has here become his human existence and nature itself has become human for him. Thus *society* is the accomplished union of man with nature, the veritable resurrection of nature, the realized naturalism of man and the realized humanism of nature.

Such a description of communism as the resurrection of nature and the restitution of man to authentic humanity, in community with all men and nature, is scarcely less transcendent to the present historical condition of man's existence than biblical eschatology. It is both the rescue of man and nature from their bondage to alien powers and their transfiguration in a new communal life. How can the process of history itself produce this final transcendence of historical conditions? This was the "riddle of history" with which Marx struggled all his life. The transition from the final stages of capitalism to communism always remained vague and rudimentary in his thought. He supposed that capitalism was creating a proficiency that would provide the material basis for this higher stage of life in which man would be freed from producing for the sake of *means* of existence and could be free to create simply as the *expression* of his being. Thus some kind of highly developed technology that would free men for purely creative labor is part of his view of the historical work of capitalism.

Initially he believed that the socialist revolution could not take place until this high level of industrialization was fully developed within the womb of capitalism. At the same time, however, from a social point of view, capitalism dug its own grave by radicalizing the antithesis between objectivized wealth and the impoverishment of the worker. The middle class destroyed each other through competition and the larger part of their number sunk into the proletariat. Capital thus became concentrated in the hands of fewer and fewer capitalists and, by the creation of combinations and monopolies, the way was prepared for the expropriation of capital at a single blow. The proletariat became increasingly impoverished, and increased in numbers until they included virtually all of humanity. Armageddon was being prepared in the womb of the capitalist system, and, like the biblical apocalypse, the last stage of world history would necessarily sink to the lowest possible point before the final reversal. Then, in a sudden climactic act, they would rise up and expropriate the expropriators. The proletariat would become the new ruling class, but since it comprised virtually all humanity, the dictatorship of the proletariat was the direct rule of the vast majority of mankind over the few remaining exploiters, and thus was the highest expression of democracy. Under the dictatorship of the proletariat, the final acts of abolishing private property and the transition to higher communism were accomplished. As Engels describes it,

The proletariat siezes political power and turns the means of production into state property. But in doing this, it abolishes itself as proletariat, abolishes all class distinctions and class antagonisms, abolishes also the state as state.

The state hitherto had been the organ of the exploiting class. With the abolition of class, the state necessarily vanishes as well.

The first act by virtue of which the state really constitutes itself as the representative of the whole of society—the taking possession of the means of production in the name of society—this is, at the same time, its last independent act as a state. State interference in social relations becomes in one domain after another superfluous and then dies out of itself.... With the siezing of the means of production by society, production of commodities is done away with and simultaneously production is replaced by systematic definite organization. The struggle for individual existence disappears. Then for the first time man is finally marked off from the rest of the animal kingdom and emerges from mere animal conditions of existence into really human ones.

Man becomes the lord of nature, the lord of his own social organization, which no longer confronts him as an alien law, but becomes the result of his own free action. History passes over into the control of man.

Only from that time will man himself more and more consciously make his own history—Only from that time will social causes set in movement by him have, in the main and constantly growing measure, the results intended by him. It is the ascent of man from the Kingdom of Necessity to the Kingdom of Freedom.[13]

Marx in the *Economic and Philosophical Manuscripts* had seen that mere socializing of property could not of itself bring higher communism, because property itself was only the expression of the alienation of man. It was this inner alienation, the root of reified alienation in private property, that had to be overcome. Marx then asked the question: Why does man alienate his own labor?[14] This question remained unanswered, and instead Marx turned from the search for the Achilles heel of man within man's self to its analysis in social relations. By abolishing these social forms, at the moment prepared by history itself, the inner alienation of man would disappear as well. Thus Marx ignored his earlier insight that the external alienation was based on the inner one, and believed that the inner one could be overcome by abolishing the external alienation. This unanswered question stands as the unbridged gap separating the "Kingdom of Necessity" from the "Kingdom of Freedom."

To have pursued further the question of why man alienates himself would have suggested that man is involved in a dilemma within his own nature that he therefore cannot abolish. If the abolition of private property did not also overcome the inner dilemma of man, then this dilemma would simply take a new form of alienation and exploitation in any new society. Marx himself recognized the need to go beyond crude communism of

public property and state capitalism to the inward root of alienation itself, but he had no suggestion of how this was to be done
since, clearly, this inner alienation was not accessible and trans-
formable by a mere change of external social and economic conditions.

This dilemma of man, unsolvable within the critique of political economy, thus forms the point of mystification of Marx's
thought into an ideology, as that thought became the basis of the
ruling parties of actual socialist states. The dilemma of Marxism
as an ideology of a party in power was prepared before these
states came into existence. Already by the 1880s, as Marx lay on
his deathbed, the tide of economic development was disproving
his schematization. The capitalists were not getting fewer but
larger in number and diversifying over a variety of intermediate
classes. The working class was not becoming more impoverished, but was raising its standard of living and integrating itself
into the present system through political power and reform. The
chaos and desperate squalor of the working class and the revolutionary ferment of the 1840s that Marx had taken to be the death
throes of capitalism were increasingly seen to be merely its birth
pangs.

Edward Bernstein and other revisionists began to redirect
Marxism from the path of violent revolution to that of democratic reform. Marx himself began to have many second
thoughts, suggesting that the transformation from capitalism to
socialism might be one of gradual development rather than
apocalyptic nemesis and reversal. In the 1882 Preface to the new
edition of the *Manifesto,* he even suggested that socialization
might begin in a backward country like Russia, which could pass
over the stage of private property by going directly from peasant
communalism to communism. In the twentieth-century revolutions carried out in Marx's name, beginning with the Russian
Revolution in 1917, the principle that communism arises in the
most advanced capitalist nations as a leap beyond the highest
stage of industrial development was more and more contradicted
in practice. Instead, Marxism became an ideology of preindus-

trial states that were attempting to pass with rapid strides to industrialization by means of collectivized property and centralized control. In practice communism came to mean, not an advance beyond capitalism, but a way of introducing capitalism, bourgeois values, and life styles by political force. Not the higher communism, in which all alienated authority disappears, but the most authoritarian type of economic and political life in the form of state capitalism was the social reality of the Marxist states. But since this social reality was in fundamental contradiction to Marxian eschatology, and since the claim to be on the road to the achievement of this eschatology was the basis for the legitimacy of the party's power, the result was an extraordinary and intricate mystification of Marxism as a party doctrine.

From a purported science, Marxism became an orthodoxy to be accepted on the authority of the ruling magisterium, with the further complication that this orthodoxy had no higher revelation but had to be declared on authority to be purely scientific. Purges, executions, cries of heresy—all reminiscent of the inquisitional tactics of the medieval church—accompanied this effort of the party to shield from its own eyes the contradiction between its theory and its practice.[15] Like the early church, the party suffered from the ideological dilemma created by the "delay of the Parousia." The dictatorship of the proletariat became, in Lenin's revision, a dictatorship *over* the proletariat by the party. Even the party itself became increasingly subservient to its hierarchical leadership, until finally the dictatorship became concentrated in a single tyrannical figure. The party threw itself into the tasks of industrialization on the good Marxist faith that they were preparing those higher material conditions of existence that would lead to full communism and the withering away of the state. As full industrialization approached, however, the state showed no signs of withering away, but of ever tightening its dictatorial control. The material conditions of the society itself became ripe for liberalization along the lines of Western democratic socialism, but to take this road would have been to throw into question the orthodoxy on which the legitimacy of party control was based. Thus the party, far from relaxing its control, had to foment new crises and international triumphs in order to justify its own power. Every movement of liberalization from within was taken as a direct challenge to the authority of the party.

The dilemma of the party rested directly on the contradiction between its apocalyptic understanding of its role as the means of transcending the historical situation of man and its ongoing relation to history. Marx had seen the "revolution" as the beginning of a real transcendence of present historical conditions. When this Parousia failed to appear on anything like its proper schedule, the party was left up in the air, unable to relativize itself without losing its own claims to authority as the avant-garde of the new humanity. As its inherent credibility waned, it substituted the "adherence" of brute force and compulsion. Its greatest fear was that it would lose faith in itself, and to prevent this dawning of self-doubt, it had to force itself on everyone else. Deviation within the party hierarchy became the greatest and most dangerous offense.

Since 1956, with the death of Stalin and the confession of the Stalinist atrocities by the party leaders, a progressive demythologization of the Communist party has been taking place in Marxist thought. The repudiation of party-Leninism has sent the Marxist revisionists back to Marx's early writings in search of a Marxist humanism. The problem of alienation as the root of the later dialectic of the class struggle has been uncovered, and with it, the uncovering of the question that remained unanswered in the early manuscripts and buried in later Marxism: "How does it happen, we may ask, that man alienates his own labor?"[16] This is the still unanswered riddle of history wherein lies the key to the nonemergence of that higher communism that still eludes the world and mankind.

Part II

THEOLOGICAL REFLECTIONS

ON MODERN SOCIETY

Chapter 7

Crisis Theology and the Attack on Liberalism

The two decades that followed the First World War saw a sharp break with the liberal theology of the nineteenth century. Christian theologians drew back from the Christian Socialist and Social Gospel traditions and mounted a concerted attack on all the presuppositions of liberalism, progressivism, and evolutionary optimism upon which the Social Gospel had been based. The attack began in Europe, specifically among German-speaking Protestant thinkers, and did not come to the United States until about a decade later; however, it never wholly supplanted the indigenous American Social Gospel tradition that was so deeply rooted in American psychology and historical experience. In Europe the leader of the attack on liberalism and the founder of what became known variously as "crisis theology," "dialectical theology," or "neoorthodoxy" was Karl Barth (1886–1968). Barth's colleagues in this enterprise comprised a group of brilliant minds, whose names read like the roll call of the theological giants of recent Protestantism: Emil Thurneysen, Friedrich Gogarten, Emil Brunner, Rudolf Bultmann, and Paul Tillich. Barth concentrated his attack on liberalism on the foundational issue of revelation: the question of the source and basis of man's knowledge of and relation to God.

The target of the Barthian polemic was the mystical, pietistic "culture Protestantism" that seemed particularly exemplified in the line descended from Friedrich Schleiermacher (1768–1834). Schleiermacher had assumed a direct access of man to God through man's innate religious consciousness, in which revelation became naturalized and universalized. It was based on the universal nature of man's existence, which rested at its roots upon divine being. Man had only to go down to the depths of his inward self to make contact with God. The organ of our knowledge of God was this religious experience, i.e., the experience of the grounding of our existence upon the Being of God, or what Schleiermacher called "the feeling of absolute dependence."[1] Doctrine or revelational truths were simply our cultural representations of this primary religious experience. In practice Schleiermacher's approach tended to eliminate any tension between God's revelation and man's religious culture. God was domesticated in the depths of man's religious experience; revelation was domesticated in man's religious culture. As crisis theology saw it, such a view of faith could no longer speak to man from outside his present state of cultural awareness. It represented a closed system of revelation and culture without any radical transcendency that could break in from beyond man's field of consciousness to reveal truths and possibilities beyond them, to break apart present cultural assumptions, prophecy against them, and to open up a world beyond them.

For Karl Barth, as a young pastor in a Swiss Alpine town during the first World War, the defects of this liberal theology came as a personal, existential problem. A Christianity identified with immanent religious culture had nothing to say in the face of the breakdown and discrediting of that culture. Barth had received his theological nurture from the great liberal teachers of the turn of the century and also belonged to that generalized Christian Socialist milieu that found its source in Ritschl's restatement of the doctrine of the Kingdom of God. But he found that this theological and cultural currency left him without a prophetic word to preach in a time of profound crisis and reversal of that optimistic faith. In short, for Barth and others, the Great

War functioned as the concrete crisis that threw into jeopardy those notions of the innate goodness of man and the possibility of the progressive betterment of mankind through the extension of human rationality and education. Culture, reason, science— all appeared impotent to save man as the heartland of Christian society opened up and revealed a demonic chaos beneath.

Barth and the others that belonged to his circle set themselves to separate what cultural Christianity had joined together, to distinguish the spirit of man from the Spirit of God, to distinguish religious consciousness from revelation, to distinguish religion from the gospel, and to distinguish man's word from God's Word. In Barth's famous commentary on Romans published in 1919, he made his foundational assault on religious immanentism. Here he sought to reverse the whole psychology of liberalism by emphasizing the unbridgeable distance between man and God and the futility of all human ways to God through legalism, moralism, or mysticism. Revelation is God's Word that breaks in from the other side of this unbridgeable chasm after all of man's ladders to Heaven have fallen short and given way. Revelation is the story of God's ways with man, not man's ways with God. Only from such a vantage point can the gospel be recovered as a new creation, as a new word from beyond man's present situation that man cannot say to himself, but that comes to him from beyond the limits of his own aspirations and powers. Only such a truly new word can convert, revolutionize, and recreate him. Crisis theology thus took its stand on a radical recovery of the Reformation sense of God's transcendence, man's sinfulness, and the tension and antithesis between the gospel and culture. Thereby it raised the possibility of the church not simply as the ally of established culture and the bearer of the ideology of the society in religious terms, but the church as critic of culture and even a standpoint for protest and resistance against society.

Vis-à-vis society, crisis theology assumed a double possibility. On the one hand it could counsel a detachment of the gospel from the world, a rigid separation of revelation from culture that would seem to suggest an irrelevancy of the church to society, at least as far as the aspirations of society were concerned. But on the other hand, the dissolution of the ties between the church and culture might also suggest a prophetic relevancy of the church to society of the type that had been lost in the amalgamation of the church into the social currency since the time of Constantine. We must remember that the theology that sought to break the closed circle of revelation and cultural currency was also the basis for the Confessing Church of the Nazi era. It was that part of the German church imbued with dialectical theology, led by such figures as Dietrich Bonhoeffer and Barth himself, that refused to bow to the demand of the state to place the church's preaching at the service of Hitler's fascist national culture. The extent to which the church had indeed become the tool of the dominant society is revealed by the fact that the greater part of it, the "German Christians," did indeed go along with this amalgamation of Christianity and Nazism. But the Confessing Church, which went underground and formed a resistance movement to Hitler, testifies to the power that theology gained through Barth's insistence on the disparity between revelation and culture, between the word that God has to speak to man and the word that man wishes to hear.

Crisis theology was suited to such a resistance and gave Christians a new authority and confidence to challenge the power structure and assert that the gospel has a "No" of divine wrath that it must speak against the world. Crisis theology, through its reassertion of the radical transcendence of God and the incapacity of man to save himself through his own powers, thereby recovered an independent basis for revelation, apart from current culture, including the religious currency of the church. It sought to free the gospel to speak a new word to man from beyond his present situation. Therefore it was radical in the double sense of being a recovery of fundamental doctrines that had been eroded by liberalism as well as a basis for a revolutionary power of criticism of present social structures. Its orthodoxy did not have to be socially conservative in character, but could be the basis from which theology could continually challenge present human systems in the name of the Word of God. It did not legitimate but challenged the status quo. On this basis not only present secular society but the culture of the church itself was subjected to continual prophetic scrutiny.

Yet the principles of crisis theology, generated in a time of crisis and breakdown of the cultural synthesis, seemed to feed upon and demand this condition as a permanent presupposition. It seemed to flourish best in an atmosphere of catastrophe, when the church, deprived of all social currency, withdrew to the splendid purity of a gospel that stood ever poised to negate man's pretensions. Indeed, we might as well ask to what extent the antiliberal radicalism, which reigned not only in theology but in German political and cultural life in the late twenties and early thirties, did not generate something of a self-fulfilling prophecy of doom, which, by undercutting and eroding the fragile synthesis of liberal democracy, opened the way for the illiberalism of the right.[2] The absolutism of the transcendent standpoint tended to level and render irrelevant all relative differences between human systems and cultural syntheses and almost to prefer a totally demonic world against which the church could take its uncompromising stand to those ambiguous syntheses of man and God represented by "Christian culture" or "reformist liberal democracy." Thus crisis theology, powerful in the attack on cultural religiosity, was typically silent when it came to a new synthesis or reconstruction. Its eschatology tended to undercut and invalidate this or any possible cultural incarnations.

Barth's *Letters to East German Christians,* written after the Second World War,[3] illustrates the catacomb view of the social order that seems congenial to dialectical theology. Here Barth argues that it is preferable for a Christian to live under atheistic Marxism than under liberal democratic society in the West, because in a Marxist land the state makes no pretense of being an ally of Christian values, but frankly and openly reveals itself for what it is: the opponent of the gospel, the reign of the "prince of this world." In the West, however, society still poses as Christian; the state still pretends to be an ally of the church, converted to and furthering the ideals of the gospel. The church and the world have nothing in common; they live from opposite and antagonist principles of existence. Hence it is better to live in a state where this opposition is uncompromisingly revealed than in a state where it is masked by Christian culture. The church witnesses best to its own truth when it has nothing to do with such compromising syntheses, so it gathers out of the social currency, standing uncompromisingly over against it and living out of the salvation won for it by Christ.

In Barth's later theology the stress on the "No" of God's wrath was to an extent complimented by a greater stress on the answering "Yes" of divine grace. The two sides were implicit in the dialectical structure from the beginning, so the difference between the early Barth of the *Commentary on Romans* and the later Barth of *The Humanity of God* is a matter of emphasis rather than a change of thought.[4] Man could freely discard all of his ladders up to Heaven with their inadequacies because God had built a ladder from Heaven to earth in Jesus Christ and, in him, what is irreconcilable from man's side is reconciled from God's side. Yet this new emphasis on incarnation or condescension of God to man remained suspended in the unique person of Christ, whose victory was juridically "imputed" to mankind, but whose fruits might not enter into and transform history and the created universe itself into a "new creature" without flaunting that negative estimation of man's capacities that is fundamental to Barth's system.[5] This hiatus between Barth's Christology and anthropology is undoubtedly the root for that peculiar silence and abstention of Barthianism from any questions of the positive reconstruction of society through the gospel of redemption. The dialectic of fallen man and transcendent God remained permanently poised over against each other in a crisis relationship that could only throw down every synthesis that emerged between the two as the opening for a new idolatry.

Neoorthodoxy began to enter American thought only in the late twenties, and rose to significant influence with men like the Niebuhr brothers and Paul Tillich in the thirties. Here it rubbed hard against the traditional American religious activism and the tradition of alliance between Christianity and social reform. It is not surprising, therefore, that it was on American soil through a man nutured in the Social Gospel tradition that there should be the particular effort to demonstrate the relevance of crisis theology for politics.

Reinhold Niebuhr shared the active concern with politics characteristic of the Social Gospel tradition. He, too, was a socialist, a firm proponent of the rights of labor and a man who looked to the working class for a reconstruction of society. The Social Gospel tradition had its broadest effect on American society in the period after the First World War, when its spokesmen spearheaded the passage of the Prohibition amendment and the defeat of Al Smith for the presidency. But precisely in these two crusades it revealed all too clearly how social Christianity in practice tended to become reduced to the dominant currency of the Protestant cultural community. The Social Gospel had simply taken the Protestant churches for granted as the great central stream of an already achieved moral society, and they hoped to absorb industrialism into this same Christian cultural synthesis. In the Social Gospel the utilitarian and the idealistic were fused together. To pursue justice for the working class and democracy in industry was simultaneously to achieve a more personal, loving community. It never occurred to them that there might be any disparity between these two ideals, or that justice and equality might be achieved, not as an expression of a more loving personal society, but through even greater depersonalization. That revelation waited upon the works of twentieth-century Marxist states.

It was the particular task of Reinhold Niebuhr to break apart this fusion of political utilitarianism and personalist idealism, and to disabuse American Christianity of the idea that the gospel of love was also a social success philosophy. The thrust of Niebuhr's thought broke apart the Social Gospel fusion of political progress and the doctrine of the Kingdom of God.[6] In vindicating the autonomy of the gospel, however, Niebuhr also sought to vindicate the autonomy of politics as well, and to show that neoorthodoxy could provide a basis for political activism. The Christian could and should be involved in the political arena, but his politics should not be based on a utopian fusion of what was possible in the world with the transcendent goals that were possible only with God.

Niebuhr began his attack on the cultural synthesis of Christianity and social progress in the late 1920s as the high tide of the Social Gospel tradition was breaking. In his first book, *Does Civilization Need Religion* (1927), he particularly underlined the impotency of cultural Protestantism to lead American society to the redemption that the Social Gospel had promised. The Protestant churches could not reconstruct society from a socialist standpoint because they were themselves the captives of the capitalist classes, who had a vested interest in the present system and would oppose or subvert any radical reconstruction of society for the benefit of the workingman. The Social Gospel synthesis of religion and society was simply an expression of this identification of the church with the culture of the middle class. In the first chapter of *An Interpretation of Christian Ethics* Niebuhr sums up this theme.[7] The church had lost an independent ethic because of its identification of Christianity with modern culture, the culture of capitalism and liberal progress that was the creation of the bourgeois class. In order to recover an independent ethic that could issue in prophetic fruitfulness, the church had to break with this identification of the gospel and bourgeois culture and reestablish the sense of the tension between the historical and the transcendent. The idea of the Kingdom of God was the symbol of this transcendent ideal that could be truly relevant to history only when it was clearly distinguished and set over against all historical achievement. The Kingdom of God was the absolute future and ultimate goal that transcended every particular historical achievement. To fuse the Kingdom of God with the progress of history was to lose the prophetic tension between the two.

Modern culture is compounded of the genuine achievements of science and the peculiar ethos of a commercial civilization. The superficialities of the latter, its complacent optimism, its loss of the sense of depth and of the knowledge of good and evil ... were at least as influential in it if not more influential than the discoveries of science. Therefore the adjustment of modern religion to the "mind" of modern culture inevitably involved capitulation to its thin "soul." Liberal Christianity in adjusting itself to the ethos of this age, therefore, sacrificed its most characteristic religious and Christian heritage by destroying the sense of depth and the experience of tension, typical of profound religion. Its Kingdom of God was translated to mean exactly that ideal society which modern culture hoped to realize through the evolutionary process. Democracy and the League of Nations were to be the political forms of this idea. The Christian ideal of love became the counsel of prudential mutuality so dear and necessary to a complex commercial civilization. The Christ of Christian orthodoxy ... became ... [the] symbol of human goodness and human possibilities without suggestion of the limits of the human and the temporal—in short, without the suggestion of transcendence.

Failure to recognize the heights led modern Christianity to an equal blindness toward the darker depths of life. The "sin" of Christian orthodoxy was translated into the imperfections of ignorance, which an adequate pedagogy would soon overcome. ... There has been little suggestion in modern culture of the demonic force in human life, of the peril in which all achievements of life and civilization constantly stand because of the evil impulses in men may be compounded in collective actions until they reach diabolic proportions. ... Modern culture, both Christian and secular, was optimistic enough to believe ... that the forces of reason had successfully chained all the demonic powers.

It is by faith in transcendence that a profound religion is saved from complete capitulation to the culture of any age, past or present ... the more realistic portion of the church which recognizes the weaknesses and limitations of a liberal culture, inclines to substitute a radical Marxian world view for the discarded liberal one. ... The attachment of radical Christianity to Marxian viewpoints ... represents a gain in religious as well as moral realism. But Marxism is as naturalistic as modern liberalism. It is therefore deficient in an ultimate perspective upon historic and relative moral achievements. Both liberalism and Marxism are secularized and naturalized versions of the Hebrew prophetic movement and the Christian religion. But Marxism is a purer derivative of the prophetic movement ... its dialectic is much truer to the complex facts of history than the simple evolutionary process of liberal naturalism. It has a better understanding of the depths of evil which reveal themselves in human history, and hence its philosophy of history contains a catastrophism, completly foreign to the dominant mood of modern culture, but closely related to the catastrophism of Jewish prophecy. ... In common with apocalyptic religion it transmutes an immediate pessimism into an ultimate optimism by its hope in the final establishment of an ideal social order through a miracle of history. ... The weakness of the Marxian apocalypse is that its naturalism betrays its utopian fantasies. Whenever naturalism appropriates the mythical symbols in the religion of the unconditioned and the transcendent, to make them goals in time and history it falsely expects the realization of an absolute ideal in the relative temporal process. ... Utopianism must inevitably lead to disillusionment. Naturalistic apocalypse is unable to maintain the moral tension which it has created. ... Both liberal and radical naturalism have moral beauty when they are waiting for their "word" to "become flesh," but they are betrayed into lethargy and hypocrisy after the incarnation. ... The significance of Hebrew-Christian religion lies in the fact that the tension between the ideal and the real which it creates can be maintained at any point in history, no matter what the moral and social achievement, because the ultimate ideal always transcends every historical fact and reality.[8]

In Niebuhr's well-known book, *Moral Man and Immoral Society* (1932), he tries to clarify the distinction between the ethic based on the transcendent principles of the gospel and the ethic appropriate to social morality. The ethic of love or *agape* is the ethic that rests on the transcendent principle of God and his Kingdom. Love is the transcendence of self-interest and a self-giving to the needs of the brother without regard to one's own reward. This ideal of selfless love finds its only complete expression in the selfless love of God for man in Christ. Christianity prescribes that men love each other in the same manner as much as possible, but this transcendent ideal for man cannot be a norm for society. Groups, by their very nature, cannot live selflessly. The very basis of group life is self-interest and self-perpetuation. And the highest goal that groups can achieve is not love but justice. Justice is a rationalized balance of power against power, self-interest against self-interest, resulting in each group receiving proportionately equal opportunities and satisfactions. To pursue social reform on the basis of love is utopian, and prevents the employment of realistic strategy for the realization of those proximate goals of justice that can be realized in society. The clear distinction and separation of the transcendent ethic by which man is ultimately judged from those proximate ideals that society in history can achieve is both a vindication of the autonomy of politics from impossible idealistic hopes and the delimitation of a sphere of achievement within which a realistic political ethic can be employed.

An example of Niebuhr's construction of a realistic political ethic tailored to approximatable goals rather than impossible hopes is found in the chapters on "Justice through Revolution" and "Justice through Force."[9] Whether a Christian could accept violence in the pursuit of social justice was a topic hotly debated in the thirties. Niebuhr broke with the idealists of the Fellowship of Reconciliation (FOR), resigning from its membership, over this issue. The FOR was the leading organization for liberal Christian idealists in this period, and Niebuhr's rejection of pacifism and, by implication, all efforts to apply an absolute ethic of love to politics, was symbolically his break also with the Social Gospel mixture of politics and the ethics of the "Kingdom." In opposition to the leading lights of the FOR, Niebuhr endorsed the possibility of a just use of violence, even to the extent of armed revolution as morally defensible in situations of extreme oppression. Justice is a higher value than peace, and in the efforts of oppressed groups to throw off their shackles, the righting of wrong is more important than the preservation of peace at any price.

Playing the pragmatist, however, Niebuhr argued that violence is essentially a tactic relative to its context. It should be used judiciously, not indiscriminately, and in a way not likely to result in a massacre of the oppressed by the oppressors. For example, in the case of the rise of the Indians against British imperialism at this time, Niebuhr judged that the Gandhian tactics of nonviolence and passive resistence were preferable to force. He also speculated on the possibility of such tactics of passive resistance as an appropriate tactic for a revolution among the American Negroes as well. However in both cases, Niebuhr suggested the appropriateness of passive resistance, not on absolutistic grounds, but on the pragmatic political grounds that a minority group or a disarmed colonial people could not expect to win in a violent confrontation with the oppressor; hence the tactics of passive resistance were, for them, a more possible scheme for attaining social justice within existing power relationships.

... the differences between violent and non-violent methods of coercion and resistance are not so absolute that it would be possible to regard violence as a morally impossible instrument of social change. ... The advantages of non-violent methods are very great but they must be pragmatically considered in the light of circumstances. Even Mr. Gandhi introduces the note of expediency again and again and suggests that they are peculiarly adapted to the needs and limitations of a group which had more power arrayed against it than it is able to command. The implication is that violence could be used as the instrument of moral goodwill, if there were the possibility of a triumph quick enough to obviate the dangers of incessant wars. This means that non-violence is a particularly strategic instrument for an oppressed group which is hopelessly in the minority and has no possibility of developing sufficient power to set against its oppressors.

The emancipation of the Negro race in America probably waits upon the adequate development of this kind of social and political strategy. It is hopeless for the Negro to expect complete emancipation from the menial social and economic position into which the white man has forced him merely by trusting in the moral sense of the white race. It is equally hopeless to attempt emancipation through violent revolution.

As nonviolent tactics that might be developed for the self-emancipation of the Negro in America, Niebuhr suggested boycotts against banks that discriminate against Negroes in granting credit, against stores that refuse to employ Negroes while catering to Negro trade, against public service corporations that practice discrimination, and refusal to pay taxes in states that offer an inferior education to Negroes. Niebuhr expressed confidence that such a campaign, once developed, could be waged successfully because of the particular spiritual gifts of the Negro race. It waited only upon an effective leadership that would fuse the aggressiveness of the new, younger Negro with the strength of character of the older Negro.[10]

Niebuhr's polemic against cultural Christianity led him to a certain emphasis on catastrophe during the early thirties. Such dwelling upon crisis and imminent catastrophe had its source in meditation upon the Great War, but for Niebuhr this emphasis was sharpened especially by the Depression. Niebuhr, still a socialist and somewhat under the spell of Marxian rhetoric, believed that Western capitalist society stood on the brink of a catastrophe that was built into the very logic of its economic structure. In *Reflections on the End of an Era* (1934), he discusses the brink toward which Western society is headed and asserts that America, although temporarily shielded from this catastrophe that was overcoming the West by her particular social fabric, would not ultimately escape this common fate. However, Niebuhr's vested interest in this prophecy of doom was not primarily Marxian. He also had a theological interest in catastrophism that survived his critique of the utopianism of Marxist socialism. He believed that Western liberal society was based on an illegitimate faith, a naturalistic modernism which immanentized and domesticated the transcendent and identified the Absolute, the Spirit of God, and the Kingdom of God with its own cultural spirit and historical goals. He looked to the Western man's experience of catastrophe to unmask this domestication of deity and to discredit the implicit theology of liberal progressivism.[11] Catastrophe would operate in the history of society as the tragic experience of the personal despair of one's own capacities to save oneself by good works operated in personal conversion, as the revelation of man's sinfulness, his finitude (crisis theology tends to identify the two), and the unmasking of the pretensions of self-salvation. It would act as an experience of judgment to open up the heart of Western man to the workings of divine grace and the life of faith.

What Niebuhr was trying to say to modern Western man is that the conditions that have frustrated the building of utopia since the French Revolution are not accidental or surmountable by greater rationality. They will not be overcome by better organization and planning, better education, or by some evolution that will take place in human nature to make the future radically different from the past. The conditions that frustrate the realization of the Kingdom of God on earth are fundamental and permanent factors in the nature of man, in the nature of creaturely, finite temporal existence. The very structure of man's historical existence is a dialectic of nature and spirit, of necessity and freedom, of finitude and transcendence. It is the nature of man in history to remain unfinished, incomplete, always on the move. Every attempt to find a final resting point within history is always an apostasy of the spirit and a betrayal of man's freedom for transcendence. Man domesticates the absolute and identifies his particular achievements and goals with the absolute Spirit of God and the ultimate Kingdom of God only at the price of losing the true transcendent and so by losing his own freedom. When man believes that he has the final Word of God in some cultural system or social structure, he freezes these vehicles into static authorities and so loses his ability to hear the real Word of God that comes to him in the freedom of the Spirit, "blowing where it lists." When man identifies the goals of technological development and democracy with the Kingdom of God, he fails to appreciate the relativity of these structures. He sets up a golden calf out of his particular historical conditions and falls into bondage to it. These deities then reveal their hollowness at times of catastrophe to all the hopes pinned upon them. Indeed, the things that earlier generations identified with the absolute often appear. absurd after their hour is done. It seems laughable that thousands of Anabaptists would have seriously thought that the New Jerusalem was about to be revealed in the town of Münster in the sixteenth century or that the Prussian state could be thought to be the final goal of the historical dialectic in Hegel's philosophy of history. These fusions of the absolute with relative points of achievement or aspiration in history are properly called idolatry. Indeed, for neoorthodoxy, idolatry became the central symbol of the persistent sinfulness of human nature and history. History is a trail of idolatry, a long tale of man's self-absolutizing of his finite cultural expressions and his preference of bondage to idols to the freedom of the sons of God.

The way to life for man, then, is through repentance. Only by freeing himself from his idolatry, through that historical grace that overturns and dissolves the credibility of these idols, can he be delivered to a new life that can transcend the works of his own hands. The source of this grace is the absolute transcendent, which goes beyond history, beyond every finite achievement. When man can live in faith, trusting in God alone, the chains that bind him to his past can be broken and he can be delivered to a continual openness to the new, to the future, to genuine historic existence. This is the structure of human existence that emerges in Niebuhr's more developed statement in *The Nature and Destiny of Man* (1941). Here it becomes evident that the human dilemma is not between moral man and immoral society. Man is not moral and society immoral, but rather the social, historical context is where man projects and expresses his root immorality. But this immorality is rooted in his nature and the structure of his historical existence, not in society as something distinct from human nature. The relation of the ethic of justice and the ethic of love is worked out on a higher level.

In *Moral Man and Immoral Society* one was left with the suggestion of a somewhat static separation of love as the private morality of man and justice as the attainable ethic for society. Now the dialectical interplay between the two ethics is more developed. Justice stands for the proximate ethic toward which man works in history, but love is the transcendent ethic that is never fully achieved in history and is ever being thwarted by the egoism of man. But this transcendent ethic is of the greatest historical relevance as the expression of the dissatisfied "still more" that stirs men up beyond their proximate goals and achievements, opening up visions of ever greater goals. The ethic of love corresponds to the ideal of the Kingdom. It cannot be completed in history, but it stands as a mandate upon history. It is the vision of ever greater possibilities in the light of which our present works are judged and found lacking. It is the critical standard by which our justice is judged. The Social Gospel fusion of politics and the ethic of the Kingdom are dissolved, but only in order to give them a new relationship. The human spirit and God's Spirit, democracy and the Kingdom of God are related dialectically rather than by a naturalistic fusion. The Kingdom is the absolute standard that reveals the sinfulness of our proximate achievements, stirs us to dissatisfaction with them, frees us from attachment to them, and gives us the power to move beyond them. This is what it means to "live by faith, not by works": to be constantly willing to leave our works behind us and count them as worthless, and thus be ever open to new possibilities.

The traditional doctrines of original sin, faith, and salvation by grace alone are interpreted in crisis theology as a key to human freedom in history. Implicit in this view is a corporate and secular perspective on the meaning of salvation that would lead thinkers such as Friedrich Gogarten to formulate this interpretation of Christian doctrines as a "secular" theology.[12] Freedom for futurity can be said to be the fruit of the neoorthodox message about redemption. Confrontation with the absolute, expressed in the demand of the ethic of love, the Spirit of God, and the Kingdom of God, shatters man's idolatrous self-absolutizing of his finite achievements. But when man accepts this judgment, he finds a power to relativize his own works and thereby be restored to a life that is ever free for the future and its possibilities. This existential structure of neoorthodoxy was to be particularly developed by the Bultmannian school in Germany, but the basic direction can be found in Niebuhr as well.

Niebuhr turned this critique of social religiosity against not only bourgeois liberalism but against Marxism as well. The truth of Marxism lay in its prophetic judgment of capitalism and its sense of the catastrophic failures of this society. Its truthfulness lay on the side of apocalyptic wrath leveled on man's present exploitive relationships and its projection of an ultimate future hope to be achieved through profound revolution. In this respect it reproduces the structure of biblical apocalypticism. But on the other side of the revolution, Marxism falls into illusory self-deception because of its naturalizing of the final eschatological "revolution." For this reason it inevitably turns totalitarian and despotic through absolutizing the new regime that emerged from the revolution. The classless society and the withering away of the state belong to the ultimate paradisaic hopes. This transcendent ideal, by its nature, goes beyond the conditions of finite historical existence. Therefore the party as the transitional means to the final state becomes itself finalized. The Kingdom never comes, but instead the party replaces it, taking into itself the finality and absolutism that belongs to the Kingdom. Marxism, for Niebuhr, revealed more than ever that the crisis of modern Western society was a crisis of confusion of politics and religion, and in Marxism it was brought to its ultimate despotic expression by raising absolute politics into absolute religion.

The answer to this dilemma of Western man, for Niebuhr, was the old-fashioned prescription of repentance, not just as a private act, but as a social, historical conversion. Repentance means faith in an absolute that is truly transcedent to history. The God who is beyond history, who ever transcends our historical processes, is the only God who can save us. Only the radically transcendent can keep us from being trapped by our works, can relativize even the boldest of our answers, and thereby keep us constantly open to the future. Does this process itself move toward any goal? For Niebuhr and the neoorthodox this process itself generally had no goal. It was the permanent situation of man within history. The transcendent stood over against history in a dialectical relationship with it, but, by the very nature of historical reality, there could be no final synthesis of the two. The function of the Kingdom is not to literally come but to keep us from stopping where we are. "History does not solve this basic dilemma of human existence, but simply reveals it on progressively new levels."[13]

Chapter 8

The Mood of the Resistance:
Rebel Against God

If the experience of the First World War was the occasion for theological attack upon the naive optimism and progressivism of the liberal tradition, the experience of the Second World War was more cataclysmic still. That experience was truly one of hell on earth, spiritually as well as literally. A demonic abyss seemed to open up and engulf the foundations of Western civilization itself. Those who lived through this period and most deeply assimilated the import of its horrors found it difficult to find any values at all on which to stand and from which vantage point to initiate a critique of this society that had been brought to the denouement of total calculated destruction of life and value in the bomb and the extermination camps.

Albert Camus, perhaps more than any other thinker, caught the mood of this denouement of the Western tradition. He especially retained an impeccable honesty in the face of this madness and tried to look face to face at the variable modes of the insanity, to probe it to its roots, to discover its sources and contradictions and to come out of this descent with some modest resurrection that could again sustain life on this planet. Camus's first experimental principle by which he sought to wrest value for man in a world rushing toward destruction was the absurd, which he explored in *The Myth of Sisyphus* (1942). Here Camus examined the possibility of suicide as a response to the incoherence of the world. But this revolt was discovered to be itself based on a demand for value, unity, and coherence. The absurd is born of the contradiction between human expectations and the condition of the world. The question is whether this contradiction renders existence untenable.

Camus insists that we face and take upon ourselves the burden of the dilemma of the absurd. The leap of faith both in a transcendent God and a heavenly future hope evades the reality of the dilemma. But suicide is also a way of evading it. In the contradiction between his demand for coherence and the insufficiency of reality, man finds that he is affirming a value inherent in his own nature, but a value that the world does not confirm. Man therefore finds that he is a stranger in the cosmos. To live is to take up the burden of affirming the dignity of human life in a world that remains cold and unresponsive to this value. Affirmation of human dignity in a world without God or transcendent principles to answer and ground this affirmation—this is the stark humanism that Camus maps out as the path for man to follow in the conclusion of the absurdist investigation.

I leave Sisyphus at the foot of the mountain! One always finds one's burden again. But Sisyphus teaches the higher fidelity that negates the gods and raises rocks. He too concludes that all is well. This universe henceforth without a master seems to him neither sterile nor futile. Each atom of that stone, each mineral flake of that night-filled mountain, in itself forms a world. The struggle itself toward the heights is enough to fill a man's heart. One must imagine Sisyphus happy.[1]

The theme of man's revolt against the absurd through self-affirmation is taken up into a larger principle in the study of rebellion, *Man in Revolt* (1951). The investigation of man in revolt raises the question of the value of individual life to the level where it includes the value of all life. The rejection of suicide implies the rejection of murder as well, and the affirmation of the life of the neighbor in that of the self. In his essay "Remarks on Revolt" (1945), Camus makes clear the transition between the absurdist line of thinking and the later philosophy of revolt.

Here at last we have the first bit of progress that the spirit of revolt brings to bear on a reflection which was first penetrated with absurdity and the apparent sterility of the world. In the absurd experience the tragedy is individual. With the movement of revolt it is conscious of being collective. It is the adventure of all. The first progress of a mind struck by this estrangement is to recognize that he shares this estranged condition with all mankind.

In the first chapter of *Man in Revolt,* Camus develops this theme. The movement of rebellion is shown to be implicitly an affirmation of the equal human dignity of all mankind, not mankind as an abstraction or a universal essense, but all living human beings. The rebellion of the oppressed against the oppressor is an implicit value judgment. It is a declaration that there is a limit of one's toleration of debasement and that there are values in oneself that must be respected. "You have gone too far"; this is the declaration of the slave that initiates the revolt. The slave begins his revolt by discovering a value in himself that he will not allow to be violated. As long as the slave remained silent under oppression, it could be assumed that he acquiesced and accepted the judgment of the oppressor that he was no more than an object to be used. To revolt, therefore, is to overturn this assumption and declare a value in oneself that defines one's dignity and declares a limit to use by others. Revolt is born as a moment of self-awareness. It corresponds with the birth in the slave of a sense of his own personhood. This value of himself, once grasped by the slave, grows until it becomes all-important, more important than his own life. It becomes a value for which he would be willing to die. So the movement of revolt moves toward universalization and implies a value in human nature that is larger than the individual and confronts and limits the invasions of the oppressor.

Here Camus shows his independence from existentialist ontology by postulating the existence of a universal human nature that is the common ground upon which all men, including the oppressor, have a community. The affirmation of the dignity of man that is inherent in the individual movement of revolt against oppression postulates the common humanity of all men, and this commonality sets the limits to men's dealings with one another. It is in terms of this community of man that the rebel demands respect for himself. This also suggests that any movement of revolt that expresses itself by impuning or negating the humanity of the oppressor undermines the ground upon which it itself stands, and delivers the affirmation implied in rebellion over to destructive nihilism. The slave rejects the master as a master, not as a man. But in so doing he postulates a common humanity on which all men stand and that is the ground of his own self-affirmation.

Rebellion, then, is the breaking of silence between man and man. It is the beginning of communication for the first time, and this communication also points to the common humanity between slave and master. "If men have no commonality to which they can refer, then man is incomprehensible to man." In demanding the recognition of this commonality, the slave is actually demanding rather than resisting order, for the oppressive situation is not true order but systematized disorder. The revolt implies a demand that all recognize a common principle and a rejection of the disorder of a universe in which some men have rights of personhood while others are treated as objects. The slave does not demand to be given a value that he does not presently possess, rather, he affirms that he already has this value, and he demands recognition of it on the grounds of a universal truth equally applied to all.

It is not enough simply for the slave to recognize his own worth. "Human being" is precisely that form of being constituted by mutual recognition. Camus refers to Hegel's distinction between conscious and unconscious nature as the difference between human nature and that of the inanimate object.[2] It is the distinct human mode of existence as distinct from the existence of the thing or the animal; it exists only in and through the recognition of another consciousness. "He must be acknowledged by other men. All consciousness is, basically, the desire to be recognized and proclaimed as such by other consciousnesses. It is others who beget us. Only in association do we receive a human value, as distinct from an animal value."[3] In the master-slave relationship such mutual recognition is denied. The slave recognizes the master without himself being recognized in turn (this is why slaves typically know so much about their masters while the masters know nothing about their slaves). In being denied a corresponding recognition, the slave is used as an object. The master's prestige is built up from his recognition by their consciousnesses, while he recognizes none of them in return. But this also makes for a truncated existence for the master as well. Even the universal obedience accorded the absolute monarch finally reveals this hollowness. "Obey," said Frederick the Great to his subjects; but when he died his words were, "I am tired of ruling slaves."[4] Because the master is recognized in his autonomy by a consciousness that he does not recognize as autonomous, his own autonomy is purely negative. Mastery thus reveals itself as a dead end. Rebellion stands as the basic act of awareness by which mutual recognition and autonomy is demanded. Rebellion in the realm of human affirmation plays the same function as the *cogito* in the realm of thought: "I rebel, therefore *we* exist."

Nevertheless rebellion has not been universal in all times and places, but has in fact occurred in the West, more specifically, in that Western secular society where the sacred has been dethroned. In a world sanctioned by sacred mythology, inequality is blessed by the gods and receives its reward in heaven. Consequently the question about inequality is cut off at the root. Only in a secular society where the sacred myths of inequality have been dethroned, and where the theoretical equality of all men conflicts with the actual enormity of their inequality, does the spirit of rebellion arise. The value raised in revolt is universal and essential to human nature, but it is brought to the surface only under the historical conditions of secularity. The overthrow of the sacred corresponds to a demand for a human order in which all actions and relations are justified in reasonable terms. This is the dividing line between the two basic periods of human history: the period of the gods, in which every act is grace, and the period of secular man, who has overthrown the gods and whose spirit is rebellious, i.e., self-affirmative in his proper autonomy. There is no possibility of a return to the world of the sacred once this transition has been made. The world of rebellion, which has no recourse to grace, is irretrievably our present historical actuality.[5] But rebellion itself is creative, or rather, "revelatory" of values. Consequently it is within this experience that we must find the values for our times. Revealed within the movement of rebellion itself, a new ethic must be found without absolutes or divine sanctions that can stand as a self-sufficient humanism.

Man's solidarity is founded upon rebellion, and rebellion in turn can only find its justification in this solidarity. We have then the right to say that any rebellion which claims the right to deny or destroy this solidarity loses simultaneously its right to be called rebellion and becomes, in reality, an acquiescence in murder. In the same way, this solidarity, except in so far as religion is concerned, comes to life only on the level of rebellion. And so the real drama of revolutionary thought is announced. In order to exist man must rebel, but rebellion must respect the limits it finds in itself—a limit where minds meet, and, in meeting, begin to exist. Revolutionary thought, therefore, cannot dispense with memory. It is in a perpetual state of tension. In studying its actions and results, we shall have to say each time whether it remains faithful to its first noble promise, or if, through indolence or folly, it forgets its original purpose and plunges into a mire of tyranny or servitude.[6]

Camus thus announces the subsequent purpose of his study of the historical experience of Western man in revolt. He examines first the spiritual revolt of man against heaven, and then his translation of this revolt into historical action in the period since 1789. Camus poses the question to this cultural and historical experience of modern Western man: Did he remain faithful to the original value of human solidarity uncovered by the act of rebellion or did he betray it? Camus stands at the moment of the denouement of Western man's search for secular salvation, and sums it up in a penultimate judgment. Since we, from a vantage point of some twenty-five years more of historical experience, are trying to make a similar appraisal, it is not inappropriate to summarize his judgment here.

The rebel against Heaven opposes the author of an unjust universe in the name of a demand for order and justice that he feels in himself but finds unreflected in a disorderly and unjust universe. The metaphysical rebel is not an atheist so much as he is a blasphemer. In the name of justice he denounces an unjust Creator and stands in judgment upon the Maker of a universe in which evil, catastrophe, and senseless slaughter reign. The metaphysical rebel begins by confronting God as an equal and denouncing Him. But such a stance suggests that the principle by which God may be denounced is itself superior to God, and so the metaphysical rebel becomes a dethroner of God. He throws down the throne of an evil and murdering Creator in order to become the creator of his own values. Metaphysical rebellion begins with a cry for justice and order and an affirmation of solidarity with creation against an unjust and tyrannical Creator. But these values are now seen as having lost support in the "grounding" of the universe, and so the rebellion against Heaven, instead of being the beginning of autonomous values, tends to fall into cynicism, despair, and loss of all values.

Camus's most important examples of the rebel against Heaven are the Marquis de Sade, Ivan Karamazov (of *The Brothers Karamazov*), and Nietzsche. De Sade is the metaphysical rebel for whom the denunciation of God the Murderer becomes a mandate for unbridled libertinism. But unbridled license proves to be incompatible with human liberty, and so the darkly fertile imagination of the imprisoned Marquis de Sade conjures up a convent and prison-house discipline turned upside down as the arena of boundless lust. The logic of total libertinism creates a rigid system of absolute subjugation of the victims. All recognition of personal contact between sadist and victim must be banished. The objects of sadism must never be allowed to appear as persons. The logic of oppression demands total dehumanization and objectification of those who are used. The rebel against the impersonalism of Heaven capitulates even more narrowly to the same relationship between himself and those subjected to him. Not only does the victim lose all personhood, but the sadist is finally frustrated in his own quest for pleasure by this relationship. Sex and murder intermingle until finally a rule of total slaughter engulfs the whole picture, leaving de Sade alone and defiant in an empty universe.

Ivan Karamazov begins and remains a far more human rebel. Much more clearly than de Sade, Ivan revolts against God in the name of all humanity. Faith in immortal life is rejected because no future Heaven can compensate for the evil and injustice of the world. No salvation that is not a salvation of all men can cure Ivan of his anger. Grace is rejected in the name of justice. The tears of little children and the slaughter of innocents cry out from the earth and thunder against heaven, and they cannot be satisfied by any gratuitous condescension from above. No sop of grace can make up for a child's tears. But Ivan's revolt also turns nihilistic, and he who trembled at the thought of children's tears becomes the accomplice of his father's murder. The murder of the father is both the murder of God and the annihilation of the ground of all values. Ivan does not descend into nihilism as deeply as de Sade. His rejection is far nobler and more searching in its compassion, but he fails to find a new affirmation that can balance his negation.

Nietzsche, Camus feels, was the most constructive thinker among the metaphysical rebels and a figure who has been misunderstood and misused by later nihilism and Nazism. Nietzsche does not seek to kill God. He simply finds Him dead in the hearts of his contemporaries. He constitutes himself as the announcer of the death of God that has already taken place. The death of God means that the efforts to find redemption through world renunciation are a sin against the earth. On these grounds Nietzsche angrily rejects Christianity. But God having died, the universe itself takes His place, not an ideal universe, but the universe as it is in all its suffering and inconsistency. It is the suffering, insufficient universe that actually exists that is the only divinity and the ground of man's being. It is through identifying with the world as it is, as a true son of the earth, that man becomes the creator of a new ethic. Man himself, as the one who springs from and participates in the suffering divinity of the world, becomes its conscious expression and the creator of the new values. But only the strong can take up this challenge. It belongs to the supermen who stand on their own ground to take up the challenge of ethics in a world after the death of God. But this compassionate, affirmative side of Nietzsche was ignored by his followers, who were attracted only by the idea of the superman. So Nietzsche, too, became another source for modern nihilism and Caesarism.

Beginning with the French Revolution metaphysical rebellion in literature and philosophy passes into metaphysical rebellion in action. The third part of Camus's book concerns itself with the story of historical revolution. The anarchist and terrorist rebels, particularly in nineteenth-century Russia, express this rebellion in the form of personal heroics and self-immolation. The Jacobins of France are the starting point for this story while its conclusion is found in the denouement of Marxist revolution in Russian totalitarianism. Nazism also figures as a theme in this movement, but, based as it was on totally nihilistic principles, it could be nothing more than a passing nightmare that came and littered Europe with corpses and then disappeared, leaving no lasting memorials of its presence except a hastily buried question mark in the souls of a generation. Because of its total nihilism, Nazism offers less of a challenge than Marxism, which is built upon the positive principles of rebellion, but represents the tragic corruption and contradiction inherent in rebellion that makes it possible to erect a deep and lasting system of slavery upon the erupting demand for freedom and justice. So it is Marxism particularly that poses the question mark over the head of all revolutionary movements of modern times.

The movement of historical rebellion from 1789 to 1917 exhibited a twofold assault upon Heaven. First there was the destruction of God and then the death of transcendence in the form of eternal principles. The dethroning and killing of the absolute monarch ruling by divine right was the primary historical expression of the murder of God. The Jacobins dethroned and killed God in the person of the representative of divine sovereignty on earth, but they did so in the name of transcendent principles: reason, justice, liberty, fraternity, and equality. God was thrown down, but the eternal principles remained in Heaven as the guide and ground of action. "Reason and transcendent principles remained as the residue of the old transcendent divinity which the Jacobin revolutionaries" disincarnated, cleanly detached from any relation to the earth, and "like a balloon, sent back into the empty sky of great principles." Kings had been killed before, but only to be replaced with other kings, while the revolutionaries in 1793 intended to empty the throne forever and express the total overthrow of divine rule itself by killing its incarnation.[7] Rousseau's *Social Contract* was the philosophical underpinning of Jacobin revolution as Hegel was to be for the Marxist revolution. In Saint-Just's speech at the King's trial it was clear that the King must die in the name of the social contract.[8] Yet the doctrine of the General Will, which cannot be known simply by polling the "will of all," but was discerned by the charismatic understanding of the popular leader, became the opening for a new and more rigorous form of terror and boundless despotism.

The philosophy of Hegel completed the death of God by the destruction of transcendent principles. The eternal truths that had remained as the fixed stars in the Jacobin heaven were now hurled into the immanent dialectic of history. Thereby the principles ceased to be a criterion and basis for action and henceforth became the goal of action and the end of the historical process. Consequently the revolution sold out the present for the future. To work for present amelioration even became counterrevolutionary. Men were commanded to endure indefinite and even worsening misery, injustice, servitude, and murder for the sake of that liberty, fraternity, and equality that would be produced out of the historical dialectic in some paradisaical future. Since the transcendent principles no longer remained in Heaven as continual sources of judgment upon the methods of action but had fled into the future as goals, there ceased to be any criteria by which the present conduct of the revolution could be judged. Any means, even unlimited murder, were justifiable to bring about the goals of the revolution. Lenin could advocate every kind of falsehood, terrorism, and death for the sake of the revolution, where, ultimately, truth and justice would prevail.

When all the economic predictions of Marx had been overturned by the course of events, it was precisely this messianic, apocalyptic nihilism that remained. Marx rejected all gradualism and progressivism. There could be no attempt to build a future utopia from the gradual amelioration of present conditions. All reformism was a sop to capitalism, resulting in a postponement of the day of reckoning. Trade unionism and reform of working conditions were opposed because it was believed the great reversal could only come when present conditions had been brought to their lowest nadir. This was not realism, however, but apocalypticism. The progress of modern societies show a continual improvement of the conditions of the working class through trade unions and parliamentary reform, whereas Marxist countries have totally suppressed free trade unionism to a system of state capitalism, which represents the final expression of industrialist subordination of the worker to the system of production. The revolution does not quickly lead to the worker's paradise; rather, the emergency repression of all freedom demanded by the revolutionary process itself becomes indefinitely prolonged until it itself emerges as the new system. The revolutionary process becomes institutionalized, and yet continues to justify every form of servitude and murder in the name of that final state of freedom and justice that is to be its outcome. Thus, as in Christian history, Marxism begins in the announcement of the apocalyptic day of wrath and the speedy advent of the Kingdom of God, but ends in the indefinite prolonging of the era of the church, which can justify all persecution and suppression of liberty in the name of that final liberation that never comes but to which it is the exclusive gateway.

Camus, however, does not recognize the older version of this

tradition, but finds its root in the Hegelian dialectic, which immanentized the transcendent principles in the historical process
and thereby deprived the process itself of a present judge. Camus
sees Leninism as the expression in action of this Hegelian logic,
which turns values into historical goals and banishes all criteria
of values by which the means of the revolution are judged, only
to announce the reappearance of these values, as if by magic, as
the future outcome of this trail of murder and slavery. Thus
Marxist revolution, although aiming at the future reign of all
good things, justifies a nihilism toward human values in the
means by which the revolution proceeds.

These are the major outlines of Camus's critique of the perversion of the spirit of revolt. The rejection of disorder fails to grasp
and uphold its affirmative principle and so descends into nihilism and unprincipled Caesarism. Camus then sketches the basis
for a critical reconstruction of the philosophy of rebellion as
distinct from this corrupt revolutionary ideology. The first principle lies in the rejection of murder. Murder can be justified in
no way by the spirit of rebellion, because rebellion itself rests on
the affirmation of the solidarity of all men. To say "I rebel" is to
say "we exist." It is to recognize a value inherent in humanity as
the ground upon which one's own rejection of injustice rests. Any
rebellion that is carried out through murder undermines the basis upon which the rebellion itself is grounded, and this ultimately falls over into the extension and totalizing of all those
conditions of injustice against which one originally rebelled.
Thus the spirit of rebellion does not demand unlimited aggran-
dizement of the rebellious self at the expense of all others, but
it demands precisely the spirit of moderation that is born of
respect for others. The rebel must take his stand not upon a
supposed future value of men that is to be brought about through
revolution, but upon the present value of man that is the ground
and basis of rebellion. He rebels against injustice, not in order
that *we shall be,* but because *we are.* Whenever the "we shall be"
grows so domineering as to cancel out the "we are" and becomes
a rationale for oppression and murder, then the rebel has lost the

basis of his original rebellion and has no alternative but to die himself.

Camus identifies this spirit of limit and moderation as the Mediterranean spirit as opposed to the Germanic spirit of historical absolutism. It is also the classical spirit that looks to nature as the guide as opposed to the Judeo-Christian spirit that exalts history. The authentic philosophy of revolt is not a philosophy of unlimited means for the sake of an absolute end; it is the philosophy of limited means for the sake of an uncertain end. It rests on fidelity to the present, to nature, to one's existing fellow men. It is rebellion that must be carried out in the spirit of uncertainty and risk, a risk whose consequences the rebel must take upon himself and not project upon others. Its purpose must be to extend, even by a little bit, that currency of hope, justice, and brotherhood which is presently found among men, knowing that the outcome always remains uncertain and the battle for a better world has no end. Man must dedicate himself not to the utopian end but to the present duration of history. He must work in the moment and in the place where he is to lessen, even if by a little bit, the suffering of children. Anything more grandiose than this is contradictory, and ends in rationalizing excess contributing to the growth of institutionalized evil. To be human we must refuse to be God; only in this way can we serve the earth and our fellow man. Real generosity to the future lies in giving all to the present.

He who dedicates himself to history dedicates himself to nothing and, in his turn, is nothing. But he who dedicates himself to the duration of his life, to the house he builds, to the dignity of mankind, dedicates himself to the earth and reaps from it the harvest that sows its seed and sustains the world again and again. . . .

The men of Europe, abandoned to the shadows, have turned their backs upon the fixed and radiant point of the present. They forgot the present for the future, the fate of humanity for the delusion of power, the misery of the slums for the mirage of the eternal city, ordinary justice for an empty promised land. They dispair of personal freedom and dream of a strange freedom of the species; they reject solitary death and give the name of immortality to a vast collective agony. They no longer believe in the things that exist in the world and in living man; the secret of Europe is that it no longer loves life. Its blind men entertain the puerile belief that to love one single day of life amounts to justifying whole centuries of oppression. That is why they want to efface joy from the world and postpone it until a much later date. Impatience with limits, the rejection of their double life, despair at being a man, have finally driven them to inhuman excesses. ... For want of something better to do, they deified themselves and their misfortunes began. These gods have had their eyes put out. Kaliayev and his brothers throughout the entire world, on the contrary, refuse to be deified in that they refuse the unlimited power to inflict death. They choose and give us an example of the only original rule of life today; to learn to live and to die, and, in order to be a man, to refuse to be a god.

At this meridian of thought, the rebel thus rejects divinity in order to share in the struggles and destiny of all men. We shall choose Ithaca, the faithful land, frugal and audacious thought, lucid action, and the generosity of the man who understands. In the light, the earth remains our first and our last love. Our brothers are breathing under the same sky as we; justice is a living thing. Now is born that strange joy which helps one live and die, and which we will never again postpone to a later time. On the sorrowing earth it is the unresting thorn, the bitter brew, the harsh wind off the sea, the old and the new dawn. With this joy, through long struggle, we shall remake the soul of our time.[9]

Camus's resolute agnostic Hellenism would seem to be at the farthest possible distance from dialectical theology, with its Barthian thundering against man in the name of the majestically transcendent God. Yet, when we look at these two movements more deeply, ignoring certain linguistic underpinnings, but analyzing the life style that they would decree for man, we see a rather startling similarity. From opposite ends of the idological spectrum they seem to come around and meet each other on the nether side of the circle. Dialectical theology rejects the Greek world for the Hebrew. Camus rejects the Hebrew world for the Greek. Dialectical theology takes its stand on the sinfulness of man and the earth and the radical transcendence of God. Camus proclaims the goodness and beauty of natural man that emerges in rebellion against transcendence. Man's hope lies in a firm faith in the nonexistence of God and all aspirations to divinity and heavenly worlds beyond this earth. Yet these contradictory foundations nevertheless converge on a similar conclusion. For dialectical theology, the radically transcendent principle that can never be domesticated in history acts as a permanent limit upon man's megalomania. It cuts off and strikes down his Heaven-storming and returns man to his finitude. Humanized man is man living by faith, rescued from his idolatry, and returned to his creaturely limitations. Grace is the power to relativize his works and accept the temporality of his frame of reference. The absolute acts as a guarantee of man's limit. In a peculiarly similar way, Camus's empty sky and absence of God operates as a guarantee of man's limit. The nonexistence of God cuts off his Heaven-storming and throws man back upon his finite existence, where he must make his own values in a radically finite, temporal frame of reference.

For both points of view the source of all man's evil is his self-absolutizing of his historical projects. Redeemed man is man returned to the earth to live day by day, no longer identifying his being with an absolute behind him or ahead of him, but living in that creaturely present that is rescued from both diabolic depths and divinizing heights. Dialectical theology hurls man back to earth with a wrathful judgment, while, for Camus's man, Heaven-storming simply bursts in thin air like an empty bubble; in either case man is enjoined to repent of his self-deifying folly and return to where he is, to live day by day in faithfulness. Even Camus's choice of his cultural locus is less in opposition to dialectical theology than might be imagined. Both choose the early classical period of their respective traditions against the "Hellenistic" flight from this earth to a heaven above and beyond. Dialectical theology implicitly prefers the thoroughly mortal man of the original Hebrew tradition as against a Persianized apocalyptic hope of later Judaism (and early Christianity!). Camus returns to that measured and balanced man of Hellenic classicism as against the orientalized flight of the soul of the world of eternal Being of neo-Platonic Christianity (which Camus, being a good Catholic, assumes to be the Judeo-Christian tradition!). In both cases a prescription of acceptance of limitations and a humanizing through return to finitude is the path to salvation for a generation meditating upon the disasters wreaked upon the modern earth by the boundless aspirations of modern man.

Chapter 9

Secular Theology: Man, History, and the Church

In the mid-1960s the theme of secularity burst upon the popular theological scene as the keynote for analyzing the situation of Christianity in the modern world. The new twist to this theme, however, was that secularity was described not primarily as the situation of *the world* in which Christianity found itself, but as the method of describing the way in which Christianity should live in this modern world. Secularity was now taken as a theological keynote in itself, not as something alien to Christianity and the church, but even as the product of Christian faith and, understood properly, the modality of life demanded of us by Christian faith. All this was in startling contrast to the still dominant way of using secularity vis-à-vis the church, as the enemy and rival of Christianity that sought to challenge and displace it with a worldly, nonreligious view of man. Moreover, secular theology did not deny that secularity was worldly and nonreligious, but, instead of viewing it as the red flag of combat, it was potentially seen as the authentic expression of faith, whereas otherworldliness and even "religiousness" were judged to be contrary to Christian faith. To understand this remarkable about-face among churchmen, we must return to Karl Barth and the school of theology that arose through and around him, for the contemporary theological celebration of the secular takes its parentage directly from Barth, however much they may disavow each other.

Barth's insistence on the radical transcendence and "otherness" of God was aimed at cutting all links between God and the world by way of *analogia entis,* and hence of abolishing all remnants of a metaphysical view of God that could be erected upon a natural theology. The gospel is to be clearly distinguished from all metaphysical systems and worldviews. This means the final repudiation of the alliance of Christianity with Hellenism upon which traditional Christian metaphysics was based. It means that the God of Abraham, Isaac, and Jacob can, in no way, be described in terms of Being, Highest Being, Ground of Being, or any other such ontological category, because all such views fail to take seriously the meaning of creation and the radical otherness of God from the nature of the world. All such metaphysical descriptions of God bring Him down from his true transcendence into a system of being in which He is a part, a thing among other things, a level of being within the cosmos, even if this is understood as the highest level of being that grounds all other levels of being and from which they spring. In other words, all systems that describe God as Being are implicitly emanational rather than creational in their view of the relationship of God to the world. God and the world are described within a closed system of metaphysics in which worldly being evolves out of divine being by way of some process of emanation, and therefore God, instead of being truly transcendent, is immanentized so that God and the world form one cosmos understood on levels and ontological relationships with each other.

Barth insists that the Christian doctrines of God's transcendence and the created status of the world demand a breaking of all such ontological descriptions of the relation of God and the world that would place them within the same closed metaphysical framework. This radical otherness of God expresses the freedom of God and necessitates a description of the relation of God and the world in terms of faith and grace, not in terms of relational structures of being.

The end of metaphysical worldviews also brings to an end all confusion between the gospel and religion. Religion, in Barth's language, depends upon a metaphysical analogy of being between God and creatures whereby the creature, by some process of detachment and contemplative ascent, rises to unity or direct communion with God. Such a view rests on the underlying assumption that there is a ladder of being between God and creatures by which the creature can thus ascend to God by proceeding down into the depths of his own being. Barth sets out in his pioneering commentary on Romans to kick away this ladder. Man can in no way relate himself to God by some ascent through his own being to its source and foundation. The true relation between man and God is the reverse of this religious worldview and system of sanctification. Man does not stand in a right relationship to God by descending into the depths of his own soul and thereby rising to Heaven as though he were himself, in the depths of his own being, eternal and divine. Rather, he relates to God by remaining on the earth where he is and accepting his finitude and creatureliness as the status in which God has made him and that is always and everywhere "very good." Man does not ascend to God; God comes down to man and becomes present as the true man and the head of authentic humanity and creation in Jesus Christ. It is precisely as the power to be authentically human, rather than as the power to be supernatural or religious —in the sense of rising to some status beyond that of creation— that man experiences the meaning of Christ. God is not being, but *presence.*[1] God is the presence of transcendence that breaks apart all of man's metaphysical and ideological constructs by which he seeks to deify himself and his historical projections and expectations. The presence of God breaks apart these religious and pseudo-religious structures, restoring man to where he should be; to authentic creatureliness and finitude. The God of Barth, therefore, is the iconoclastic God, the God who overturns man's religious idols and self-projections. He is the redeemer precisely as the restorer of man to his authentic created existence. Barth thus set the basic themes for the theology of secularity as a description of God as transcendent presence rather than Being and a description of the redeeming work of God as iconoclastic and humanizing. He firmly established the polemic against the confusion of the gospel with religion and Christian theology with metaphysics.

These themes have been continued by numerous disciples of Barth. They found tentative new extensions in the famous notes on worldly theology that Dietrich Bonhoeffer made in prison.[2] But the theologian who, from the thirties on, has systematically tried to develop the implications of the gospel for secularity, has been Friedrich Gogarten. Although little of his work is as yet in English, Gogarten's influence has come into American theology through various interpreters, such as Harvey Cox in his widely read *Secular City* (1965).[3] Secularity, as Gogarten understands it, is basically the historical working-out of the doctrine of justification by faith alone. Secularization is implied in both the doctrines of creation and of redemption. The doctrine of creation, as contrasted with metaphysical systems of the universe that enclose God and the world in a fixed system of being, means that the world is genuinely open and provisional. The system is not fixed; the future is not fixed; but it is open to be created out of no prior materials. This is the meaning of genuine creatureliness, finitude, and authentic historical existence. But man ever seeks to evade this freedom of the sons of God by seeking to draw God down as the ground of some fixed system that thereby receives a divine ground and sanction and makes the future predestined. Redemption is experienced existentially most especially as iconoclasm. Redemption is made possible through the overturning of those sacred order and systems. It is the overcoming of the world construed as an emanation of divinity. But this iconoclasm as the work of God's wrath against man's idolatry is, at the same time, the work of God's grace. It is the restoration of man to that open situation that is the proper stance for authentic human existence.

Secularity is the expression of what it means to be restored to our original created nature. But this created nature is found in freedom and lordship over the world. It means that man is responsible for the creation of history rather than simply a product of a divine cosmos. To be authentically human is to be freed from all enslavement to closed worldviews and to stand before a future that is open and undetermined as one who is ever ready for new life. Man is no longer encompassed by the world, but he is responsible for it. He is free from all world systems that would enclose him, including ideological systems that seek to predetermine and possess the future in a fixed system of predictions. Man is free and responsible for the world because the future is open and radically undetermined. This is the situation into which Christian faith releases man. To walk in this world as a free man without succumbing to some new system of security is what it means to walk by faith alone. Existence by faith is the basis for authentic historical existence, and so secularization is the basis for the emergence of genuinely historical man. Secularity and historicity are the descriptions of the modality of Christian life that is given in faith, or, put the other way, faith is the freeing power for secularity and historicity. This is the modality of authentic human existence into which we are restored by God's grace. Consequently the coming of the gospel spelled the end of sacred societies and the overthrow of the mythological view of nature. Nature and society are demythologized and desacralized. With Christian faith we have the beginning of the end of mythological man and the advent of secular, historical man.

It is the radical transcendence of God that guarantees this freedom of man; this secularity and historicity. This means that God cannot be described as behind us as the divine ground of our being, but he is ahead of us as the "God who comes." The coming of God into the present from beyond shatters the past being of the world, opening a path to new possibilities that man has obstructed through his closed systems of life and thought. God is "ahead of us" in the sense of being a power for self-transcendence that is ever coming to us from beyond where we are. Only because God is beyond us can he be a power of self-transcendence for us. This view leads Gogarten to describe God as the "coming one" and the "Beyond in our midst," and to speak of God as the "presence of futurity." A power for the future becomes the central category for describing the locus of man's experience of God. This is how the transcendent is "present" for man in his concrete historical life.

For this reason eschatology has become very important in post-Barthian and post-Bultmannian thought. Eschatology existentialized becomes a way of expressing the doctrine of God experienced as the end or limit of the world. But eschatology is not used as a symbol of a future goal of a historical process. Such a notion would be a way of immanentizing the eschatological just as the description of God as Highest Being immanentized God. The *eschaton* is God or the transcendent, experienced as the ultimate future. The eschatological God is not the source or goal of a world system emanating or developing through some straightline process. The eschatological God is that transcendent otherness that comes in judgment upon such closed ontological or historical systems and restores us to freedom without a divine ground and before an undetermined future.

Gogarten's use of a future-oriented, eschatological language is to be sharply distinguished from nineteenth-century liberalism or from Hegelianism, which incorporated the idea of the Kingdom of God into a system of immanent progress toward a final perfecting of the world. The *eschaton* does not refer to a distant Kingdom that comes about through an evolutionary process; it is God himself encountered as the end of history. God is the end of history, not as processional goal, but as the present shattering of the closed world that man has built up and in which he has become enslaved. The concept of God as the *eschaton* is thus used existentially as the experience of the overturning of closed systems of life. It is a power for freedom that applies not only to our past, but to our past projections of our future as well. It overthrows our past self-image and the expected goals projected out of that self-image, restoring us to humility, which is to say, freedom and faith to walk in creative insecurity. God or the presence of the *eschaton* is symbolized by the future, not because

God is the conclusion of any past projection of ourself upon the future, but because historically we experience the future as the arena where our self-images and their self-projections are shattered. Therefore, to encounter the future is again and again to encounter some radically new thing that acts iconoclastically upon our finalized self-image. This is why the future is the special modality of our experience of God. The coming of the future is our historical experience with transcendence both as judgment and as grace. The future comes as judgment in the sense of overturning our systems. It comes as grace by acting as a power that forces us to make constant reevaluations of ourselves. Such an encounter, if received in faith (i.e., by those who can "hang loose" from themselves) can become a power that can ever more deeply teach us how free we can be.

Existential theology of the post-Bultmannian school (in which Gogarten himself stands as an older member) particularly likes to describe God as "event," and to talk of salvation as the "eschatological event." God is experienced as an eschatological event in the sense of a "happening" of the unexpected which overturns our self-image and challenges us to "hang loose from ourselves" (live by faith alone). This is what Gogarten means by the Pauline categories of the Old Adam and the New Adam. The Old Adam is the mythic, metaphysical, religious, or ideological man. He is the man who clings to closed systems of life grounded on sacred orders encompassing Heaven and earth, the beginning and the end in a single system in which all is fixed and there is nothing new under the sun. The New Adam is the man of faith, for whom this history of man's self-projection and this world of fixed systems has been brought to an end and who lives an open, provisional existence of radical freedom.

What precisely does all this complex demythologizing of religious language really mean? In order to give a vivid historical example of the sort of "event" that is being pointed to we might look at the present shattering of the American self-image by the impact of historical contingencies. The United States has been operating in a foreign policy that has led to various interventions around the world, most especially to that of the Vietnam War, out of the projection of a certain self-image and a certain set of expectations and goals based on that self-image. The self-image set the United States up as the champion of democracy and self-determination against "godless communism." American foreign policy was based on pragmatic calculations of self-interest only on a secondary level (the same might be said of Soviet foreign policy). These calculations of self-interest, however, were themselves based on an implicit kind of messianic self-image of the American mission around the world. Our might necessarily must be right because our might was *Good.* It was founded upon good principles and directed toward good ends.

But the Vietnam War turned out to be far different that the calculations based on these expectations. Both our might and our right have been, thereby, radically called into question. Our might is very fearsome indeed, but it has nevertheless not succeeded in overwhelming a ragged army of guerrillas shod with sandals made out of our airplane tires and armed with weapons stolen from our soldiers. Our might has proven astonishingly impotent before the determination of a band of ideological nationalists filled with a superior confidence in the righteousness of their own cause. Our ability to kill has collided unexpectedly with their superior willingness to die. Consequently our might has proven the creator of a sickening slaughter of everyone—soldier and civilian, child and old man—and the harbinger of an almost total and irresponsible chaos that strips the land itself of its capacity to reproduce while being unable to advance any significant distance toward the accomplishment of our goals. In this fearsome happening, the rightness of our might has thus been called into question. Before the determination of the Viet Cong and North Vietnamese and the evident corruption and lethargy of the regime we support, our claims to be the champions of self-determination grow increasingly hollow. In short, the experience of the Vietnam War has been an iconoclastic event for the American self-image, with its idolatrous messianism and identification of might with right.

So far this encounter with the unexpected is simply a challenge and an implicit judgment. Whether we can accept this calling into question will determine whether the implicit judgment becomes an opportunity to free ourself from our present presuppositions and find a new freedom for the future. A new future cannot be found without a willingness to stand in radical judgment upon our self-mythology and the structures of self-aggrandizement built upon it. Grace and judgment are bound inextricably together as death and resurrection, Good Friday and Easter Sunday. It is in this manner that the event character of historical experience becomes a concrete expression of the theological categories. The happening of the unexpected that comes to us from beyond where we are is, concretely, our experience of God and our encounter with the *eschaton*. The event calls our present existence into question. This is the historical experience of judgment. It becomes an opportunity for the surrender of our presumptions and the gift of a new life beyond the mythologies that have confined the old self. This is the historical experience of grace. To be empowered to accept it is the historical meaning of faith. To learn to live by faith is, therefore, to learn to live historically. This does not imply a divinizing of history, but on the contrary, a desacralizing of history and an acceptance of finite, creaturely existence as the sphere of provisionality and openness to temporal contingency. Faith is the mode of living in radical freedom, freed from predetermined patterns of expectation and ready for the gifts of life.

The future is one modality of experiencing the transcendent. Gogarten and other followers of this school also use another model of the experience of transcendence that has perhaps been even more important in the formation of recent theological language. This is the experience of transcendence through interpersonal encounter. The transcendent Thou or Otherness of God finds its concrete expression in the encounter with the Thou or the radically "other" subjectivity of the other person. Like the historical event, the event of the other person encounters us as a concrete experience of transcendence. Idealistic systems of philosophy always try to annihilate the autonomy of the other person and incorporate the whole world into a system that emanates from the self or the one central ego, just as metaphysical systems of being try to annihilate the genuine otherness of God and incorporate God into a single system of being with the world. But the doctrine of creation and grace demands an understanding of God as the Thou who is truly other and who breaks through the closed world of the ego, presenting us with an experience of a self that is truly beyond and other than ourself and that cannot be incorporated into and subjugated to our ego. The encounter with the Thou challenges and calls into question the world built upon the projection of our own ego.

Here again there is a good example in contemporary American social experience: the emergence of Black Power and black consciousness in the black American. The black man has characteristically been the slave in America. Even after formal civic servitude was abolished, the habitual relationship between white and black persisted. The black man was the invisible man, the man with no ego, no subjectivity, no identity of his own. He had no name of his own, but only those names given to him by the white man. He had no identity of his own, but only the identity given to him by the white man. Until recently the whole image of the Negro in American society was nothing else but a pastiche of stereotypes created by the white man's projection of himself and his own attitudes upon the black man. The black man was the dangerous beast, about to revenge himself for centuries of physical abuse and exploitation of himself and his women by some violent attack upon the white man's wife or sister. Or the black man was the shuffling, smiling watermelon-eater who bobbed at the end of the white man's yo-yo, an amusing pet, a fall guy for superior humor, never a person to be confronted and taken seriously in his own right.

When the civil rights movement began, it attracted a great deal of white support because, in part, it did not radically challenge this traditional role of white toward black. The black man still, in effect, stood hat in hand at the white man's back door asking for admittance. Humanity was still achieved basically by sitting next to, relating to, and being accepted by the white man. The black man had no humanity of his own to assert, but only one dispensed by association with white humanity. Then came Black Power, a complex movement for political and economic rights, but its core is psychological and cultural. The center of Black Power is black consciousness, a rejection of the servile incorporation of the black man's soul into the white man's soul and the black man's assertion of his own autonomous subjectivity. Thus the subjectivity of the black man now encounters the closed humanity of the white world as a shattering iconoclastic force, calling into question the whole world that has been made in the image of the white man's self-projection. In the black consciousness, the white ego is broken and forced into an encounter with a black subjectivity that is truly beyond, autonomous, and transcendent to the white ego. For many whites, this judgment has been an offense. They have not been able to tolerate the black man's transcendence of the white ego. But for others who have experienced and accepted this judgment, black consciousness has been the event of grace, a breakthrough to a new understanding, a new humility, and the possibility of authentic dialogue between black and white people for the first time.

The idea of the Thou or the otherness of the neighbor as the concrete expression of a transcendence beyond one's own ego that challenges one's self-enclosed world, calling one to repentance and to a loving, selfless style of life demanded by authentic relationship, has been a central theme for the existentialist school of theology. Not only Gogarten, but also Bonhoeffer, Brunner, Buber, and others give it a central place, and it becomes for them the chief model for constructing their Christology. The neighbor is where the otherness of God meets me, therefore the neighbor represents Christ. The neighbor represents Christ made present for us. This does not mean that the neighbor becomes metaphysically divine. The existentialist understanding of Christology rejects metaphysical Christology just as it rejects metaphysical divinity. The neighbor represents Christ as the specific manifestation of a transcendent self that breaks through one's self-enclosed egoism and calls one into a new, open relationship to the other man, but the neighbor in his own existence remains completely finite and human. This is the way the Chalcedonian formula of Christ as wholly God and wholly man is to be understood, not as a metaphysical doctrine of substances, but as the understanding that, in the gracious event, the neighbor becomes the place where God meets me while the neighbor himself remains wholly human. The mediation between God and man has been removed from all sacred settings, persons, and sacraments, and become the secular sacrament of the encounter with the neighbor that cuts across our self-enclosed egoism and opens us up to a new possibility of an open, loving relation with our fellow man. In this Christ event the alienation of man and man is overcome and the possibility of community is founded.

Secular theology has had its greatest impact on popular theology through its implications for ecclesiology. Perhaps in no area has its iconoclasm been greater or its insights more intriguing to many than the opening up of the idea of a secular theology of the church. A very sizable proportion of recent theological writing reflects this secular ecclesiology.[4] This theology has as its context the effort to get the church out of the old fixed postures of an institution that was originally formed in another, different society, and now stands in an anomalous relationship to a new society that arose by negating and bypassing the worldview of the church in Christian society. In order to recover for a new age the tension and relationship between church and world, it becomes necessary to overcome these inherited boundary markers and stand in the world as it now is. By taking as the point of reference modern technological society with all its wonder and danger, its threat and its promise, Christians ask how this world can be a place where men can communicate, be reborn, and become that New Creation for the sake of which God came into the world. It is no longer in terms of Roman world empire, feudal chivalric society, the rural life of the farmer, or even the town life the bourgeois that we have to ask where the church is happening, because these worlds are gone or all but gone. Rather it is in terms of technopolis and metropolis, the Cold War and the arms race, developed nations and the Third World, napalm in Vietnam and riots in American cities that we have to ask how the world can become a New Creation. This is the arena in which men must overcome alienation and be led into new forms of reconciliation.

The church in its biblical definition is "the community of the New Creation." This new creation is creation itself redeemed and made new. Therefore if the church is the community of the new creation it is not basically a special ecclesiastical world of its own raised up in a sacred social structure beyond the life and destiny of creation; it is simply creation and human society considered from the point of view of where God's activity is renewing the world. Secular society proposes a radical testing of the church that dissolves the claim of that structure that calls itself by ecclesiastical titles to any monopoly on being the place where this renewal is most likely to be happening. If the church is human society considered from the point of view of God's renewing action in history, then it is basically a secular reality. Wherever the Spirit is stirring the waters and groups of men are on the rise to overcome alienating and false modes of existence and form a more authentic life of brotherhood, that is where the church is. This view supposes that the Holy Spirit as the presence of Christ and the power of the New Creation is not somehow the captive of ecclesiastical ministries and channels, but is a free spirit abroad in the land and whose presence is recognized wherever alienation is being overcome and human community built up.

This demythologizing of the church, however, has been a source of considerable confusion because it seems as though the obliteration of the distinction between the sacred and the secular also dissolves the more fundamental distinction between the church and the world in the sense of the line between the arena of redemption and the arena of false, fallen modes of life. In order to clear up this confusion it is necessary to clarify certain distinctions that the writers of this school seem to leave unclear. We must define the authentic theological distinction between church and world as principles of life and differentiate this distinction of theological principles from the institutional line between ecclesiastical organizations and those nonecclesiastical or so-called "secular" organizations that encompass the greater part of our social life.

It is important to realize that many of the social forms that we think of as secular were once seen as sacred. Economics is usually thought to be the very epitome of the secular, but in ancient societies the economic realm was under a special relation to the sacred. Much of the religious cultus was built around the economic cycle of sowing and harvesting. The rebirth of the land from winter was the expression of the victory of the gods over death and chaos and the recreation of the world. The economic cycle was linked to and dependent upon the sacred rites that assured its continuation. In ancient Babylon the land was owned by the gods, and administered for them by the temple priesthood. Economic life was not only dependent on sacred rites, but directly controlled by sacred personnel set aside for that purpose.

Political life until recently was a sacral function. Political power emanated from God and was vested in the sovereign, who became thereby the representative of God's sovereignty on earth, if not an incarnation of God in person. The assumption is that political power is close to divine power and an expression of divine power on earth, and he who exercises it is more than a man. The realm of the sacred then is not divorced from what we call secular processes but is a way of lifting up those secular processes to point to their source and meaning. The process by which this sense of the depth and divine grounding of secular processes was lost in modern times is often called secularization. Secular theologians are fond of attributing the source of this process to Christianity itself, but this assertion leaves out several vital links in the history of modern secularization.

Secularization does appear in the sphere of modern Christian culture, but only some seventeen hundred years or more after the

birth of Christianity and as a byproduct of technological forces
and rationalist philosophies that arose both outside of the Christian worldview and in opposition to it. Historically secularization
arose in the West as something experienced by the church as a
losing rear-guard battle against the rising tide of rebellion that
deposed the church from one sphere of influence after another.
Economics, politics, education, culture, and finally even the
family were secularized by a process of deposing the influence of
the ecclesiastical institution and pushing it back step by step
until finally it appeared primarily in the privatized form of personal relationship with God that lay in the realm of subjective
feeling, having lost contact not only with the social structures
that surround the remainder of life but even the larger intellectual world as well. This is what is popularly called churchgoing
in modern society.

The ancient distinction between sacred and secular had nothing to do with any such distinction between society and life processes at large and an institution that ministered to men only in
a private, subjective dimension. Rather, the social and cosmic
processes were themselves sacred from the point of view of their
ultimate source of power and efficacy. The modern shrinking of
the sacred to a privatized institution and the enlarging of a secular sphere to cover the rest of life appears peculiarly within
Christian societies in the West, but one that by no means flowed
by a straightline development out of the church itself. The primitive church understood itself in an apocalyptic light as a revolutionary beachhead of a new world and saw itself as standing over
against worldly society that was demonic and ripe for destruction. Yet by the fourth century it had become so acculturated in
this society that it could amalgamate with it and create a sacred
society based on a fusion of Christianity with classicism and
Roman world empire. In modern times the church has been gradually displaced from this role of religious sanction and guardian
of society and has retreated to a diminishing sphere of influence.
But since the religious institution retained its claim to be the
sphere where man was related to God, this diminishing sphere

of influence meant that less and less of man's life was seen as related to God. Relation to God shrunk to the proportions of the Sunday gesture, and the rest of man's life was seen as secular. Secular then meant self-grounded and self-sufficient, having no source or goal in any transcendent realm. The theologians who want to celebrate the secular do not really want to celebrate this kind of secularism but to combat it. This is what they call secularism and is to be sharply contrasted with biblical secularity. What they want to do is to dissolve the delimiting boundaries of church and religion that relegate these to an insignificant corner of man's life and to recover the biblical sense of the gospel as a message about the whole of life. In Bonhoeffer's words:

> How do we speak in a secular fashion of God? In what way are we in a religionless and secular sense Christians, in what way are we the *Ekklesia,* "those who are called forth," not conceiving of ourselves religiously as specially favored, but as wholly belonging to the world? Then Christ is no longer an object of religion, but something quite different, indeed and in truth the Lord of the world. . . . I would like to speak of God, not on the borders of life but at its centre, not in weakness but in strength, not, therefore, in man's suffering and death, but in his life and prosperity. . . . It is not with the next world that we are concerned, but with this world as created and preserved and set subject to laws and atoned for and made new. What is above the world is, in the Gospel, intended to exist *for* this world.[5]

Secular theology thus, in a certain sense, might be considered neocatholic, and certainly one of its precursors, F. D. Maurice, would have preferred the word catholicity to secularity. There is the desire to recapture the view of the ancient Patristic theologians of the gospel as a message about all mankind and all history, about society and creation in all of its aspects. But recent secular theology also wants to avoid the past mistake of relating social structures to God by making them sacred, holy, and immutable. They want to recover a sense of the universality of the catholic vision but without its sacralism. And so they would distinguish secular catholicity from older concepts of Christian society in this way. Ancient sacred societies and worldviews, including that one formed in the name of Christ, were built on an emanational view of the universe. The world arose by flowing out of the divine and imitating it as an image founded on a divine likeness. Divine reality was the primordial pattern of which creation was the image and likeness. Society, too, shares the immutability of the divine by constituting itself in the image of the primordial pattern. Christian sacralism took over this view from Platonizing gnosis of the ancient world and overlaid it upon the biblical doctrine of Creation.

The secular theologians wish to banish the last remnants of this emanational view of the relation of the world and society to God. This is what they mean by the desacralization of the world. The world must be desacralized in order to reestablish the biblical view of the relation of the world to God. Christian secularity rests on the biblical view of God's radical transcendence and is thus radically different from a self-enclosed secularism. When we say that the world is Creation, we say that it is truly finite and historical. It is not finished or predetermined in its movement, but provisional and open-ended. This is the modality of being of the creature as one who is contingent and yet free. The creature stands before the Creator with his own distinct being and personhood to make his own decisions maturely in response to the life given it by the Creator. As a radically temporal being he is not bound back to some eternal pattern of being that fixes his possibilities. He exists precisely as Becoming. He is a distinct, nondivine reality responding to the work of the Creator by living responsibly in his own temporal frame of reference.

Secularity, then, means radical creationalism. It is used to break down the last remnants of Hellenism and sacralism and to overcome the impasse created by the retreat of the church's frame of reference to a privatized segment of man's life. Just as Bonhoeffer spoke of the cosmological God being edged out of the world, so the secular theologians would edge the ecclesiastical institution out of the world, but only to release its original meaning and so interpret all of reality back in relation to Christ and the redemptive community. This relation to God does not abolish but sustains the finitude, historicity, and temporality of the world.

In order to complete this picture, however, we have to relate this understanding of Creation to redemption as well. Man who is created free and called into responsibility is also free to be irresponsible, to surrender his freedom to the works of his own hands and so to fall into alienation and a false, demonic mode of existence. God then acts as the redeemer of Creation, rescuing man from this alienated form of existence and restoring him to responsible freedom. This fall of Creation comes about precisely through the effort to abolish the free finitude of created being for divinization, to become "like gods." But this effort to abolish the created status of being for self-deification is also the loss of its relation to the authentically transcendent and so its fall into demonization.[6]

In the New Testament "the world" does not stand for the nature of the original Creation; it refers to Creation as fallen, existing under the servitude to man's idols and given over to an oppressive relationship between man and man. This is the theological identity of "the world." The problem in the differentiation of church and world comes from a confusion of this meaning of world with that of Creation. "This world" is creation considered from the point of view of the Fall, while "the church" is this same Creation considered from the point of view of redemption. But redemption is precisely the restoration of Creation; hence the church is not a community of redemption that removes men from Creation but restores man to it. Secular theology rejects all supernaturalist separation of redemption from Creation and thereby also rejects the idea that redeemed life has as its purpose the raising of man to a destiny beyond history. Redemption is a redemption to rather than from finitude. Redemption restores man to the open, temporal, provisional mode of existence that is his authentic nature. Redemption is humanization, while sin is a demonic dehumanization that comes about through rejection of creational existence for self-absolutization.

Therefore the theological meaning of "world" is not to be identified with secular structures of society in any unequivocal sense, and still less is the "church" to be identified with ecclesiastical structures. Rather the theological principles of church and world cut across all social structures, including those that call themselves "church." "This world" is the sphere governed under the law of alienation and oppression, under the dominion of the powers and principalities. The ecclesiastical institution, far from being exempt from this sphere, can become one of the principal exemplars of it. This is what the Reformers of the sixteenth century meant when they called the Church of Rome the church of the antichrist. They were expressing the horrified discovery of late medieval man that the ecclesiastical institution was in no way especially exempt from sin, but could become one of the principal exponents of that evil principle of life that the gospel calls the domain of the antichrist and that the gospel itself comes to overthrow. It is in this sense that the gospel can become a power to overthrow the church and proclaim the death of its gods. But the theological reality of the world as well as the theological reality of redemption cut across ecclesiastical and secular institutions. Redemption happens wherever men are being recreated in freedom, truth, and responsible relationships. The gospel overthrows the ecclesiastical institution whenever it interprets itself in a self-deifying fashion; it overthrows the secular world when it interprets itself as self-sufficient and capable of creating a true Kingdom of God without reference to God. The gospel is the idol-smasher in both cases. The gospel restores the church to its secularity as simply that place in history where mankind is being redeemed and it recalls secular institutions to obedience to God.

What, then, is the role of the historical institutional "church." The institutional church does not monopolize the reality of redemption. It is not "The Catholic Church," for this includes all mankind and all aspects of life in its intentionality. Instead its role is to display as best it can the paradigm of the redeemed society and to act as the servant of the whole church of mankind. The historical church has a special self-consciousness as the bearer of this message of salvation, a reflector and interpreter of it, but, from the point of view of where redemption is happening, it has no special rights or priorities. The message is not exclusively about itself, but it is about mankind. The mission does not exclusively emanate from itself; it is already abroad in the land at work among men, and those who call themselves Christians simply try to join God wherever they discern this action to be happening.[7] They may help to formulate a part of the mission according to their lights, but they by no means dominate or promulgate the mission as a whole. The mission is much bigger than they, and the most they can do is to try to be part of it rather than irrelevant or contrary to it. So when the church is considered from the point of view of where historical redemption is really happening, the ecclesiastical community can best be the church by recognizing that it is only one place where, by the grace of God, the church might be happening.

However the walls that define the ecclesiastical institution are themselves a falsification of what the church really is, and so those who try to live in terms of the reality of the redemptive community must try to dissolve these walls and create a new consciousness that allows men to see the renewal and humanization going on in all spheres of life as expressions of it. In this way Christians also help to break down the secularism of secular institutions and to spread among all those engaged in renewing the world a consciousness of a deeper plane and meaning of their work. This does not mean any effort to spread the influence of the ecclesiastical institution as a particular power structure that would again imperialistically dominate all spheres of life. The church as a power structure must become more and more unpretentious and let its borders be overrun, so that groups with no sociological membership in the church can find church people and church property usable resources that will not try to control them. This means that the church can open its doors and resources to whoever is doing redemptive work without attaching some price tag of allegiance. Churchly realities also must overrun their borders in the other direction, so that the forms of preaching, celebration, communion, and ministry can be recognized as happening in all kinds of contexts that bear no ecclesiastical banners. Liturgy ceases to be an ecclesiastical rite and becomes a celebration of a breakthrough in human existence wherever this may occur. By letting the frontiers be invaded and the boundaries overrun, the historic church both helps the metropolis to recognize itself as the place where repentance and resurrection must occur and also recovers its own power to relate to the whole universe and to celebrate in the midst of the whole redemptive process happening in God's world.

Chapter 10

Post-Christendom
and the Death of God

The concept of "the Death of God" burst upon the popular media several years ago as the *enfant terrible* of the theological world, yet the lineage of this recent speculation can be found in a revival of various nineteenth-century radicals. Its intent was to give an analysis of the theological meaning of that dissolution of Christian culture that had been going on since the seventeenth century. Thus, despite the esoteric appearance of this short-lived movement for the general public, it probably expressed deeper and more pertinent trends for the long range of Christian history and in the broad popular experience of religion in modern times than the obscure squabbles of the established theologians over "demythologizing" and "hermeneutics." Particularly in the person of William Hamilton, the Death of God movement tried to break the ivory tower of professional theology and to theologize in the midst of the popular culture that expressed the actual existential situation of the times.

Within the ranks of the immediate theological heritage as this had been reconstructed by dialectical theology, the Death of God movement represented a rebel offspring. It represented a crisis in the very project of theologizing itself that had been building up among the disciples of the German school who had followed the line of thought that led from Barth's rejection of natural theology to Bultmann's demythologizing to Bonhoeffer's religion-less Christianity and Gogarten's secularization of history. The unmasking of this crisis by the sudden eruption of the scandalous phrase, "Death of God," provoked much soul searching and a rash of books exploring the possibility of "God-talk."[1] As might be expected, God was never talked about so constantly and earnestly than when the possibility of talking about God had been thrown into question.

This crisis emerged out of the womb of dialectical theology itself. Crisis theology had applauded the breakup of the fusion between the divine and culture that is the root of the sacred. All sacralizing of cultural forms was to be rejected. The relativity, finitude, and temporality of the world that appeared after the breakup of the sacred manifested the true created nature of the world and, far from being the enemy of the gospel, it was the God of the Bible who affirmed and sustained this secularity of the world. In other words, dialectical theology tried to affirm at the same time a secular world and a radically transcendent God and set these in a polar tension with each other, so that openness to the radically transcendent God was at the same time the power for authentic secular existence. The biblical God was the iconoclastic God who shattered man's self-deifications and set him back into the condition of secularity that was his true created form of life. The God of dialectical theology was, therefore, a God who could not be described in terms of any continuity with the being of the world whatsoever. He is the "wholly-other." He cannot be metaphysically described because his being exists in no analogical relation to that of the world. He is that transcendent otherness that stands over against mankind and the created world.

But this otherness is also described as intervening in history, and experienced by men as the incursion of the unexpected that cuts across his tendency to become self-enclosed in his world, that restores man to that open, finite condition whereby he can relativize his past and become open to new future possibilities.

The God of dialectical theology could, therefore, not be described as being. He cannot be metaphysically contemplated as an object of knowledge. In Buber's language, he is the transcendent "Thou" without any "it." He can be known only by experience of his workings in history. In Melanchthon's words, "to know God is to know his benefits." We do not know God as a being in and for himself, but in his self-manifestation as Jesus Christ, as his workings in history for us in grace and judgment.

But, in this description of God as a transcendence that we experience in grace and judgment, God seems to have no ontological base. If being was denied to him, it was hard to know in what way he existed. As we saw in discussing of Camus, no God at all did about as well as a radically transcendent God to return man to finite, secular existence.[2] There then broke out, especially among the right- and left-wing critics of Bultmann, an argument over the ontological status of God. Some, like the left-wing Bultmannian, Fritz Buri, wanted to go on from "demythologizing to dekerygmatizing," and to frankly annex the word "God" to an intrahistorical experience of transcendence.[3] More conservative critics such as Gerhard Ebling and Helmut Gollwitzer insisted on the reality of God as the independently existing ground of the human experience of transcendence, although this could not be described metaphysically through any analogy with the being of creation. The existence of God must be described nonobjectively and always *pro nobis*.

It is illegitimate to make statements which fit God into a theoretical view of the world and make him an object among other objects, a thing among other things, fitted into a general concept of Being, even as a Being which is viewed as the cause of other beings. In regard to God, statements are illegitimate which do not affect our own existence, which can be equally understood by believer and unbeliever, which are existentially neutral in relation to our own existence.[4]

The vulnerability of the dialectical concept of God to such a critic as Fritz Buri, however, showed that the dialectic of transcendence and secularity was threatening to collapse into an intraworldly, historical form of existence that contained its own transcendence but that, in fact, did not really reckon with a God or a final transcendent goal of history that was beyond historical existence itself. The concept of God had been appropriated into a description of man's existence in history and the wholly-other God of Barth had vanished into an empty sky. The God who was not Being but transcendent presence began to appear more and more as a Cheshire cat.

The cat vanished quite slowly, beginning with the end of its tail and ending with the grin which remained for some time after the rest of it was gone. "Well," said Alice, "I have often seen a cat without a grin, but a grin without a cat! It's the most curious thing I have ever seen in my life."[5]

Finally the grin itself faded, leaving an empty hole where it had been, which William Hamilton, in a kind of negative Methodism, called "the experience of the absence of God."[6]

The cultural experience of the disappearance of God is well described by Wallace Stevens:

To see the gods dispelled in mid-air and dissolve like clouds is one of the great human experiences. It is not as if they had gone over the horizon to disappear for a time, nor as if they had been overcome by other gods of greater power and profounder knowledge. It is simply that they came to nothing. Since we have always shared all things with them, and have always had a part of their strength and their knowledge, we shared likewise this experience of their annihilation. It was their annihilation, not ours, and yet it left us feeling that in a measure we too had been annihilated. It left us feeling dispossessed and alone in solitude, like children without parents, in a home that seemed deserted, in which the amicable rooms and halls had taken on a look of hardness and emptiness. What was most extraordinary is that they left no mementos behind, no thrones, no mystic rings, no text either of the soil or of the soul. It was as if they had never inhabited the earth. There was no crying out for their return. They were not forgotten, of course, for they had been a part of the glory of the earth. At the same time no man seemed to be muttering a petition in his heart for the restoration of these now unreal shapes. There was always in every man the increasingly human self which, instead of remaining the observer, the non-participant, the delinquent, became more and more all there was—or so it seemed. And whether it was or merely seemed so, it still left it for him to resolve life in the world in his own terms.[7]

However, since theologians have a professional stake in not going out of business even though their God had disappeared, there then came about various efforts to describe this death of God "theologically," to create a new theological school around the death of God and to see in this school the new basis for the religious culture of post-Christian man. Already William Hamilton could expansively declare in the first announcement of the existence of this school "the death of God tradition is beginning to see the work laid out before it: historical, exegetical, apologetic, ethical."[8] The different members of this "tradition," however, soon proved to be so disparate that it became hard to find any basis for even describing them as a school—perhaps at most a "groupuscle" of two. Paul Van Buren, who set several of its themes by his rejection of the meaningfulness of God-talk and his embrace of Jesus as the historical datum of Christianity,[9] steadfastly refused to include himself under the banner of "Death of God." Gabriel Vahanian, the only other writer to openly embrace the term, used it in a way diametrically opposite to that of Altizer and Hamilton. We might conclude that in a world where God is really dead, iconoclasm no longer stirs up any excitement, just as the impact of the curse depends on the continued existence of prayer. As a movement, then, Death of God theology died early. As a brief pointer to what could be said in Christian language in the mid-sixties, its fingers pointed in opposite directions.

Death of God theology, as it was described by perhaps its most determined spokesman, Thomas J. J. Altizer, is a religion of "radical immanentism." Altizer shares something of the "Jesuology" of Hamilton and Van Buren. The God to whom Jesus pointed and whom he was believed to reveal in accordance with the words of the Gospel of John, "to see me is to see the Father," this Father had vanished into an empty sky, but Jesus himself remained as a vibrant reality. It is Jesus and not any transcendent God who is the proper focus of the gospel. Jesus reveals the truth inherent in man and in the universe itself. This is the fundamental datum of a religion of the earth. The secularity of Gogarten here becomes fully self-sufficient and, à la Feuerbach, takes back the divinity that it had "alienated" into the skies. Thus in Altizer we have a new secular "sacrality." The world, humanity itself, becomes the arena for a new theophany:

It is in Christianity and Christianity alone that we find a radical or consistent doctrine of the Incarnation. Only Christianity can celebrate an Incarnation in which God has actually become flesh, and radical theology must finally understand the Incarnation itself as effecting the death of God. Although the death of God may not have been historically actualized or realized until the nineteenth century, the radical theologian cannot dissociate this event from Jesus and his original proclamation.

The radical theologian has a strange but compelling interest in the figure of Jesus. This must not be confused with the nineteenth century liberal quest for the historical Jesus. The new theologian has died to the liberal tradition and is in quest of that Jesus who appears in conjunction with the death of God. Radical theology is peculiarly a product of the mid-twentieth century; it has been initiated by Barth and neo-orthodoxy in a form of theology which can exist in the midst of the collapse of Christendom and the advent of secular atheism.[10]

For Altizer, Death of God and radical immanentism are two sides of the same message. We must reject the transcendent Father God of the Old Testament. In the Incarnation, the Creator-God who stands above and outside his creation as its Lord, sovereign, and ultimate judge is overcome. Such a transcendent Father God is a projection of man's self-alienation and self-hatred. The Creator God before whom man bows and confesses his sin is an alienating projection of man's self-hatred upon the skies. In so doing man abdicates his freedom and autonomy and subjects himself to a degrading subservience to this own self-projection. The wrathful God of judgment is the ultimate expression of this human self-estrangement. Here, although Altizer cites Hegel, Blake, and Eliade as his mentors, his thought seems more in line with the Feuerbachian reversal of the Hegelian dialectic. Citing Blake, Altizer even refers to this God as the Devil, a diabolic tyrant that curses and estranges man from himself. Man must kill the Satanic Father God that steals his liberty in order to recover his proper autonomy and dignity, even his immanent divinity.

This death of God takes place preeminently in the Incarnation, which happens archetypically in Jesus although only gradually realized in history. It is described as truly a "cosmic" and "historical event." The Incarnation must be allowed to stand in all of its radical immanence. It is not to be seen as surpassed and negated by some new escape of divinity into transcendence in concepts of resurrection and ascension that stand, as a new, "transcendent source in the past," for the foundation of a new, alienated religion. This is what took place in the founding of Christendom, but this construct is now fading, allowing the true religion of the Incarnation to flower in modern times. The Incarnation is the whole and complete message and stands as the end, once and for all, of all divinity beyond man and the world and the beginning of divinity in a wholly human form. Altizer fused crucifixion and incarnation together along the lines of Pauline *kenosis* theology (Phil. 2:6–11). The crucifixion is God's death or self-emptying of himself into creation. The self-immolation of the Father into the incarnate Jesus is not simply a self-emptying of God's word, but of the Father or the transcendent godhead itself. Dying to transcendent, alienated existence, God comes to birth in Jesus in a wholly immanent form.

The self-emptying of God into Jesus does not stand as any new foundation for religious institutions, but abolishes all static foundations into radical historicity. The event does not have its locus in any elevation of a past particular, but exists in the particularity of every present moment. God dies into Jesus, liberating man from the oppressive power for primordial being. Henceforth God is incarnate in every human hand and face. With the death of God, primordial being existing as its own ground has been shattered and, with its dissolution, every form of alienation and otherness loses its intrinsic ground. Now a new humanity and a new world arise that can give themselves to the immediate actuality of the present moment, a doctrine Altizer links with the radical spiritualism of the medieval proclaimers of the Third Age. Altizer thus interprets the birth of modern secularism—in its self-sufficient form from which all transcendency has vanished—as the radical coming of age of Christianity and the religion of the Incarnation. The modern secular consciousness is the consciousness that is realizing historically this gospel of the Death of God and the Incarnation. It is a consciousness born of the eclipse of the transcendent realm and so freed for the appearance of God in a wholly human form.[11]

The death of God is interpreted as a religious and salvic event. Altizer commits what is evidently high blasphemy against neoorthodoxy with full recognition and—"consent of the will"—and no little enjoyment. The thinking that had become unimpeachable since Barth is impugned and even reversed. The Barthian transcendent God that released the world to be secular and nondivine and Christianity to be nonreligious is turned to its opposite, and in place of the religionless Christianity there emerges a godless religiosity. Where dialectical theology sought to distinguish ultimately between God and the world, Altizer seeks to create the ultimate "coincidence of opposites."

Once Altizer's drift became fully apparent, the theological establishment was not slow to the attack, but perhaps its most stinging expression came from the one other thinker who had even earlier made the term Death of God an important theological category for himself. Gabriel Vahanian, in his two books that appeared before the public furor, *The Death of God* and *Wait Without Idols,* had used this term to express an analysis of the human, historical situation that followed out of the Barthian dialectic of the transcendence of God and the finitude of the world.[12] For Vahanian, the death of God is in no sense to be interpreted as a religious event in itself; it is the experience of the dissolution of our religious culture. It is not the death of the transcendent God, but the death of our past cultural images of God. This dissolution restores the true transcendence of God and reveals the relativity of the religious systems and images whereby we seek to domesticate God in our cultural creations. The experience of the death of God expresses particularly the cultural failure of the church and Christian society. What we experience in it is the death of Christendom, the death of that cultural, societal form whereby the gospel was translated into an institution and social ideology. These outworn structures of Christendom have now become incredible. They are empty and dead, and therefore the God they sought to reveal no longer appears through them. The churches, the religious services, the places where preeminently this God of Christian culture should have appeared are precisely the places where nothing happens. This description of the churches from a recent book makes the point.

> Go to the churches. Note the atmosphere of tired inertia, the sort of vacuum of complete powerlessness that sometimes overcomes one there. Nothing happens in the churches. There are no manifestations there; no theophanies; no revelations; no encounters with the power of life and death in such a way that the church becomes the most important and the most powerladen place. For many of us, the church functions in a rather different way—more as a place to withdraw temporarily from life, from death, from power. It is a place to withdraw in order to get a perspective, but a place therefore where it is important for nothing to happen, and therefore the place where the only god one can let in is a god who is too impotent to bother you.[13]

It is this experience of the deadness, the powerlessness, the nonrelevatory existence of our religious symbols and inherited Christian communities that Vahanian is talking about when he speaks about the death of God as a cultural event. This death of Christian culture reveals the ambiguity of all human religious culture. Far from being an event that undermines biblical faith, it is an event that biblical faith is especially equipped to interpret. Because the biblical God is not the God of religious culture he gives no finality to any sacred society, but he is the prophetic God who is radically transcendent to creation and available only through a free grace which shatters man's religious and moral works. For Vahanian there is no alternative between atheism and theism because man is an incorrigibly religious animal. He is always creating gods. The only real alternative is between idolatry and iconoclasm.[14] The biblical God is the imageless God who has no sacred image and commands man to make no sacred image of him. He is present to man as the image-smasher who throws down the golden calves by which man seeks to capture the divine and put it at his own disposal.

Culturally, man stands between the poles of incarnation and transcendence. God's transcendence is not to be understood as absence or other-worldliness; God's presence is not to be appropriated a unitary immanence. God's spirit is to be described as one of transcendent presence. He is the Creator and yet beyond the creation. He is neither simply to be appropriated into creation as its divine ground and foundation, nor can we find God by fleeing Creation. There is no other world beyond creation to which we can turn to find God. Creation is the only world there is. God's creation is the arena of the manifestation of God's glory, and apart from creation there is no accessibility to God. But creation remains a place of disclosure of God only by knowing that it is itself not divine. God is present to his creation. He is not his creation. Rather, he is the transcendent presence who is disclosed through creation only when creation itself is openly finite and creaturely. We experience God's word and God's presence through the audible word, the visible image, and the created work, but not *as* the created word and work. Only by not deifying and finalizing itself can the created image be a place of the disclosure of God. As soon as creation is set up as a sacred being in itself, it becomes an idol that, by appropriating God's being, drives out God's presence. Only by existing iconoclastically toward himself can man recognize the created being as a place of disclosure of God and keep from turning it into an object which alienates the reality toward which it points.

It is the work of the Holy Spirit constantly to shatter this tendency of man to turn his culture into a god. The Holy Spirit relativizes the world and therefore opens it to constant new moments of divine disclosure. This does not mean that man in the Christian community is to remain cultureless, without words or images. The attempt to sweep away all representation in the name of the purity of God's word misunderstands the iconoclastic function of biblical religion. The presence of God must be expressed in visible, communicable form. God's presence has no reality for us except as it is incarnate in historical expression. The encounter with the transcendent must be spelled out, danced out and worked out in images and forms of expression in order to have a being and power for our lives. But this cultural expression remains powerful and revelatory to the extent that we do not try to absolutize the expression itself and turn it into the final, infallible definition. We must express our experience of God in order to make it real for us, but, at the same time, refuse to cling to these cultural expressions and let them go when their hour is done. In this way our cultural celebration of God becomes a constantly renewed improvization upon the theme of God's presence.

This, then, is how Vahanian's describes how man should live authentically before God. But man fails to do so because he cannot tolerate this freedom. He tries to institutionalize his experiences of God and turn them into the final infallible revelations that found structures and systems intended to last to the end of time. And so, in the course of time, his religious culture stiffens and dies, and he finds himself straining to catch a sound of heavenly music from an organ that has fallen toneless. The death of our religious culture and the incredibility of the official God of this culture is simply our present experience of this universal situation of man. We have built a great religious edifice in which we can no longer believe, and this means nothing less than the loss of faith in the whole cultural creation of the past two millennia of Western civilization. These towering self-images that we have projected upon the face of the earth, not merely to express ourselves, but to incarnate our historical experience of God, have become enslaving idols. We experience them as walls that cut off and eclipse our ability to feel the presence of the living God. They have taken on a life and power of their own that holds us in chains. Our cultural expression of God stiffens and dies, and we are left with the ominous work of our own hands from which the life-giving spirit has fled.

Vahanian so describes our post-Christian cultural situation. We live at a time of spiritual interregnum, a time when the old cultural expressions of God are dead or dying and we can get no nourishment from them, but a time when this death of our religious culture is also releasing the "other God" whom we never succeed in simply domesticating into our religiosity. This transcendent Spirit is going on ahead of us into the desert to lead us out of slavery and toward a new promised land. In the collection of essays entitled *No Other God* (1966), which Vahanian published immediately after the Death of God furor, he makes clear the distance between his and Altizer's understanding of this term. Altizer's religion of radical immanence he labels as exactly that apotheosis of man's idolatrous religiosity that he himself had denounced in his two previous books. It is this idolatrous religiosity that Vahanian had interpreted as the source and basis of the death of God and the incredibility of our religious symbols.

Taken as nothing less if nothing more than a cultural phenomenon, the death of God signifies the transition from radical monotheism to a radical immanentism and marks the birth of secularism as the vector of the new religiosity. More simply, it announces the advent of a new culturally Christian paganism, even while theology is busy overlooking its indigence or covering it up with a glorified but amnesic vocabulary. Indeed, accustomed to thinking of theology as an ecclesiastical task, as the self-critical task of the Church, we failed to realize that it had stopped speaking to the outside world and, *ipso facto,* to the Church itself, for the Church cannot understand itself unless the language of its self-understanding speaks to the world and unless the world itself can use the same language.

But what I have denounced elsewhere as the charter of an incipient post-Christian idolatry is now proclaimed as the first article of an immanentist religiosity. So-called "Christian atheism" glories precisely in what I deplored when I first used the term 'death of God'; and it can do so, furthermore, only by appealing to the disaffected, though still residually Christian, religiosity of Western man. What I denounced, the "Christian atheists" now advocate, but only because they have, in effect, turned Sartre's definition of man as a useless passion into a soteriological program, not realizing that if godless man no longer needs God to understand himself, neither—as Sartre and Camus show—does he need God to establish himself as his own contradiction. I should have hoped the "Christian atheists" would not lag so far behind the real atheists, at a time when even these admit to the superannuated character of the conflict between theism and atheism.[15]

Vahanian here sets himself against any attempt to interpret the death of God as a religious event and the ground of an immanentist metaphysic. The death of God is the death of man's superannuated religious culture, not the death of the transcendent Spirit. Indeed, the death of Christian religious culture is possible precisely because God remains transcendent to the world. Altizer wars against God's transcendence in the name of the immanent divinity of man. Vahanian wars against man's acculturated immanences in the name of God's transcendence. For Vahanian man must be prepared to see his cultural expressions of God die so that, in this judgment of the Spirit upon his dying religiosity, he may fall into the hands of a living God. For Altizer this whole function of God as transcendent maker and judge is an alienating self-projection and an assault upon man's autonomy. The God of law must die to come to birth in the immanent divinity of human love and reciprocity. The redeeming God abolishes the God of creation and releases the divinity of the world inherent in every moment of experience. These two theological analyses of man's present situation could not be more diametrically opposed.

The difficulty with Altizer's position is that it appears to be good for only one revolution. The Creator God can be killed only once; then, having abolished this principle from one's reckoning, one is left with a human divinity that has done away with the power of self-transcendence and self-judgment. These are the functions of a God who is beyond creation. Having killed the principle of transcendence and judgment, one would also have killed the principle of renewal, thereby bringing to birth a god-man that would shortly become the ultimate tyrant, since there would be nothing beyond him that could judge him and toward which he would point. This is precisely what had happened in history when a theology of radical immanence became the ruling force. We can see the potential for this in medieval and Reformation radical sects that believed that God had become totally and finally incarnate in themselves. Marxist societies that see themselves as the bearer of the final age of the historical spirit suffer from the same defect. Societies formed by the death of the Father and the birth of the final immanent Kingdom in history are good only for the one initial revolution that kills off the alienating, authoritarian forces of the past against which they are rebelling, but then they themselves turn totalitarian, denying any possibility for further criticism. Radical, uncompromising criticism of the existing society leads up to the revolution, but once the revolution is over, the final truth has dawned and all criticism must cease.

Here Vahanian's perspective seems more viable for the long historical journey, since it is a theology of the relativity of all our human historical incarnations of God. It is a theology that provides the possibility of ever-renewed revolutions to come. The difficulty with Vahanian's dialectic, however, is that the two poles are so diametrically balanced against each other that one side seems to annihilate the other and then the other side seems to shatter the first, and so the process appears to be fruitless. The transcendent God stands over against us as a presence that overthrows our cultural expressions of the divine. In this experience of grace and judgment we create a new image that expresses this transfiguration. The booths set up on the Holy Mount, however, in due time become new traps and enslaving temples and are, in turn, dissolved by a new incursion of the transcendent. The pace of image-breaking and image-making seems to accelerate as we come into modern times, so that whereas once it took a millennium or two for a religious culture to run its course, we now have a new religious culture every year, e.g., since 1964 there has been a New Theology 1, 2, 3, 4, 5, and 6.[16] Vahanian's alternating rhythms of idolatry and iconoclasm allow no finality and permanence in historical experience, and even undermine any meaningful duration in historical experience as well, and so embark us on an all-too-modern quest for endless novelty, a psychedelic light show of religious shock therapy with one image after another exploding through our brains until all meaningful communication disintegrates.

This collapse of meaning at the tag end of dialectical theology seems to me by no means accidental or peculiar to Gabriel Vahanian, but simply the expression of the latent crisis of meaning within crisis theology itself. In a dialectic that forbade an ultimate synthesis, the transcendent pole has become increasingly unreal and the historical pole increasingly meaningless. It is, therefore, not insignificant that very shortly after the post-Bultmannian debates in Germany and the Death of God furor in America, there was an effort to grope beyond the evenly balanced dialectic to some restoration of hope in an ultimate future synthesis by reaching back to the liberal progressive, evolutionary, and Marxian revolutionary strains of the nineteenth century that had been out of theological fashion since the time of Barth.

Chapter 11

Christian-Marxist Dialogue

Christianity and Marxism would seem to be irreconcilable antagonists in both their intellectual systems and their historical experience with one another. From its very beginning, Marxism announced itself as the foe of organized religion in society. Existing Christian churches were judged by Marxism as the class religion of the bourgeois, and religion itself was exposed as the ultimate ideological expression of man's alienation. By definition, then, socialism was the foe of religion, and religion was due to wither away in the socialist state as the overcoming of the alienation of man from his labor did away with this alienated ideological superstructure. In practice, Marxism has established itself in technologically underdeveloped areas, first in Russia, then China, and then, as the formula for possible revolutions, in the Third World. Hence Marxism has actually been a tool for bringing the industrial revolution to areas outside its original Western European and American heartland, but it has done so through the motivation of a revolutionary antagonism to these older centers of industrialization.

This area of European civilization is also the heartland of Christian civilization. Thus the stage was set for a reaction to communism in Europeans and North Americans as the reincarnation of the barbarian foe to Western Christian civilization, and there arose a confusion between the cultural, economic, and national antipathies to communism and a crusade against communism in the name of Christianity. This crusade against communism, largely sanctified by the Christian churches, has dominated the foreign policy of the West—particularly that of the United States—for some twenty years, to the extent that the whole economy has gradually shifted over to a military basis and all aspects of life focus around a permanent state of military preparedness vis-à-vis the "Communist" East. Deep strains of Manichaean mythology have become so enmeshed in this struggle that the possibility of reexamining its very foundations has, for many Americans, become unthinkable. Yet precisely this situation has become the threat to the continued existence of the world, with two superpowers facing each other across a fortress of missiles and countermissiles with a might that could annihilate, many times over, every man, woman, and child on the globe. Such is the world crisis brought about by Christian-Marxist antagonism and one of the very basic reasons for a need to reexamine it.

On the other side of the ledger there has been a continual tradition, though one that has been submerged and without political effectiveness, of Christian-socialist dialogue and even mutual identification. On the Christian side there has been a small but continuous tradition of Christian socialism, which has seen in the Socialist critique of the dehumanization of industrial society and its hope for a world of brotherhood to come a secularized version of the gospel itself. Christian socialism sought to return socialism to its Christian foundations. The Christian Socialists that gathered around F. D. Maurice in the middle years of the nineteenth century, the revival of English Christian socialism around Stewart Headlam and the Guild of St. Matthew in the last decades of that century,[1] the German Christian socialism emanating from Ritschlian liberalism and influencing the young theologians of the early twentieth century (especially Tillich), and the American Social Gospel tradition were all the grounds of a continuous sympathetic view of Christians toward socialism. This Christian Socialist tradition usually preferred the democratic evolutionary tradition of socialism to its more Jacobin, anarchistic, and revolutionary forms, but from the last decades of the nineteenth century (and even in the writings of the later Engels himself) there was a gradual adaptation of Marxism to evolutionary parliamentary methods, and this revisionism has become the practice (and more belatedly the theory) of Western European Marxist parties.[2] Moreover there were not lacking Christians, such as Reinhold Niebuhr, who recognized in Marxist revolution a catastrophism drawn from Judeo-Christian apocalypticism, and one not without moral validity as an uncompromising judgment leveled upon the failures of industrial civilization.

On the Marxist side there has also been a submerged but nevertheless real tradition that has recognized, along with Constantinian-established Christianity, a second left-wing revolutionary tradition in Christianity that is not only congenial to but a real source of the Socialist tradition itself. This interest in radical Christianity as a progenitor of socialism is found in the later Engels in numerous essays on various aspects of religion where he took a particular interest in both primitive Christianity and the left-wing traditions of the Reformation as forerunners of socialism.[3] Indeed, one might say that the theological origins of Marxism were implict from its very beginnings in left-wing Hegelianism and Feuerbach's theological radicalism. Since Engels's death, numerous leading Marxists have written on aspects of the radical Christian tradition as a part of their own background. Ernst Bloch's work on Thomas Münzer, as well as his continual use of the religious tradition in his monumental work on the "principle of hope," Kautsky's writing on Thomas More and on the foundations of Christianity, Bernstein on Cromwell and socialism in the Puritan revolution are examples of this tradition.[4] In many ways the modern Marxist partners in Christian-Marxist dialogue, such as Roger Garaudy, Milan Machovec, and Leszek Kolakowski, continue the same tradition, with Ernst Bloch surviving as a bridge between the work of Klausky and Bernstein and the contemporary dialogue.

However, the new dialogue takes place in a situation that

makes it qualitatively different from these earlier Marxist works on Christian sources of socialism, a situation created by the historical practice of Marxism in the Soviet Union and the states and parties which have looked to it as the controling ideological center. Contemporary Christian-Marxist dialogue can be said to have its roots in Khrushchev's denunciation of Stalinism at the 20th Party Congress in 1956, which set the stage both for a post-Stalinist political struggle against the domination of the centralized Soviet party structure in Eastern Europe, and also for an ideological struggle to demythologize the "infallible" pretensions of the Leninist-Stalinist party magisterium and to recover a humanist Marxism by going behind this party tradition. The struggle then that has emerged around the new revisionism in non-Soviet Communist parties generally, but with greatest political pertinence in Soviet-dominated Eastern European countries, is in many ways parallel to the Reformation struggle to relativize the medieval papal tradition and to illegitimate its infallibility by going behind it to the sources. In 1953–56 a debate broke out in Poland, Hungary, and Czechoslovakia over the recovery of a moral humanist Marxism as against the "historical necessity" of the party tradition; this debate was the intellectual background of the Polish and Hungarian uprisings of 1956.[5] These uprisings were suppressed by the Soviet-directed power structure, but only at the price of sharpening the credibility gap between party theory and practice that had been building up, thus increasingly discrediting the Soviet-directed party as the legitimate heirs of future Socialist hopes.

The result has been an increasingly restive and revolutionary situation in Eastern European countries, as well as an erosion and gradual break of allegiance to Russia as the heartland of socialism among Western Communist parties. This revisionist revolution against Soviet direction has continued to the present day with the Czechoslovakian revival of humanist socialism, their subsequent occupation by Soviet troops (in August 1968), and the new shock and disaffiliation that this has created among non-Soviet Marxists generally as the latest act in this drama. The contemporary Christian-Marxist dialogue must be seen as a part and expression of this "revisionist" revolution against the Leninist-Stalinist party tradition. Not surprisingly it has had its chief impetus in these very Eastern European countries of Poland, Hungary, and Czechoslovakia, and the Marxist partners in the dialogue have been in the center of the revisionist struggle in their own countries.[6]

"Revisionism," as Leopold Labedz notes, is the Marxist equivalent of "heresy," and stands not so much for any particular line or content as for an "autonomous" Marxism as opposed to a Marxist line dictated by the party magisterium. The contemporary dialogue was announced by such books as Roger Garaudy's *From Anathema to Dialogue* (1965), Milan Machovec's *Marxismus und Dialektische Theologie* (1965), and the distinguished *Disputation zwischen Christen und Marxisten* (1966), where Marxist philosophers, mostly from Karls University in Prague, met with Christian counterparts on a series of key issues concerning history, human nature, alienation, sin, faith, and community. This interest among Marxists in dialogue with Christianity had, in turn, a responsive ear both among certain Catholic theologians who, from the 1950s, have engaged in ideological analysis of Marxism from a Catholic standpoint and the Commission on Marxism of the evangelical study group in the German Federal Republic, which had brought together students of all disciplines to study the questions that Marxism addressed to Christianity.[7]

Protestant attitudes toward Marxism since the 1930s had been fairly well set by the theological categories of neoorthodoxy. For Americans this view had been summed up by Niebuhr's analysis of Marxism as secularized apocalypticism, which, nevertheless, as an established historical system, was bound to fall into idolatry by its insufficient perception of the "infinite qualitative difference" between the historical and the transcendent.[8] This Barthian critique of Marxism found its most sympathetic spokesman in the Czechosolvakian theologian of the Reformed (Hussite) tradition, Josef Hromadka.[9] Hromadka defined for his

Christian brothers in Communist lands a third way between reactionary anti-Communist ghettoism and an unprincipled sell-out to the party line. This meant that quite consciously he had to procede with a criticism on both fronts, of both Christian and Communist presumptions.

For Hromadka, the Christian presumption that must be unmasked is that of "Christian civilization." The reactionary view, which regarded the old order as the norm of European society from which communism could only be viewed as a fall or deviation, and which can only think in terms of annulling recent times and finding the way back to the thread of history before 1917, must be laid to rest. Such a view contains the implicit idolatry of equating traditional European society with Christianity and tying it to an absolute relationship to the gospel. The church, therefore, ceases to have a message for all men in all times, and becomes a gospel that can only be preached in terms of a particular culture and social structure. Against this idolatry of Christian civilization, the Christian must explore and proclaim the real legitimacy of the new society. The Russian Revolution marked a new and irreversible era in the history of humanity itself. It signalled the end of Western European dominance and the retreat of the West.

Twentieth-century history, marked by world wars originating from Western European antagonisms, unmasked the moral pretentions of Christian civilization vis-à-vis the rest of the world. Western industrialism related to the rest of the world in the form of colonialism or neocolonialism, and the revolt of the non-Western world marks the demand of these other areas for the fruits of modern knowledge in an autonomous and dignified way, rather than in a chattel relationship to Western superiority. In addition, the rise of socialism as the formula for the industrial revolution in non-Western countries generally expressed the failure of liberal democracy to effect a more fundamental economic revolution for the benefit of the masses. Liberal democracy was exposed by socialism as a middle class ideology that rose in the struggle against feudalism on the part of the new economic class who wanted political power commensurate with their economic power. It had little to say to those deprived of economic power. (This limitation of political democracy might be illustrated from the American civil rights movement at that point when those who had struggled to secure for the black man the right to sit at the lunch counter found that they had accomplished nothing for those who did not have the money to buy the sandwich at the lunch counter in the first place. In effect, a purely "civil rights" struggle could only secure the rights of those who already had economic power but were illegitimately deprived of their political rights, i.e., the black bourgeois.) This is why the have-nots of the world are attracted to socialism rather than liberal democracy as the formula for change, because it gets at the fundamental economic injustices between classes that liberal democracy does not touch.[10]

Industrialization, transformation of the human environment through technology, and secularization as the new cultural style are all transforming the world into a new era, and there is no way back to the old forms of life. This new era is not automatically congruous with the gospel, but it is not automatically contrary to it either. It simply forms the new situation in which the gospel of repentence and grace is to be proclaimed. It is replete with both its threat and its promise to humanity. Rapid technological advance poses a threat to many of the natural balances of life and death, air, soil, and the animal kingdom. It puts men in a new relationship to the earth and to each other, and if this new relation is not properly mastered, it will bring the annihilation of man in overpopulation, pollution, national rivalry, and destructive wars. "For the first time in history *mankind has arrived at a possibility of suicide or self-destruction*" (Hromadka's italics).[11] On the other hand, technological life is filled with much promise of a better life for all men where hunger, disease, and impoverishment of mind and body for the first time might be overcome, not just for a few, but for all mankind. This is essentially the dream of socialism. It is precisely in the midst of this society, and not by retreat to some lost society of the past, that the gospel must proclaim its message.

If the churches have fallen captive to a nostalgic fixation in the past that prevents them from relating to the human situation in this new context, then the gospel must desert the churches so that it can fulfill its mission of proclaiming the message of liberation of men in every place. The future of the church depends on our courage to take the revolutionary changes in Eastern Europe and Asia as the opportunity to make a new beginning. The bondage of the churches does not lie primarily in the new societies but in the unwillingness of the churches to take their stand in the present time of new judgment and new grace. Nothing could be more harmful to the churches' true mission than to give these kind of churchmen a false consolation and hope (i.e., that the present society could be overthrown and the old world reinstated).

The church of Christ is on the march. It is nowhere at home. It depends on no historical institutions and on no political system of liberty. It knows only the sovereign freedom of its Lord, who continually creates ever new opportunities and situations, even on the ruins of what had been dear to our fathers and to ourselves. He liberates the souls, ears and minds of his people and makes them at home wherever he is. He may prompt his believers to revolt against many institutions and systems, but he may also help his people to work joyfully under new circumstances which may be at first frightening and yet full of promise for the future.[12]

Such a view is not to be confused with mere partisanship of a new worldview, but it is equally removed from partisanship toward the Communist worldview, as it rejects any necessary affinity and partisanship between the gospel and Christian civilization. Rather, it takes its stand in sovereign freedom toward all worldviews to bring both a necessary judgment upon them and to appraise the opportunities they may offer for a new moment of promise.

From this perspective Christians may indeed give just due to many points of real affinity between the gospel and Marxism. For example the "unity of theory and practice" is analogous to the Christian understanding of Incarnation and its insistence that faith is not merely theoretical but must be grasped as the way of life in the concrete situation. Similarly, the doctrine of historical materialism can be related to and itself understood in greater depth through the historicism of the biblical faith, which insists that revelation is not an abstract formula but an encounter of the transcendent with man in his concrete historical situation. The Marxist critique of the ideological superstructure and its foundation in class rationalization of self-interest is analogous to the biblical critique of idolatry. The Socialist challenge to the individualism of liberal democracy and its championing of the oppressed classes assert themes of the organic community of men and the call for justice that are indigenous to biblical prophetism. Finally, the Socialist future hope for a classless society and the revolutionary overthrow of the oppressing class is a page taken from biblical apocalypticism and the hope for a coming Kingdom of God.[13] Thus the Christians may find many points of affinity and even regard Marxism as a secular derivative of the biblical message at many points.

Having justly appraised both the failures of the churches and the true authenticity of Socialist hopes and possibilities, Christians are then free to exercise an authentic judgment on socialism's limitations. Christian judgment must be leveled against the historical immanentism of Marxism, which absolutizes the historical process and creates a new sacral society in the Communist state as the ultimate climax of this historical process. Here the gospel takes its stand on the radical transcendency of God and the Kingdom that relativizes all ideologies and social systems. Every revolution participates in and partly incarnates the final revolutions of the Kingdom of God, but this final revolution remains transcendent to every historical achievement as the ultimate future that can never be simply a product of historical processes but transcends history as the end of history. Communist idolatry resides in its absolutist identification of the present revolution with this final eschatological revolution, thereby absolutizing the resultant Communist society and losing freedom for self-criticism and for a continuous new future beyond its own achievements. Christianity, taking its stand on the radical transcendency of God's Kingdom, can become a vantage point from which Communist achievements are brought into judgment, relativized, and from which Communist society itself recovers a freedom for a new future.[14]

This Barthian critique of communism did not form a program for dialogue so much as a fundamental prerequisite for dialogue between Christianity and Marxism. In the new Christian-Marxist dialogue, emanating, as we have suggested, from a Marxist "New Left" that implicitly recognized the failures of Marxist society and was groping for a restoration of the themes of transcendence lost in the party ideology, we might say that this critique is already absorbed in historical experience itself. So the revisionist Marxists who are engaged in this dialogue can take this critique for granted in its call for a critical relation to Marxist achievements and go on to themes that suggest new possibilities for both Christians and Marxists.[15]

The manual for such a dialogue from the Marxist perspective might be regarded as Roger Garaudy's brief volume, *From Anathema to Dialogue*. According to Garaudy, the Marxist objection to Christianity was essentially a rejection of Constantinian Christianity, which had domesticated the church in an established relationship to the ruling classes and which had assimilated the Greco-Latin ideology with its hierarchical conception of the world. Such a church must necessarily resist change both because of its social identification with the established power structure and its metaphysical identification of the norms of human existence with a fixed system of being bound back to a primordial pattern. In contrast to this Hellenistic Constantinian Christianity, however, there is the second suppressed tradition of apocalyptic Christianity, which is the authentic foundation of the gospel and which flowed as a suppressed, protest stream within Christianity down to the present. Marxism can not only sympathize with this tradition but can even claim it as a part of its own heritage. Moreover the present era is one in which Hellenistic Constantinian Christianity has been unseated from power and theologically discredited, and a revolutionary apocalyptic Christianity has become the source for the tradition of the new theologians. Garaudy cites Bultmann's program of existentialist demythologizing of the gospel and Teilhard de Chardin's vision of faith as the forefront of evolutionary progress as evidence of a conversion of the church to the hopes of the earth.

Here is a synthesis of the Christian "God of the Above" with the Marxist "God of the Ahead" with which Marxism can speak in authentic dialogue. Such a Christianity rejects the Greek metaphysical concept of being that binds human possibilities to a fixed and already existing system, and instead opens up a view of human life liberated from bondage to the cosmos and nature to live a life of free decisions and new possibilities. Only in such a view does true history become possible. The recovery of the apocalypticism of primitive Christianity as the religion of protest against the established order and hope for a coming Kingdom are the prerequisites for the possibility of Christian-Marxist dialogue from the Marxist side. Such a dialogue is no mere luxury of a few intellectuals, but it is a necessity for continual human survival. Only a common understanding and united front of Christians and Marxists can prevent the annihilation of the human race. The continued misunderstanding, rivalry, and antagonism between Christian and Marxist society poses a threat to human existence itself, whereas together Christians and Marxists could remake the face of the earth.

Having accepted the possibility and the commonality that makes such dialogue feasible, both Christians and Marxists have essential questions to ask each other. The Christian question to Marxism is summed up for Garaudy in the challenges posed by Karl Rahner and Johannes Metz (both Roman Catholic theologians) at the colloquy in Salzburg on "Marxists and Christians Today" (1965). There Rahner replied to Garaudy's definition of Marxist humanism—as the methodology of historical initiative for a realization of the total man—by challenging Marxists to recognize the necessity of God for an integral humanism. Rahner defined Christianity as the "religion of the absolute future." Far from sacralizing the present, such a view teaches us "to understand everything on the basis of what is in process of arrival."[16] But such a view of continually self-transcending history is only possible if historical process is not itself self-enclosed and self-grounded but is grounded in an absolute transcendent existence beyond history, i.e., God. By making this essential distinction between every human project and the absolute future, Christianity also makes it possible to affirm the partial but real value of every achievement, and so avoids the temptation of "brutally sacrificing each generation in favor of the next succeeding and of thus making of the future a Moloch to which the real man is sacrificed in favor of a man who is not real but is always still to come."[17] In a similar way in his queries to Marxists Johannes Metz tried to show that the dialectic of the future of man gives birth to the question of the future of God as the absolute transcendence beyond history that grounds and makes possible the relative transcendency within history.[18]

Garaudy replies to these questions by first defining the nature of historical dialecticism as an empirical existential method rather than as a materialism in the philosophical sense. Marxist methodology intends to reject all purely theoretical answers for models that direct man to a grappling with his concrete historical conditions. Existence precedes essence in the sense that ideas become real only through historical *praxis*. In an earlier era myth and ritual were primitive forms of science and technology by which the imagination was led into a forward-moving practice through analogy and symbol. Theories are not absolute, therefore, but models to be tested in historical practice. Today Marxism needs a plurality of models to fit the historical needs of revolutionaries in non-Western countries with widely different circumstances and backgrounds from that of the European experience where socialism originated.

But Communist future hope, for Garaudy, is not merely a revolution in environment and institutions but an inward transformation of man and the creation of a new society in which love ceases to be a mere promise or moral law and becomes the objective law of the entire society.

If we are communists, it is precisely because we are struggling for this classless society. .... Our task as communists is to draw near to man in his most glorious dreams and his most sublime hopes, to draw near to him in a real and practical way, so that Christians themselves might find here on our earth a beginning of their heaven.[19]

This Communist society is not the "end of history" but the authentic beginning of history for the first time. Alienated man is overcome, and authentic man makes his first appearance on the earth, not as a static achievement but as the basis for a continual struggle for the conquest of nature and the perfection of man's communal dialogue. Thus the immanent transcendence within history is not a limitation because it is itself infinite. History contains its own dialectic of the finite and the infinite and thus does not need to look beyond history to ground this infinite future hope. Once alienated and hostile "prehistoric" man is overcome, then truly historical man can flower in a never-ending aspiration toward infinite perfection. "The endless dialectic of freedom made one with creation will flower."[20]

The problem that Communists have with the Christian dialectic of the finite and the infinite is that it takes as a dogmatic answer what is, in fact, only a question addressed to man in his historical situation. The Marxist lives under the same historical exigency and the same tension between the finite present and the infinite future as the Christian, but he does not mistake an exigency for an answer or a lack for an existing being. God as the absolute future of man is not, therefore, established as an existing being that grounds and necessitates the success of this project; God is precisely an aspiration of man, the not-yet-fulfilled being of man that is not thereby an existing being, but a nonexisting hope. Transcendence is man's self-élan rather than God's presence and summons. The absolute future is precisely this endlessly expanding horizon of man's future aspirations. This future, open on the infinite, is the only transcendence known to the Marxist.

We reject the name of God because it purports to claim that the answer to our need already exists, whereas it is only an exigency which we live, a never satisfied exigency of totality and absoluteness, omnipotence and

perfect loving reciprocity of consciousness. We live this exigency but we
cannot hypothetize it under the name of transcendence. Regarding this
totality I can say everything except: it is. For what it is is always deferred
and always growing, like man himself. If we want to give it a name, the
name will not be that of God, for it is impossible to conceive of a God who
is always in process ... of being born. The most beautiful and most ex-
alted name which can be given to this exigency is the name of man. To
refuse it to him is to strip him of one of his dimensions, and his essential
specific dimension, for man is precisely he who is not. This exigency in
man is, I think, the flesh of your god.[21]

We cannot say that God as the symbol of the absolute future of
man is already existent and we already move within him because the project of the future is not predetermined, but is truly
open. The making of the future of man is one carried out in real
uncertainty and risk, without any a priori divine being that assures its success. Thus, whereas the Christian sees transcendence as an existing being and a guarantee of the future, the
Marxist can only define it as an exigency and an absence for
which there is only demand but no guarantee. Christianity has
been a traitor to the real future of man by locating this absolute
future in Heaven as a transcendence divorced from history and
for the sake of which endless servitude may be endured on earth.
It must, therefore, realign its future hope with the future hope
for the world. On the other hand, Marxists can learn a deeper
appreciation of both transcendence and subjectivity from its dialogue with Christianity. It is in these areas particularly that
Marxism is indebted to Christianity and stands in need of continuing Christian instruction. What matters is that human faith
not mutilate any of the dimensions of man that have been won
through faith in God, and that faith in the transcendent God not
mutilate faith in the human task. These are the mutual fruits
that each can hope to win through a dialogue between Christian
humanism and Marxist Promethean humanism. "If each of us
take stock of what is basic in his convictions, he will discover, the
one in his faith in God and the other in his faith in his task as
a man, a mutual willingness to stretch man's creative energies
to the maximum for the sake of realizing the total man."

Garaudy assumed that the Christian definition of God was necessarily tied to an identification of God with "being" or at least an already achieved existence, and thus that here must be a fundamental clash with the Marxist view of transcendence as absence and aspiration. In fact, as our discussion of secular theology has shown, such questioning of the idea of God's existence was already prepared by crisis theology; thus it was not at all impossible for a school of Christian theology, in the form of "theology of hope," to move rapidly toward an acceptance of this challenge of Marxism by a definition of God as the "future of man" and "he who is not yet." Marxist queries to Christianity tended to center on somewhat theological themes such as subjectivity and the definition of transcendence, while the Christian partners in this dialogue soon showed a desire to move off this ground to questions of "revolutionary praxis."

Thus, not surprisingly, Christian-Marxist dialogue vindicated its authenticity precisely by the fact that each side showed less of an interest in defending their own special tradition than in themes that might be thought to have been more the prerogative of the other side, i.e., Marxists wishing to learn about transcendence and Christians wishing to learn about revolutionary practice. Hence Jürgen Moltmann reported a reversal of fronts between Christians and Marxists. Marxists responded to the Death of God movement by asserting in a series of articles "God is not quite dead." At the meeting of the Paulus Society in Marienbad, Czechoslovakia, the Christian concern was primarily in terms of the engagement of the church in society and the necessity of a Christian alignment with the hopes of the earth and a struggle against unjust social conditions, while the Marxists were involved in more theoretical questions that had traditionally been the sphere of the theologian.[22] Both Thomas Ogletree and Paul Lehmann, in a recently published Christian analysis of the dialogue, see its fruits primarily in the formation of a methodology of redemptive action rather than in the theoretical sphere:

Without obscuring the significance of man's personal life, openness to dialogue with Marxism requires Christian theologians to develop the meaning of Christianity's redemptive promise to men in terms of the structures that order men's life in society. ...

Attempts to interpret Christian faith in relation to social processes, particularly those involved in the struggles of oppressed peoples to bring into being a more fulfilling social order, have important implications for theological method. They call into question methodologies that view theology as a self-contained intellectual discipline. ..., They point instead to a way of doing theology that is shaped and conditioned by the concrete commitment of a community of faith to play a healing, reconciling role in the social and political struggles of man. ... Theology that follows this "reflection-in-action" model has many affinities with the Marxist view of the relation of thought and being.[23]

Thus Christian-Marxist dialogue can count as its achievements on the Christian side a theological reformulation that moves away from the more static dialectic of the finite and the infinite of crisis theology, with its tendency toward social conservativism, to a more progressive, action-oriented theology of hope. This is accompanied by a turning from purely theoretical formulations to a theologizing "in the streets," which constantly tests its theory against concrete practice. But the orientation toward a theologizing in the context of revolutionary *praxis* also has the effect of turning the younger and more involved theologians, particularly those of the American activist tradition, away from the original locus of the dialogue among Eastern and Middle European intellectuals toward those spheres where new revolutionary movements are developing, such as the American black liberation movement, and Asian, African, and Latin American revolutionary struggles. Here there might be an arena where such dialogue could bear fruit in Christian-Marxist revolutionary practice.[24]

Chapter 12

The Theology of Hope

The emergence of "the theology of hope" became the theological fashion of the later 1960s, following the publication of Jürgen Moltmann's landmark book of that title in 1967. It was quickly said that the theology of hope was superceding secular and Death of God theology, and pointed to a reemergence of questions about God and history. The sequence of "secular theology," "Death of God," and then "hope" is perhaps something of a "media sequence," but it does point to a deeper crisis within crisis theology itself that the theology of hope sought to overcome. Crisis theology or dialectical theology—and its later forms in Barthian theology of the "word" and Bultmannian "kerygmatic" theology—cut off the old liberal theology of progress. The nineteenth century had taken its stand on a secularized version of Christian future hope, and crisis theology arose as a very real critique of its naive optimism, its lack of a sense of radical evil, and its deification of its own cultural trends. Crisis theology then insisted on the radically transcendent nature of the two poles of God and the Kingdom. These represented the absolute that stands ever over against finite man, relativizing his projects and opening him up to new possibilities. The "future" was used as a key theological category, but to embody a new chance rather than a chance that could be projected into an ultimate fulfill-

ment. The literal pole of historical consummation was eliminated for an ever-unattainable symbol that could never come,
but functioned in history by keeping men from remaining where
they were. Christian life was simply this life of faith. The transcendent Kingdom was that absolute that was ever beyond the
finite, which judged and renewed it, but, by the very nature of the
finite and infinite, could never "come"; i.e., it could never achieve
a completed synthesis within created, temporal reality.

This concept of the Kingdom as the source of crisis but never
of fulfillment gradually eroded the nerve of social expectation.
Here theology was probably not so much the instigator as simply
the reflector of the erosion of optimism in Western society generally. What appeared a striking judgment upon overconfidence in
1920 by 1960 appeared a gratuitous slap at a civilization groping
to recover some straws of meaning. Niebuhrian realism gradually gave way to a complacent satisfaction with minimal expectations that all too easily supported the conservative status quo.
When that faith in the impossible possibility of a real kingdom
in a real future disappears, faith in man's ability to change his
situation fades as well. Thus, out of the dying embers of the old
liberal society there comes a demand to recover a new basis for
hope. One sign of this is a reaching back to nineteenth-century
theologies of progress themselves to see what can be recovered
from them in a new and more chastened way that will take into
consideration the intervening lessons. Neo-Hegelianism and
neo-Marxism, the vogue of nineteenth-century thought among
radical theologians, seem to be a part of this effort. Marxist humanism, the New Left and Christian-Marxist dialogue also are
a part of this effort to recover the roots of an earlier historical
faith. It is in this context that the theology of hope crystalizes as
a particular movement.

Two of the main sources for the theology of hope are the Catholic philosopher-scientist Teilhard de Chardin and the Marxist
philosopher Ernst Bloch. Teilhard de Chardin represents nineteenth-century man in his most sweeping cosmic and world-historical vision, not yet really shaken by twentieth-century doubt.

Teilhard, to be sure, only became available to the reading public in the 1950s, but his mature thought was developed decades before, and his philosophical structure looks back to Bergson. So although chronologically he intrudes into the twentieth century, his usefulness to the present lies precisely in the fact that he represents the last great nineteenth-century thinker. Bloch, on the other hand, represents an independent and humanistic Marxism that has shaken off the chains of party dogma and exposes the vital possibilities of this tradition in a new way. He bridges the time of the great Marxist revisionists of the turn of the century and the new post-Stalinist revisionism that forms the background for Christian-Marxist dialogue. When Bloch is assimilated into Jürgen Moltmann's theology of hope, we have no longer simply a stance for further dialogue, but a Christian-Marxist synthesis on the basis of which a new Christianity questions the adequacy of its recent theological heritage, and tries to recover anew the literal faith in the biblical Kingdom to come. Here we will look first at Teilhard and then at Moltmann in order to point to the problems of historical futurism in both its undialectical nineteenth-century form and as it restates itself after having passed through dialectical theology.

Teilhard's progressive vision of the universe, and that of nineteenth-century philosophy in general, rested on the older tradition of Christian history that viewed world history as a single drama of salvation beginning with creation and ending with the Kingdom of Heaven. Teilhard's achievement was to combine the nineteenth-century doctrines of historical progress and scientific evolution into a single cosmic drama, thus obliterating the distinction between nature and history by making nature historical and incorporating human history into the processes of nature. The universe is seen as a total system that ascends upward in systems of organization from the atomic to the planetary level and that is also engaged in a forward developmental movement extending from its primal form in the energy field, which forms its basic unity, to its final spiritual unification in what Teilhard calls the "omega point." There is no duplication in any level of the system, however. One cannot pass from the atomic to the molecular to the organic to the planetary levels simply by changing coefficients. Nor, as we move forward in the evolution of matter, is there mere change in quantitative organization, but, at set stages, there are qualitative leaps to new levels of existence. Thus the system must be seen as the universe as a whole, and the total meaning of this universe must be seen in the entirety of its evolutionary drama from beginning to end, i.e., in the perspective of cosmogenesis. But this universe is a closed quantum of energy that appears infinite only because we cannot go outside of it, but each new synthesis is created as the price of loss of energy. Thus the universe reveals itself as finite, spatially bounded, and temporally limited. It is a historical and not an eternal being, and takes its place among the realities that are born, grow, and die.

The universe evolves along the axis of complexification of matter. This is expressed outwardly in increasingly complex forms of organization and inwardly in intensified "radial energy." It is this interior aspect of the complexification of matter that Teilhard believes is responsible for certain breakthroughs to new levels of existence at specific "boiling points," first of life and then of consciousness. Everything that appears in the process of cosmogenesis is latent from the beginning, but this does not do away with the reality of its historical birth, which appears only when a certain critical level of evolution is reached. The link between the geosphere and the biosphere, i.e., between chemistry and biology, is the organic cell, which is the highest unit of the molecular structure and the lowest unit in the biological structure. It represents a buildup in the organization of molecular energy to such a level of tangential and radial energy that there is a "leap" or "boiling point" achieved in which a new level of existence, namely life, appears. The molecular structure is organized mechanically. It can be split up, and any of its parts will survive. This breakthrough to life represents a new level of centeredness and unification in which the whole structure becomes an organism participating in a common center and a common life, and not just a mechanical organization. If it is cut at its vital center, the whole structure disintegrates. Teilhard believes these breakthroughs are truly historical in that they took place at a specific *kairos* of the process of cosmogenesis that was unique to those times and is not repeatable at any time and place. Thus the universe is a truly historical organism that passes through stages that are not repeatable any more than the stages of the development of a person from foetus to childhood to adulthood can be repeated.

Once animate life appears, its profusion immediately ramifies into ordered types. The phyla become self-perpetuating along the lines laid out by their specific type, and they cease to be able to cross-fertilize with each other. Teilhard compares the evolution of species with the laws of human invention. First there appears a rudimentary type, then a series of rapid modifications and experimentations until the most efficient species is reached, at which stage it is stabilized around the reproduction of a single type. The less successful experiments die out, and evolutionary change within that species ceases. Again it is a historical process that has its own specific *kairos,* and is not repeatable at any later time. The suppression of the penults gives the impression of a greater distance between the phyla than originally existed when the evolution was in process. The younger phyla naturally exist in more profuse species than the older ones, with mammals, as the youngest branch on the evolutionary tree, existing in the most profuse numbers of species.

The evolutionary tree does not favor all phyla equally, but moves down a specific privileged axis. This axis, like that of cosmogenesis generally, is toward increasing interiorization and centricity, toward increasing coordination around a directing center of the organism. Thus with the vertebrates we arrive at an animal, not held together by external shells, but held together from within by the nervous system. As we move down the axis of vertebrates from reptiles to mammals, we find the nervous system itself developing a unifying center in the brain. The increasing size and convolutions of this brain corresponds to increasingly intelligent species of mammals until finally we arrive at man, where a new breakthrough in psychic energy takes place to a new level of life, namely, thought. Again the axis is one of increasing complexification of exterior organization, accompanied by rising centricity and intensification of interior energy (not as two things but as the "inside" and the "outside" of the same thing). Finally this intensified radial energy, which has first broken through to the level of life and then risen along this axis of biopsychic energy, finally breaks through to a new level where life energy doubles back on itself and becomes thought or self-consciousness.

From that point on man is the privileged axis of cosmogenesis, to the point where the animal kingdom from which he arose increasingly dies out around him. The earth more and more becomes a human earth, with the animal kingdom first subdued and then, in our times, confined to small preserves and reservations to keep many types from dying out altogether. The age of animals is over, and man has inherited the earth! Once the level of thought or the "noosphere" is reached, cosmogenesis now moves socially rather than organically. Organically man has a "stripped-down chassis." He had little external tools and devices of protection such as a hide or horns built into his organic structure. He is an animal equipped with hand and brain alone, and thus he can improvize his technological equipment indefinitely in constant new forms instead of having a static technological equipment built into him. The technological, cultural development of man becomes the new axis of cosmogenesis. Morphologically the transition from higher hominoids to man is very slight, but this slight increase in the convolutions of the brain presents a new threshold in which a new breakthrough of thought takes place. The higher mammals have increasing levels of instinctual intelligence, but only in man does this buildup of psychic energy reach the level where it breaks through to reflection.

With the birth of reflection, all the specifically human expressions of language, art, and science become possible. This is a revolutionary new threshold, which is only comparable in magnitude to the appearance of life itself from the inorganic envelope. Like the previous threshold, it is a critical boiling point that is crossed at a single stride. Although the lower mammals increasingly approximate intelligence, there is an infinite qualitative difference between intelligent animality and reflective man. Only in man does the centered surface become a true center or a person. With the advent of personhood, there is a decisive mounting of the individual over the species; this does not just fragment into chaotic individualism but points toward the evolution of a new collectivity—society.

With the birth of thought, a new tool of evolutionary change and transmission appears: technological invention and learning. Learning becomes the new tool for transmitting acquired characteristics in a much freer and more rapid way than the processes of organic experimentation, biological heredity, and suppression of unsuccessful types. Organic evolution is virtually complete, and now developmental processes are carried by the cultural envelope of reality. The cultural evolution begins when man socializes himself to the point where he can transmit the collective memory of his achievements to the next generation. This has grown increasingly complex as we move from recitation of traditions around a campfire to writing, to books, to printing, and finally to computers, which can store and transmit infinite amounts of information. The evolution of civilization depends on this ability to collect, digest, store, and transmit increasing amounts of information. Since none of this cultural envelope makes significant biological modifications in man's structure, if the cultural processes broke down, i.e., the flame of learning was not passed on for only one generation and all books destroyed, man would be immediately returned to his primitive state.

The shortness of time, relatively speaking, of this historical evolution of man is shown by the fact that there are still today surviving neolithic groups. Man, however, is not a phylum with species; he is a single species that can all intermarry despite minor differences in appearance. The cultural-technological evolution of society flowers in five great basins of civilization, but it is the Mediterranian basin that becomes the privileged axis of human development that is destined not to suppress other human experiments, but to gather them up together into a single synthesis. Here Teilhard was an undisguised partisan of the superiority of the West, but he thought this was a reasonable scientific projection, both from the general tendency of evolution to move down a privileged axis after a period of variegated experimentation, and the processes of westernization which were affecting all parts of the world. Even though this westernization might take autonomous national and cultural forms, it was working everywhere to transform man into an increasingly unified community around a common modern, Western, technological culture.

Cultural evolution moved out of the original neolitic revolution that gave birth to social organization and cultural transmission toward the development of a limited number of great classical civilizations. But the period from the Renaissance to the nineteenth century saw a new development beyond the level of classical civilization. Modernity began by transcending Western classical culture in its Greco-Roman and Judeo-Christian forms, and now is reaching around the globe to lift all of the areas of civilization to this new postclassical culture. Each area of culture transcends its classical civilization in its own way with reference to its own background, but the process is similar and the new technological culture of the "modern earth" is universal in scope. Teilhard believes the leap from classical to modern culture represents a cultural threshold not unlike the thresholds of life and thought. From the industrial revolutions and the Enlightenment to the French, Russian, and now worldwide revolutionary movements, we are seeing the birth of a new man, a new humanity transcending human culture.

Teilhard believes this new threshold is represented both by the rise of systematized technology whereby man is gradually gaining control of the processes of nature itself and by the rise of historical consciousness that represents on an interior level the historical process of evolution now become conscious of itself. In effect, modern man represents the point at which cosmogenesis becomes conscious of itself and in control of its own processes, so that, instead of being merely the subject, he becomes the agent of evolution. The classical consciousness lacked specifically these dimensions of historical consciousness and technological mastery. As late as the seventeenth century our ancestors still lived in static cubic space. The fourth dimension of time entered only with the birth of modern humanity. Even now only the most avant-garde men are fully modern; most still live in a static, prehistorical state of consciousness.

This new historical state of consciousness is not merely a theory among theories but is the new substratum and ground of all thinking. It is the place where cosmogenesis itself as a continuum of space and time gains conscious mastery of itself. Man as the tip of the soaring arrow of cosmogenesis now, as it were, assumes the driver's seat. The explosion of this new sense of immensity and responsibility is the source of the malaise and anxiety that affects modern man. Modern man has a sense of being lost in immense new possibilities for which he can conceive no suitable outcome. He lives in fear of cosmic catastrophe, which now becomes conceivable for the first time. On the edge of his vision looms the spectre of the collapse of all this development into nothing, a vast cosmic experiment with no meaning or goal.

This anxiety is the birth pangs of modern man coming of age. Man himself is both the player and the stakes in this last stage of cosmogenesis. No longer dependent on outside forces, the final leap of world evolution must now take place as a voluntary act of man's own will. Hence there enters an entirely new possibility that man might refuse this ascent, and thus refuse his own future and the future of the world. Evolution become self-conscious now depends on self-consciousness to carry it forward. But the will to carry us forward also depends on a faith in a reality not yet seen, but only dimly intuited as a force beckoning from beyond. Man can complete the building of the modern earth only through a faith in this transcendent point. Openness to this transcendence beyond present existence is the life force sustaining man's ability to press forward. Without this faith in a higher future, man loses the will to live and the whole process of cosmogenesis will come crashing to a halt, for this faith has now become the life force of evolution.

The axis of the evolution of the modern earth is toward increasing unitary personhood in which each individual becomes self-conscious at the same time his self-consciousness grows through an expanding consciousness of his fellow man. All the new techniques of travel and communications, the flooding of the consciousness with an expanding sense of the history, culture, and developmental state of every other human center expresses this movement toward a unitary humanity that is both increasingly personal and increasingly collective. The second aspect of this revolution in collective self-consciousness is the technological revolution whereby man increasingly gains control of all the world processes: reproduction, atomic energy, the very basis of all cosmic processes, even the reproduction of the evolutionary processes themselves in the mutation of genes and the creating of life. The entire universe increasingly becomes a single organism ordered and controlled by the collective human community as its self-conscious head.

Teilhard believes this growth toward increasing collective consciousness and control (omnipotence and omniscience?) will move toward a new critical point where the collective consciousness of man will break through (take off) from the finite substratum, which has been its evolutionary body, to achieve a completed state of transcendent communion. This is the point traditionally figured in the Christian tradition as the messianic community. Although Teilhard would not venture such unorthodox language at this point, this "hominization" of God and deification of man not only completes man but in a real sense "creates God." This, of course, is precisely how traditional Christian theology (i.e., the patristic period) spoke of *Christ*. This omega point is both the apex of the evolutionary series and a final leap that is transcendent to the whole series and goes beyond the space-time limitations of the finite universe itself. The finite gives birth to the infinite, time to eternity. The universe falls away and dies after having given birth to God; the ultimate communal consciousness in which nothing that has gone before is lost.

Most of the objections of Teilhard's thought are usually directed to this final projection. Undoubtedly at this point he passes beyond scientific knowledge, although he believes that it offers convincing pointers to this transcendent culmination. Two objections are often raised. One is that Teilhard lacks a sense of radical evil. His broad canvas tends to relegate details like atom bomb devastation and inhuman collectivist states into temporary unsuccessful experiments that are nevertheless leading in the right direction toward authentic mastery and community. Teilhard's optimism tends to make man's capacity for radical evil, even to the point of final refusal of the future, inconceivable. Therefore, in the last analysis, one might say that man is not truly free but is simply a part of an inevitable process that must lead towards its goal. But this criticism is not quite fair. Teilhard, as a matter of faith, had to believe that man would ultimately choose his authentic future over various inauthentic ones that presently tempted him in his experimental groping. But his theoretical system itself postulated that the last leap of cosmogenesis, which brought the whole development to its consummation, was now in the hands of man's free decision, and so, theoretically, the alternative between final salvation and final annihilation and collapse of the whole process into meaninglessness was open and possible. Teilhard did not choose in his systematic exploration to dwell on this negative possibility (his fear of it appears much more in his personal letters), but he clearly knew and recognized it to be there.

Secondly, one might criticize Teilhard's system for finally rejecting its own presuppositions at the point where the radial energy effecting the complexification of matter finally takes off from this material substratum and exists by itself. Nowhere in his system has there been any hint of a distinction of matter and spirit as two separate substances; rather, they are simply the inside and outside of each other. Thus there seems to be no basis in his previous analysis for this transcending of matter and the finite temporal universe by the interior radial energy of the universe itself. The whole process has been presented as totally temporal and historical in its very nature. Therefore, there seems to be no basis by which it could suddenly leap beyond this nature to a nontemporal condition. In partial reply to this criticism we can note, however, that this gap in logic is true of every projection of man's aspirations to the ultimate point. The inner contradiction of man's historical nature is that it presses toward a consummation that annihilates man as a historical being. Man's nature, pressed to its ultimate conclusion, reaches a point where, in order to realize himself, he must cease to be himself, and there is always a gap in logic as one tries to conceptualize the relation and transition from one to the other. The gap in logic at this point is not peculiar to Teilhard but rather to the human condition itself, and, if one would resolve it on the other side by taking man as a totally historical being that will perish with the perishable dimension of nature, then one has to explain this thirst for the eternal which the world cannot quench. Either way man is partially an alien in the universe, or, to put it in Teilhard's perspective, the universe has a dimension that can finally fulfill itself only by negating its finite temporal being. Teilhard does not really try to explain how this paradox is possible "scientifically," but simply presses the analysis of the evolutionary process itself down to the ultimate point of convergence where the paradox itself appears.

Turning from Teilhard's *Phenomenon of Man* to Moltmann's *Theology of Hope,* we appear to move from an attempt to create a system of world salvation to a methodology that fundamentally rejects such systematization for an existential analysis that rests not on scientific grounding but on biblical mythology, i.e., the language of evocative pictorial symbols. Yet a similar view of God and man and the same kind of final puzzle about this relationship confronts us in Moltmann, too, although he avoids making this explicit by eschewing systematic ontological analysis. Moltmann's background is that of left-wing dialectical theology in the form of Bultmannian and post-Bultmannian thought. To the impasse created by existentialist theology, Moltmann brings new insights from a restituted nineteenth-century progressivism, especially as found in neo-Marxianism, i.e., Ernst Bloch. But then these interpretive tools are projected back upon biblical symbolism to suggest that what we are really getting is simply straight exegesis of the book of Exodus and the gospels. Good post-Bultmannians, however, know that they no longer have to feel embarrassed about this inevitable hermeneutical circle.

For Moltmann, the biblical God of revelation must be constantly distinguished from the gods of epiphanies. The gods of epiphanies disclose an existing Heaven, a realm of perfect Being with which man can commune in that ecstatic "intersection of time and eternity." The God of revelation, by contrast, is the God of promise and demand. The promise refers to a world of reconciled being that does not yet exist but is to come. The effect of revelation, then, is not to create a moment of harmony between Heaven and earth but to shatter a false harmony, to reveal the incongruity with the present, to set man against present conditions and in a state of movement toward a new age to come. In this tension between the present and the promise, there is no sharp distinction to be made between the Old and New Testaments. Both are religions of the future promise and keep men unreconciled with present conditions and in a *status viatoris* toward a world to come. The revelation in Jesus Christ, as well as that to Moses, is not its own self-fulfillment, but points beyond itself to a coming still in the future. The effect of the revelation is to expose the incongruity of man's being with his present existence so that he departs from where he is and strikes out for the promised land.

Yet this being of man itself must be seen not as a datum, but as a mandatum. In Garaudy's words, "It is an exigency which we live." Man's "being" is precisely "he who is not yet"; a demand laid upon him to become what he is not and has never been. The "existence" of God lies in this "not yet" of man's being. This reality of God does not lie in some transcendental realm over or behind the world, it lies in the future of the world that is not yet present, but is to come. But this "being" of God as the future of man is not merely an absence, but an absence that exercises its power upon man by pulling him out from where he is and setting his feet on the road to constant new possibilities. The Israelites called out of Egypt and on their way in the desert to the promised land represent man living this exigency. The resurrection of Jesus from the dead does not bring an end to this exigency—in the sense that the new age becomes present and can thereby become a hallowed moment of fulfillment in the past—but it, too, even more strongly, points away from its own moment to the future. The Risen Lord is "He who is to come"; the Messiah or Lord of the future world. His resurrection manifests proleptically this end of the world, not as a completing of it, but as a preview of things to come. The Parousia of Christ, then, is not, as in Barthian thought, an "unveiling" of what has already happened, but rather the final happening of what was foreshown, the final fulfillment of the promise given to Moses and proleptically experienced in the Christ event.

The Kingdom of God stands as the ultimate horizon of this future hope of man. It is represented in every relative horizon of man's hopes and exercises its power through them, and relativizes every finite horizon and draws man out beyond them. This means that we must take the finite horizon of our hopes with utmost seriousness. The achievement of particular goals such as racial equality or workingmen's justice, represents for us, in a particular *kairos*, the ultimate *kairos* of the Kingdom of God. The ultimate *kairos* lends power to the particular *kairos*, filling it with an attractive potency that can energize men, draw them out of their accustomed ways, and lend them wings to transcend themselves in the struggle for the new world. But, as we draw near to a conquest of the particular goal, we must always be able to look ahead and see that a new horizon has now appeared beyond the horizon that has now drawn close and become territory into which we are now entering. The particular goal never completely fulfills these ultimate hopes, but moves on to invest a new horizon with attractive power, and keeps us from sacralizing the point that we have achieved. The danger comes in man's inability to see the new horizon beyond the present one and his tendency to settle down in an oasis in the desert and attempt to pretend that this is the promised land. In this false synthesis of the ultimate with the relative hopes, sacral and totalitarian societies arise, and man loses his freedom for new futures.

This tension between history and eschatology, which has its revealed expression in the biblical *mythos,* has, in modern times, becomes the very stuff of man's experience of history. Beginning with the French Revolution, man began to experience history as crisis, as an arena in which a struggle against the old world was taking place and the shaping of man's future was in terms of hopes for things yet to come rather than of past traditions. The metaphysics and institutions of the old order collapsed, and the philosophy of history itself became the new means of reflecting on man's being. But philosophies of history are also an attempt to control and, therefore, sell out the true messianic dynamic of historical experience. They try to incorporate history into an enclosed system, grounded on a primal being underlying and reigning over history, which history can then "imitate." They still belong to the classical tradition of Parmenidean Being, but, for the authentic dialectic of history and eschatology, there can be no "logos," because the transcendent is not an existent "primal" being that encloses the possibilities of history, but the promise of things that are not yet, that have not yet existed. For that which is not yet there can be no "logos" or system. To use more Marxian language, existence precedes essence, rather than being the product of essence, as in classical thought. "The act" brings new realities into existence and, on the basis of these new realities, new theories, a new logos about what is becomes possible. Truly historical existence lies precisely in this disparity between existence and essence in which ultimate Being is not yet achieved, and so new possibilities not contained within the logos of the present reality are possible.

In this interpretation of historical existence in a messianic perspective, Moltmann returns again and again to a polemic against existentialist theology as found in Bultmann, Gogarten, and their followers. Their dialectic of history and eschatology remained essentially vertical rather than forward-moving and inward rather than outward-turning. In effect, the "echaton" of Bultmann was a timeless transcendent, equally near to and equally far from every historical moment. Its encounter with man was an "epiphany" of the eternal rather than a demand for historical action and creativity. Out of this encounter emerged an irreconcilable polarity between transcendental subjectivity and objectified form; in effect, a new form of dualism between soul and body. Salvation again became salvation by flight into the inward, nonobjectifiable realm of man by rejecting the outward structural form of social and historical life. Even the transcendental determination of "co-humanity" in the I–Thou relationship became an essentially nonobjectifiable reality that set itself against all social institutions. This polarity Moltmann sees as a part of the romantic reaction to technological civilization, whereby man, in effect, abandons technological civilization to run by its own impersonal laws, but finds freedom through escape from this whole realm of objectified relations to one of inner freedom and personhood. As a result, however, existentialist man is unable to make anything out of the realm of objects, and so existentialist theology had no prescription for the social order itself.

The messianic perspective is not a flight from the world and history, or an ending of history by a punctual escape into transcendental subjectivity; it is a mandate laid upon history itself. The struggle is carried out not against finite possibilities, but to redeem these possibilities and fill the forms of historical life with human substance. Instead of the hopeless dialectic of "community" against "institution," one must dissolve the inhumanity of institutions from within to make them vehicles and expressions of community. The struggle involves not simply dialectic but synthesis. The syntheses are always partial and inadequate, but they express the ultimate synthesis of man and God that is the goal of history, and every partial synthesis points beyond itself to this ultimate vision that both lends it power and vision and keeps it from finalizing itself. Salvation is sought neither by conforming to the world as it is nor withdrawing from it in mere dialectical negation, but rather in a real historical struggle for justice, for the humanizing of institutions, the communalizing of humanity, and for peace on earth. It is a struggle for the redeeming of the world, not simply a redeeming of the soul from the world. This struggle must be seen neither as conforming to nor withdrawal from what is but a struggle to transform what is in opposition and creative expectation in the midst of which one believes, hopes, and loves.

What we find, then, in Moltmann is an acceptance of the challenge laid down by the Marxist partners in dialogue to express in Christian terms what Garaudy believed a Christian could not say, namely, that the word "God" stands not for primordial but for eschatological being. God stands for an absolute that does not yet exist, but is experienced as an exigency out of which man lives in his historical élan toward the future as the realm of new possibilities. Moltmann has carried through the de-Hellenizing of Christian theology to a new level by repudiating even those vestiges of the God of "Being" that remained in existentialism for a throughgoing description of God as "the future of man." The project still remains highly unsatisfactory, however, because we still do not understand this new ontology in a philosophical way, but only in terms of evocative symbols and myths. Perhaps this expresses precisely the limits of logos as linked to a concept of unitary being, but even this needs to be exposed in a more analytical way than Moltmann has attempted here.

Secondly, Moltmann bases his doctrine of the future on an apparent assumption that this future has power because it will finally come. The ultimate future will finally become present, and the synthesis of God and man will be completed. Here again, as in Teilhard, we have the paradox that the final point in the series transcends radically and not just relatively the conditions of the series itself. Thus Moltmann has really not gotten beyond the dilemma of crisis theology to establish a basis for projecting the final consummation of the historical dialectic as something that could conceivably happen. The dialectic itself is perfectly adequately explained by Garaudy's description of the infinite as endless movement. The demand in human nature for a consummation of this dialectic is the *mythos* out of which he lives this infinite exigency. But that it is finally to be fulfilled? This would be the transformation of human historical nature as we have known it. Therefore, it is "impossible." Ah ha! exclaims the man of faith. It is precisely at this point that we understand the full meaning of creation *ex nihilo* and resurrection from the dead. What is literally impossible within the old creation is precisely the radically new possibility of the New Creation, and it is this new possibility beyond all present ones that is pointed to by the faith in the resurrection from the dead and life of the world to come.

Part III

CONTEMPORARY

MOVEMENTS

Chapter 13

The American Apocalypse

The apocalyptic mood is one born of despair. As a movement, it expresses the hopes of oppressed and alienated people who see no possibility of bettering their condition within the present system, within "this world" in the sense of the shape and structure of the world situation as presently constituted. Their only hope is seen as lying through a total overthrow of the present system and a reconstitution of the world on a new and radically different basis. Apocalypticism is a leap of hope and will beyond present conditions—perhaps even beyond the human historical condition itself—by people who have no power to do anything effective within the system as it is. They gather apart, both in alienation from the present world and in anticipation of some power from beyond that will deliver them, overthrow the present system, and set up a new world on a new basis in which they can assume their rightful place.[1]

In America there have been only two groups who had entertained a strongly apocalyptic attitude toward the American ethos itself. These two groups are the American Indian and the American Negro. For the immigrant groups that came to America from Europe came as pilgrims, fleeing from an old forsaken world to a new world golden with promise, the overthrow of the old, evil world had, in a sense, taken place in their departure from their native country, and they looked to America as the new world that would fulfill their hopes. The American Indian, the indigenous population that was impoverished and destroyed by this avalanche from Europe, and the Negro, brought here as an enslaved man leaving his freedom behind him, experienced the new world not as the American dream but as the American nightmare. As Eldridge Cleaver puts it, the African slaves were "a stolen people on a stolen land."[2] Excluded by nature from this new foundation, never intended, even by the liberators of the Civil War, to become a part of it,[3] specifically excluded from the "liberty for all men" proclaimed in the Constitution, they could only envision a hope for themselves by an overthrow or escape from the covenant that the colonists were founding.

In the decades before the end of the nineteenth century, the American Indian was being pushed out of his last good grazing ground, robbed of his last sphere in which to function as a proud hunter and warrior, and confined to wasteland reservations to moulder and die. As Martin Luther King once noted, "The United States is the only colonial country founded through an open policy of genocide toward the indigenous population," or, as a popular American aphorism had it, "the only good Indian is a dead Indian." In this last desperate struggle, waves of apocalyptic expectation swept over the American Indian, especially in the Northwest among the Sioux, the Paiutes, the Utes, and the Crow. The "ghost dance," as this movement is known through its prime ritual expression, derived its symbols in part from Judeo-Christian messianism, but the hopes it expressed were strictly Indian.[4] The core of the ghost dance was a hope for a time to come when the whole Indian race, living and dead, would be reunited upon a regenerated earth. The white race, being alien and hardly even human, would have no part in this world regeneration, but would be left behind when the other debased things of earth were put to an end and ceased to exist.

The Indians could remember a time when they had been masters of the land and had roamed at will over its surface, chasing the abundant wildlife that were now dying out before the white man's advance. Their hope, then, took the form of a vision of restoration of the lost paradise, including the hosts of brave warriors who had led them in their proud tribal past of whom they themselves were only a remnant and a shadow. The ghost dance was essentially an evocation of these spirits of the warriors of old, invoking their presence both in the dance and in their mighty coming as a victorious host to bring in the new restored age to come. The ghost dance was both a communing with the spirits of the dead and a prayer for them to rise and bring back the world that had died when they passed from the earth. The dancers also believed that Jesus had already risen from the dead as the beginning of this resurrection of the warriors. He had repudiated the white man because he had proved himself unworthy, and had turned instead to become the savior of the red man. Jesus was already present, going incognito among the Indians, and his presence was a token that the great dead of the past were already rising and would soon be here to bring in the regenerated earth. As one Indian document puts it:

Do not tell the white man about this. Jesus is now upon the earth. He appears like a cloud. The dead are all alive again. I do not know when they will be here; maybe this Fall or Spring. When the time comes, there will be no more sickness and everyone will be young again.[5]

The actual form of the arrival of the new world was described in various ways. In one version, the hosts of the risen warriors would advance like a cloud, bringing the new rejuvenated earth with them. The Indians would all rise in the air, and the new earth would slide over and cover the old, debased earth created by the white man, burying him and all his works. Then the Indians would find themselves in a land thick with game and would live in the happy hunting ground forever. One Indian document of the period describes the apocalypse:

All Indians must dance; everywhere, keep on dancing. Pretty soon in next Spring, Great Spirit come. He bring back all game of every kind. The game be thick everywhere. All dead Indians come back and live again and get young and have fine time. When Old Man (God) come this way, then all Indians go up to mountains, high up away from whites. Whites can't hurt Indians then. Then while Indians way up high, big flood come, like water, and all white people die, get drowned. Then that water go away and then nobody but Indians everywhere and game all kinds thick.[6]

The ghost dance inspired some disastrous uprisings, particularly among the Sioux, who were driven to the most desperate straits and began to act out the apocalyptic hopes. The Indians believed that they would be impervious to the white man's bullets if they wore the sacred ghost shirt, and the result was a pathetic slaughter of men, women, and children at the Battle of Wounded Knee on December 29, 1890. Although most white Americans remember nothing of this battle, its memory still remains vivid among the American Indians and lives in their collective memory as a day of infamy.

The uprisings were the exception in the ghost dance movement, however. Mostly the medicine men cautioned passivity. The Indians must not go to war, but remain peaceful and prepare themselves for the day of vengeance to come. This passivity is frequently found among apocalyptic movements. Because the movement is born of desperation and constitutes a leap beyond the capacities of the oppressed group, the prophets typically caution against action, knowing that a slaughter by the oppressors will result. Instead they seek to nourish hope, group rejuvenation, and solidarity in expectation of a deliverance from beyond.[7] Often when hopes of active deliverance, either by direct action or some power from beyond, have faded, the apocalyptic movement turns to some type of withdrawal, mysticism, and communalism. Such a development took place in the Indian resistance movement as apocalyptic hopes faded. The Peyote Way, both as a group mysticism and as a means of affirming Indian solidarity and resistance to the white man, became the new road to Indian salvation after the period of struggle was over and the reservation closed in on the Indian.[8]

The problem of future hope for the American Negro was, in a sense, even more difficult to project than for the Indian. Defined as three-fifths of a person for purposes of taxation and representation, in terms of civil rights excluded from all representation or participation in the American covenant, and at the same time cut off from his own African heritage with the language, family structure, and memories of his homeland crushed out of existence by slavery, he was a man with neither a past to recall nor a future to anticipate. During the slave period there were over a hundred slave revolts, as well as some forty on the slave ships themselves, yet these revolts have been largely dropped from the white man's history. One revolt that has never quite left popular memory, however, was that led by the literate preacher-slave, Nat Turner, in 1831. Nourished almost entirely on the Bible, Nat saw his uprising as the avant-garde of the avenging angel of God. As he recounts it in his own account of the revolt, written in prison before his execution, "About this time I had a vision—and I saw white spirits and black spirits engaged in battle, and the sun was darkened, thunder rolled in the heavens and the blood flowing in streams." And again in another vision, he describes:

And on the 12th of May, 1828, I heard a loud noise in the heavens, and the Spirit instantly appeared to me and said that the Serpent was loosened, and Christ had laid down the yoke he had borne for the sons of men, and that I should take it on and fight against the Serpent, for the time was fast approaching when the first should be last and the last should be first.[9]

Turner's practical impact was small, but his psychological impact was great. The terror he evoked was not simply due to the few deaths he caused but to the consciousness that he expressed thereby of being the divinely appointed agent of apocalyptic wrath, to which white society, in its guilt, could only respond in fear and fury.

At the end of the Civil War this condition of servitude was declared abolished, and, by fiat, the Negro was incorporated into the constitutional covenant. But little effort was made to undertake the kind of total revamping of the American social structure and ethos that would make this actually possible. So the American Negro was faced with a terrible impasse. He was a man without a country, an identity, or a culture of his own to which he could return. His identity was defined for him by the dominant culture almost entirely in terms of either bestial or vaudeville images. On the other hand, the future to which he was called to aspire, a place in the white man's society, lay up a staircase so closely guarded that only a fortunate few could slip through.

To this dilemma American Negroes responded in one of two ways; one way was the way of deference. The black man should look to the covenant of the dominant society as the covenant to which he should aspire for full membership. He should seek to win the white man's friendship by adopting his manners and ways and becoming as indistinguishable from him as possible. He should seek to raise himself educationally and economically, but without taking any aggressive political action, leaving the business of power to the white man. Then gradually, as he lifted himself, he would come to be accepted by the white man and would take his place in American society. This was the way of Booker T. Washington, and it is the way that has marked the black middle class up to the present time.[10]

The other way was the way that emphatically rejected the white man's covenant as one that could never become a covenant for the black man. This is the way of black separatism, black nationalism, and black revolution. The black nationalist is one who rejects the proposition that, in due time and through some process of education and progress, the Negro's dilemma can be resolved within the framework of American institutions as they presently exist. This stand, far from being a recent phenomenon, as many white Americans are apt to believe, has a long history and is a deeper and more indigenous view than the middle class view of assimilation.

During the nineteenth century, it took the form of Black Zionism, an attempt to remove the black man from white society and found a national homeland for him. Black Zionist movements arose as early as the 1830s. They continued after the Civil War and perhaps found their best known expression in the Garveyite movement of the 1920s. One of the persistent difficulties with Black Zionism was the lack of a clear homeland symbol with which the American Negro could identify. The Negro knew that he came from Africa, but he didn't know which part. His name, his tribe, his language, and his region were lost to him. Furthermore he had been taught to be ashamed of Africa, to see it as a land of naked savages. Unlike the Indian, unlike the other immigrant groups, he had no proud memories, no ideal self-image in the past to which he could refer himself, only a past image of degradation in slavery and a more remote past behind that that he assumed to be one of ignoble savagery. Consequently, although Black Zionism sought to return the Negro to his homeland and give him an identity through awakening a sense of his origins, it was ambivalent about what this homeland and origins were to be.

Some looked to Canada, Haiti, or Latin America as the place of settlement. Others, like Marcus Garvey, openly rejoiced in the name of Africa, but chose the Mediterranean Liberia as the land of settlement. The Negro knew that the Northern Mediterranean had a proud antiquity in the Arab Empire, Carthage, and Egypt, while sub-Saharan Africa he believed to be a dark land of unrelieved savagery. For this reason Black Zionism has tended to equivocate on the nature of Negro origins, and to identify with Arab Africa rather than with sub-Saharian Africa.[11] It is only in recent times, with the emergence of the new independent African nations in lower Africa, that the American Negro has been able to identify more openly with the area closer to his true origins, and to call himself proudly an Afro-American. Even so there has been a tendency to conjure up a somewhat imaginative, glorious antiquity for these African lands to satisfy the needs for a proud ancestral self-image seemingly necessary to nationalism.

Black nationalism movements multiplied in the 1940s and began to take many forms—religious, cultural, and economic—although always finding their ultimate expression in the dream of a Negro homeland. The group that particularly gathered up these hopes in a disciplined form and mediated it to the present generation of black radicals was the Black Muslims. The Nation of Islam, as it is properly called, began under the leadership of Elijah Mohammed in about 1932. It had a previous, although somewhat undetermined, root in nationalist movements of the twenties, which took Islam as the national religion of the black man. Its immediate origins are shrouded in mystery. According to the doctrine of the Nation itself, it was founded by a black Arab named W. D. Fard, who is honored as Messiah and God incarnate. He is supposed to have revealed the true faith of the black American to Elijah Mohammed and then disappeared. The existence of Fard is somewhat hard to document, nevertheless the Nation honors Elijah Mohammed as his divinely appointed and infallible delegate, the last of the prophets, and God's representative on earth. In Essien Udom's excellent study of the Nation,[12] its views are divided into two very different but complementary aspects: the esoteric teachings, i.e., the doctrines about the origin and destiny of the black and white races, and the exoteric teachings, which are the ethics and life style that it endeavors to foster in its members.

The esoteric teachings of the Nation consist in an apocalyptic world drama by which the Muslim is taught to understand his true identity, his original origins, the nature of his present debasement, and his future hope. The doctrines may appear absurd and fanciful to the unbeliever, as all religious mythology does, but they serve the purposes for which they were created, namely, to answer, in striking symbolic form, these pressing questions of the American Negro's identity and destiny. According to Muslim doctrine, the black man is the original and authentic humanity. Tracing his ancestry to the black patriarch, Abraham, he is the original People of God. By "black man," however, this teaching does not mean simply what most people call Negroes, but all non-Caucasian peoples, black, brown, and yellow.

This black race dwelt in an aboriginal paradise when earth and moon were still united. They were a gifted race, with unusual intelligence and talent. Most particularly they were brilliant scientists. The creation of the white race came about through an error or fall within this original black people. One of the most brilliant of the black scientists, Yakub, began to turn his knowledge to evil ways. Finally he conceived the idea of creating a devil through the process of scientific mutation. Secretly, over a long period of time, he evolved this devil, whose name was Adam and who is the ancestor of the white race. The white man is not a true creation or child of God at all. He is not God's creation, but was created by what might be called "a fallen angel." He is, therefore, not an authentic human being at all, but a bastard being, inauthentic and devilish by the very nature of his origins. When the rest of the black race discovered this apostasy, they threw Yakub and his followers, numbering some 60,000, out of the paradise of the heartland of Asia into the vile European wilderness. After this fall the Edenic state of the original black race disappeared, and God determined that for this sin the black race should live under the yoke of the white devils for six thousand years as a period of trial and purgation.

However, the end of this sixth millennium is fast approaching. Its termination has already been announced by the appearance on earth of God's son, the Messiah, who revealed these doctrines to Elijah Mohammed. Under the leadership of the Prophet, the great ingathering of the black nation in dispersion is beginning. This is their resurrection from the death that takes place in their ingrafting into the one body of the Nation and the discovery of their true identity. When the 144,000 elect destined to escape the holocaust are gathered together, then the great judgment of Armageddon will begin. This definitely will occur some time before the year 2000 A.D. The judgment takes place in two stages. First there is the ingathering of the elect, which is presently taking place. Then will come the day of the apocalypse. This will be announced by the appearance of planes in the sky that will drop pamphlets in Arabic and English, giving God's final warning. Then Allah will send a great airborne attack force that will destroy white civilization by bombs, fire, and poison gas. After this destruction, the world will rise rejuvenated, inhabited only by the authentic humanity of the black race, which will inherit the earth and rule in peace and felicity forever.

These teachings also include the idea that the black man is not to be called a Negro. This is an identity imposed on him by the white devil. The black man is an Asiatic man and his true religion is Islam, while Christianity is the religion of the devil designed to fool the black man and keep him in subservience. This repudiation of Christianity, however, does not necessarily mean a rejection of Jesus. Here as in many cases of new messianic sects, the figure of Jesus has a way of transcending the repudiation of historical Christianity. Muslims tend to believe that Jesus was a true prophet and a black man, but his teachings were perverted by the white devil for their purposes.

These esoteric teachings, which are seldom discussed with outsiders, are balanced by a very high and strict code of ethics that are essential to an understanding of the impact of the Nation on its followers. The Nation teaches that the white man is a devil, but the black man is dehumanized. Spiritually he is a dead man who has lost his soul. Only by discovering his true identity and by the total conversion of his life can he recover his soul and rise from the dead. This means, in practice, that he must give up dancing, drinking, smoking, and all frivolous occupations and desires. He must devote himself to a stern regime of physical discipline and education. He must adopt a strict life of hygiene and diet and become a strong family man, a loyal husband, and a dutiful father. His wife must be decorous and modest, taking on the full robed garb and veil. She must see her primary task as wife and mother. The Nation frowns on the wife working outside the home. She must see her husband as lord and master, and he must see his first responsibility as her protection and the protection of all black women. In short, the Nation adopts a highly puritanical and paternalistic concept of family life as the necessary antidote to the family dislocation and personal dissipation of the lower class American Negro, especially in the urban ghetto. In ethical terms, the Muslim is a thoroughgoing Calvinist, and he takes over in toto all the middle class norms and virtues. The result is that the Nation has a remarkable record of rescuing the down-and-out and of instilling a new sense of pride and discipline into the ex-convicts and derelicts of the ghettos. Its best proselytizing work has been done in prisons where it is generally admitted by both friends and enemies that the Muslim is an outstanding person in the prison community, deliberately eschewing the vice of prison life and protecting its own members from these destructive practices.

The convert, once he adopts the Muslim faith and discipline, soon becomes economically mobile. He gives up the habits that were destroying him and begins to build the kind of solid personal and family virtues that determine well-being and success. The Nation sponsors a certain amount of small businesses through which it employs its members, and it sees that all attain jobs of some kind. It frowns on welfare or handouts. It also requires its members to take various self-improvement courses in remedial education, hygiene, budgeting, and food preparation. These together with other evening meetings of the Nation absorb most of the members' spare time, keeping them out of the taverns and other places of dissipation in the ghetto. On one side, then, the Nation is a panorama of world history designed to interpret the ultimate meaning of things and the Negroes' place therein, and, on the other side, it is a practical and thoroughgoing project of Negro self-help. It is this combination that makes for its attractiveness and power among the Northern urban Negro poor among whom it has had its chief impact.

Although the Nation looks forward to Armageddon, it strictly rules out the possibility that the members of the Nation should begin it here and now. Its teachings are strictly pacifist. It teaches the legitimacy of self-defense but rules out any offensive warfare. The deliverance is to be by the grace of God, not by the work of men. Here and now the black man should separate himself out of the devil's civilization, discover his true self, devote himself to the disciplined life of prayer and duty, and wait patiently until the final deliverance. The Muslims have been involved in violence in two contexts. These were self-defense under assault and punitive violence against its own apostate members, the most notable example being the assassination of Malcolm X. But even in cases of assault, they have frequently preferred to sue through the courts rather than to fight directly.

Their military style and discipline thus must be seen as symbolic militancy and as a way of unifying the community itself rather than as preparation for offensive warfare against white society at the present time. It is this pacifism that has, to a large extent, discredited the Muslims in the eyes of the young radicals who have adapted much of their ethos but in a secularized and more activist form.

The transition from Muslim expectant apocalypticism to the radicalism of the black liberation movement that succeeded the civil rights movement was made by Malcolm X. He was both the Nation's greatest convert and minister and the person who transcended its limitations toward a fuller vision. Malcolm X began his career as Malcolm Little, the fourth child of a militant Baptist minister who was murdered by white racists when Malcolm was six years old. Malcolm grew up to become the typical ghetto derelict, pimping, pushing dope, and playing "tag" with the cops, until finally he found himself in prison. It was there that the evangelists of Elijah Mohammed reached him. The message that the white man is a devil and his civilization a snare and a delusion that is about to be overthrown illuminated the mystery that had shrouded Malcolm's life until then. He was converted in prison and adopted the strict regime of prayer and study dictated by the prophet. Almost illiterate, he painfully taught himself to read and then embarked on a complete task of self-education through the prison library, exploring all fields of knowledge, but especially that of world history.[13]

Once out of prison he rapidly rose to become one of Elijah Mohammed's most valued ministers, and it is through his efforts that Muslim evangelism began to draw large numbers of converts, to build a strong organization, especially in New York, and to come to the attention of the general American public. Finally Malcolm became so powerful within the Nation that he began to challenge the power of the Prophet himself. Although he made great efforts to be deferential, the Prophet grew increasingly suspicious of him. Then various financial and sexual indiscretions of the Prophet were revealed and destroyed Malcolm's belief in the/infallibility and true prophethood of Elijah Mohammed. Although Malcolm continued to revere the Prophet, he lost the innocence of his original conversion and broke with the Nation to set up his own independent organization. From then on he was a marked man.

Malcolm had ever desired to be a true son of Islam, and so in 1964 he decided to journey to Mecca to make the pilgrimage that marks a true Muslim and also to learn whether he had indeed been taught the authentic faith by the Nation. This visit to the Arab holy land was the catalyst that helped Malcolm to transcend the dogmatic racism of the Nation and to discover a new vision of humanity and a new program for the American Negro. He discovered quite simply that Islam itself is not racist, that under the banner of Islam it practiced a fellowship of all races. But he discovered this not simply as a doctrine but as a living experience. Accepted as a fellow Muslim, Malcolm experienced true fellowship with Near Eastern Arabs of the lightest complexion on the grounds of being a brother in religion. For the first time Malcolm X discovered the reality of calling a white man "brother" and being called "brother" by a white man.

In his own words, he discovered that the white man is not himself inherently evil, but rather that it is the white system, the social structure in which he was formed, that is evil. It is the system that must be challenged and changed. Malcolm also discovered a new solidarity with the nonwhite peoples of the world that the Nation, despite its doctrine of non-Caucasian unity, had never really opened up to him, because its teaching on this subject was mythological rather than political. He discovered the international dimension of the Afro-American struggle. All over the world the underprivileged, non-Christian, nonwhite people are struggling to free themselves from the yoke of Western white Christendom of which the United States is today the primary representative. Again he felt Islam was the key because it was the traditional enemy of imperialist white Christendom. The rise of the colored Asian man signals the end of the Western Christian era of world dominance.

Malcolm went back to New York with a new program in mind. First he had to raise the black struggle in America to international dimensions, to teach the American Negro to see himself as one with non-Caucasian peoples of the world revolting against colonialism. Secondly he had to overcome dogmatic racism and declare a solidarity of all humanity of whatever religion and race around the common themes of justice and brotherhood. In practice, Malcolm felt that this should be achieved by a functional rather than doctrinaire separatism of white and black America. The Afro-American should build an all-black movement, black-run and black-financed, and work to build up the infrastructure of his own community. White people of good will could cooperate with this movement, not by trying to join much less run the Negro movement, but by working to overcome racism within their own community, which they could do far more effectively than the black man. Only in this way could the two communities meet as genuinely equal partners rather than in the usual paternalistic relationship that makes the black man's rights the gift of the white man's benevolence. Malcolm saw this program as the last chance for America, and hoped that someday white Americans would come to see him as one who pointed the way to the salvation of America as a genuinely viable society of many races as equal partners.

The essence of Malcolm's program was to be self-help. No man can give another freedom and dignity; a man must be regenerated in his own soul in order to stand up as a man. In Malcolm's words:

I said that on the American racial level, we had to approach the Black man's struggle against white racism as a human problem, that we had to forget hypocritical politics and propaganda. I said that both races as human beings had the obligation, the responsibility, of helping to correct America's human problem. The well-meaning white people, I said, had to combat, actively and directly, the racism in other white people. And the Black people had to build within themselves much greater awareness that, along with equal rights, there had to be the bearing of equal responsibilities. . . . I have these very deep feelings that white people who want to join black organizations are really taking the escapist way to salve their consciences. By visibly hovering near us, they are proving that they are with us. But the hard truth is that this isn't helping to solve America's racist problem.... Aside from that I mean nothing against sincere whites when I say that, as members of black organizations, generally white's very presence subtlely renders the black organization automatically less effective. Even the best white members will slow down the Negroes' discovery of what they need to do, and particularly what they can do, for themselves.... We will completely respect our white co-workers. They will deserve every credit. We will give them every credit. We will meanwhile be working among our own kind, in our own black communities, showing and teaching black men in ways that only other black men can, that the black man has got to help himself.... Sometimes I have dared to dream to myself that one day history may even say that my voice—which disturbed the white man's smugness and his arrogance and his complacency—that my voice helped to save America from a grave, possibly even a fatal catastrophe. Every morning when I wake up now I regard as having another borrowed day. In any city, wherever I go, making speeches, holding meetings of my organization or attending to other business, black men are watching every move I make, waiting for a chance to kill me. ... I know too that I could suddenly die at the hands of some white racist. ... Each day I live as though I were already dead. ... I do not expect to live long enough to read this book in its finished form ... and if I can die having brought any light, having exposed any meaningful truth that will help destroy the racist cancer that is malignant in the body of America, then all credit is due to Allah. Only the mistakes have been mine.[14]

On this note, Malcolm X concluded his autobiography. In the next year his prophecy came true and he was gunned down at a public meeting by his former brothers, the Muslims. But almost immediately he became the patron saint of the militant young people in the ghetto, who were looking for a viable way which was neither the deference politics of the black bourgeoisie nor the fanaticism and rigidity of the Nation of Islam. The mantle of Malcolm's leadership, however, has fallen particularly on the shoulders of Eldridge Cleaver, minister of information of the Black Panther party, and currently a fugitive from injustice in Algeria.

Eldridge Cleaver was himself a ghetto castaway and prison

inmate when the Black Muslim doctrine became his way of expressing his determination to "get himself together." Like Malcolm, he then turned to a disciplined, almost monastic style of
self-education and found his new self-understanding through
writing. His prison autobiography, *Soul on Ice,* is a nationwide
bestseller. But Cleaver turned from Elijah Mohammed to Malcolm X while in prison, and followed him in his break with the
Nation. When the shock of Malcolm's assassination came to him
in prison, he was determined that he would lend his hand to carry
on Malcolm's organization of Afro-American unity and his
dream of a higher racial solidarity. After his release from prison
he carried this determination into an abortive attempt to revive
Malcolm's organization in the San Francisco area, and then
found in the Black Panther party a better vehicle for this dream
already at hand and led by dynamic young black leadership. His
meeting with the Panthers was indeed love at first sight.[15] In his
whirlwind year as Black Panther minister of information,
Cleaver gained the podium of some of the most prestigious universities in America and ran as presidential candidate for the
Peace and Freedom party in the 1968 election. The determination
of the State of California to cut off these activities by revoking
his parole coupled with Cleaver's determination not to return to
prison and fear that he would be killed once in the hands of the
prison authorities issued in his fugitive status as of this writing.

In a real sense, Cleaver began where Malcolm X left off, with
a militant program of black self-defense and social change
rooted in a deep faith in the possibility of a coalition of black and
white radicals on a revolutionary rather than a merely reformist
program for change. Cleaver was the first black radical to be able
to embrace the white radical without suspicion, without fear of
the loss of black integrity. In this respect he represents the Black
Power movement in its still-to-be achieved maturity. His black
identity is clear and undisputed, and so black separatism need no
longer be a cloak for black insecurity toward whites. Although
fully as polemical as Malcolm in his denunciation of white racist

America, his faith and even love for the young white radicals on the campus is warm and unstinting.

Whites in America really love this country. Especially young white idealists. They've always been taught that they're living in the freest country in the world, the fairest country in the world, a country that will always have to support the underdog. So when they see their government murdering people in Vietnam, the outrage flowing from that realization is immeasurable. They don't storm the Pentagon immediately; but at a distance they begin to focus on what's really going on. People go through various stages of shock after a first awareness; they get angry, then they get uptight and finally they want to do something to change what's going on. A lot of whites have already made a correct analysis of the situation. They're aware that the government of their country has been usurped and is in the hands of a clique, what Eisenhower called the military-industrial complex, which manages the political system for the protection of large corporations. Having made that analysis, there are enough people right now, I believe, who are so outraged at the way things are going that they would move against this usurpation if they knew how.[16]

Cleaver himself didn't pretend that he knew how, but he was convinced that the fragmentation of the radicals and the suspicion of blacks for sincere white revolutionaries must be brought to an end. While he continued Malcolm's belief that each group should get their own communities together, he felt that the militant blacks and whites must join hands to create a profound social revolution in America. On this basis the Panthers cooperated with the primarily white Peace and Freedom party, and the Students for a Democratic Society have responded with an almost worshipful adulation of the Panthers.

Although Cleaver was not anxious to promote it, he felt that radical coalition must be ready for violence and even guerrilla warfare similar to the struggle going on in Vietnam and Latin America.[17] Like Malcolm, he linked up the American liberation struggle with the anticolonialist struggle going on throughout the world. He was also convinced that the black struggle could not be killed by white reaction, because, if massive repression ensued against the black movement, it would radicalize even more the white population who would not stand for the conversion of their country into a Nazi state. Cleaver placed an ultimate hope in the unfailing humanity of this white majority that would not remain passive in a time of acute crisis. Although the ultimate "solution" of the Negro question might still resolve itself in the form of a Negro homeland similar to the state of Israel,[18] basically Cleaver believes that the world has become too small for any kind of ultimate separatism. The fate of all humanity stands or falls together.[19] His ultimate vision, then, is some kind of new socialist revolution that will solve not only the racial but the human problem of man toward man, and usher in an era of cooperation based on human rather than alienated values.

If the world is not to destroy itself, the concept of people going their totally separate ways is really something that can't continue indefinitely. When you start speaking in ultimate terms, I don't see any way in which the world can be administered for the best interest of mankind without having some form of world government that would be responsive and responsible to *all* the people of the world. ...

It's clear that in order for black people to have the best that society and technology are capable of providing, we need a new kind of society and a new kind of economic system. The goal must be to make possible a more equitable distribution of goods and services—but also to have a different set of values, so that things themselves don't become a substitute for life itself. In order to achieve that dual goal, we're going to have to move toward a new form of socialism. As long as there is so much stress on private property, we're going to have a society of competition rather than cooperation. ...

I want to see a society purged of Madison Avenue mindbenders who propagandize people into a mad pursuit of gadgets. They've conned people into believing that their lives depend on having an electric tooth brush, two cars and a color television in every room. We've got to rid ourselves of this dreadful and all-consuming hunger for things, this mindless substitution of the rat-race for a humane life. ... It is not limited to black people. ... White people have to disabuse themselves of the illusion that it's their job to rule and the Black man's job is to produce the labor. And the Black men have to use their minds and acquire confidence in the products of their minds. This doesn't mean that the white man has to let his mind fall into disuse, but he also has to relate to his body again, as the black man does. Everyone needs a new understanding of his total nature, mental and physical. Only when people, black and white, start seeing themselves and acting as total individuals, with bodies and minds, will they stop assigning mental roles to one set of people and exclusively physical roles to another. Only then will the primary thrust of life—the fusion of male and female—be freed of sociological obstacles.[20]

Chapter 14

The American Youth Movement from Sit-in to Be-in

For such an amorphous phenomenon as the American youth movement—the student left or white radicals—it may seem premature at this point to try to write a "history." Certainly at this moment it is difficult to assess its political importance. Pundits aplenty have come forward to give their definitive analysis. Some see it as simply an example of the eternal generational conflict.[1] Others insist on its high idealism.[2] The mood of disaffiliation with bourgeois society in a romantic, anarchistic way can be traced back to the beats of the forties, the lost generation of the twenties and the bohemians of the late nineteenth century. This chapter intends merely to trace some aspects of the youth movement as it progressed from the student wing of the civil rights movement to the current manifestations of its more personalist, anarchistic, and "hippie" side. The side of the student movement that has now turned more Marxist in its ideology and more internationalist and revolutionary in its vision will be reserved for the final chapter.

For the purposes of this discussion, the emergence of the contemporary student movement can be traced back to the catalyst provided by the civil rights movement, beginning with the bus boycotts, the freedom rides, and sit-ins of the late 1950s. Those events were pioneered by Negro church and civil leaders and

Negro college students in the South. Yet a Harvard psychology professor analyzing the mood of white Northern college students at that time reported a general sense of malaise, alienation, a rejection of American cultural values, and a search for commitment among these students. This sentiment doubtless provided the pool of unused energy that moved into radical activism in the sixties, or that, in frustration with the fruits of the movement, turned to a hippie, dropout style.[3]

The events in the South gave dissatisfied white middle class youth an outlet for their protest. They discovered a cause and a job to do, and the student movement was born. The movement gave rise to the Mississippi Summer, the all-out effort to overcome Negro disenfranchisement in the South, the voter registration drives, and the Mississippi Freedom Democratic party. A new effort to build Negro political strength was begun. The period through the summer of 1965 is now looked back upon (by white liberals) as an almost idyllic age of cooperation, when black and white marched arm-in-arm, boldly singing "Black and white together, we shall overcome." Facing very real dangers from police clubs by day and from hidden ambush by night, the long history of social antagonism seemed momentarily suspended in an experience of instant brotherhood.

Soon, however, the difficulties of social revolution via legislation became apparent. It became evident that the powerless could not achieve change from above without building power bases in their communities, and so community organization became the thrust of the movement. Mere removal of disabilities from the books had little effect as long as these attitudes were supported by entrenched structures of power. Only power among the people could challenge the power of the status quo. Economic boycotts, new independent political parties, and poor people's cooperatives became tools for bringing power to the disinherited. But, gradually, the difficult truth was borne home that the disinheritance of the black man in America was not simply a regional peculiarity of the South, but was equally or even more evident in the ghettos of the Northern cities, and the real cause of this oppression lay not simply with a few anachronistic Southern mores but with the whole socioeconomic structure of white America.

The movement began to widen its scope to include a war against the whole of white America, in its history and its present practices, which created and enforced a system that kept the black American at the bottom and excluded a whole segment of society—Mexican Americans, Puerto Ricans, Indians, and poor whites as well as blacks—from the benefits of the American economy. The movement spread to the Northern ghetto to focus on community organizing in the cities. It also began to erupt on the campuses as a challenge to the administration of higher education now seen to be an intimate part of the American power elite. The campus revolt, beginning at the University of California at Berkeley, became the new arena for the movement. Students for a Democratic Society, organized in 1962 at Port Huron, Michigan, became the organization for the white campus radical, and the antiwar movement provided a new rallying cry for dissent. With the addition of dissent against the war in Vietnam to the issue of racism, the student revolt gradually became a comprehensive attack on what was vaguely called "the power structure", the military-industrial complex with its racist domestic operation and its imperialistic wars of intervention around the world. Frantz Fanon's book describing the struggle of the black man against colonialism in the Algerian war became a student bestseller,[4] and it became common to interconnect the exploitation of the black man at home and American imperialism abroad.

In the fall of 1965, however, the honeymoon alliance of young blacks and whites in the movement broke up. The tensions between the two groups, who had been thrown together so intensively in the Southern experience of the past few years, especially in the Mississippi Summer of 1964, suddenly and rather shockingly for many whites came out in the open. The black civil rights workers, first in modified tones but then with increasing militance, let the whites know that they had not escaped the onus of their own background by marching in the South or transplanting themselves into the Northern black ghettos. The white student might be in revolt against his background, but his way was still being paid at college or even in the movement by his "white Daddy," who was a bank president, a colonel, a college administrator, or a businessman. In other words, the white youth, through his own economic and social presuppositions, was still an intimate part of the white power structure that kept the suburbs—and even the unions—firmly segregated, and relegated the black man to the bottom of the socioeconomic ladder. An alliance based on goodwill was not enough to bridge this enormous gap between the situation of the black youth outside the system and the white youth in superficial revolt against the same system, which had borne and bred him and still continued to feed him. The question of sex raised its ugly head and, with it, the complex of fact and myth in the relation of white man and black woman, black man and white woman that was burned so deeply in the psyche of every Negro that came from a Southern background, an experience from which the Northern white youth had been shielded and tended to ignore.

Understandably the white youth had tended to be aware only of the political and economic dimensions of oppression in the black experience.[5] Therefore he was insensitive to the threat he posed to the black man by his very presence as a white symbol. The white student was being roughly exposed to a whole chapter of American history, a history of midnight terrorism, castrations, lynchings, and burnings, a chapter that he had never been taught in school. The white youth was being told who he really was in a confrontation that he dimly realized was there when he came into the South, but the full implications of which stripped and unnerved him. He kept trying to point to himself and his own commitment to racial justice as evidence that he and "some white people" should be exempt from this confrontation, that he was evidence of some exceptions to this history of white exploitation. But the black student relentlessly pursued him with the evidence of the many and varied ways in which he carried his white presuppositions with him, even into the movement. The very fact that he assumed that white people had to be in the movement, that somehow white participation and integration was indispensable to the means and goals of the movement, was evidence of his inability to overcome the myth of white superiority.

Then, with the slogan "Black Power," the black movement made it explicit: "Get out, white boy—your very presence makes it impossible for us to achieve our goals." The black man had to prove to himself and to his brothers his competence and his equality by organizing and running his own movement. The mere presence of whites in the movement, especially in leadership roles, the mere goals of integration, seemed to suggest that blacks could only rise by being led by whites, that blacks could only make it socially by sitting next to whites. Whiteness still remained the standard of humanness, and blacks could only become human by being integrated into and, as it were, having this white humanness "rub off" on them by way of association. This whole myth had to be broken finally and absolutely, and to do this entailed a black movement, black-run and black-financed, a solidarity of black people together that left no doubt that black people could be and were their own leaders and the masters of their own destiny. Only in this way could there emerge a black identity that would allow the black person to recover his own soul, his own way of being human by way of being black rather than by way of acceptance by and assimilation into white norms.[6] This view was spelled out by the Vine City project paper on whites in the movement just prior to SNCC's (The Student Non-Violent Coordinating Committee) formal commitment to Black Power.

The inability of whites to relate to the cultural aspects of Black society; attitudes that whites, consciously or unconsciously, bring to Black communities about themselves (western superiority) and about Black people (paternalism); inability to shatter white-sponsored community myths of Black inferiority and self-negation; inability to combat the views of the Black community that white organizers, being "white," control Black organizers as puppets; insensitivity of both Black and white workers toward the hostility of the Black community on the issue of interracial 'relationships' (sex); the unwillingness of whites to deal with the roots of racism which lie within the white community; whites though individual 'liberals,' are symbols of oppression to the Black community—due to the *collective* power that whites have over Black lives.

... Blacks, in fact feel intimidated by the presence of whites, because of their knowledge of the power that whites have over their lives. One white person can come into a meeting of Black people and change the complexion of that meeting.... The white people should go into the white communities where the whites have created power for the express purpose of denying Blacks human dignity and self-determination. Whites who come into the Black community with ideas of change seem to want to absolve the power structure of its responsibility for what it is doing, and to say that change can only come through Black unity, which is only the worst kind of paternalism. This is not to say that whites have not had an important role in the Movement. In the case of Mississippi, their role was the very key in that they helped give Blacks the right to organize, but that role is now over, and it should be.... There can be no talk of 'hooking-up' unless Black people organize Blacks and white people organize whites. If these conditions are met, then perhaps at some later date—and if we are going in the same direction—talks about exchange of personnel, coalition and other meaningful alliances can be discussed.[7]

The emergence of Black Power created a traumatic crisis in the white student movement. The white youth had found a cause and a raison d'être in the experience and ideal of blacks and whites working together to overcome an evil system. Now they found themselves forced back into their own white backgrounds by the black movement and told rather forcefully that the best thing they could do for the Negro was to get out of the Negro community and go back and clean up their own yards where, after all, the responsibility for the trouble really lay. Moreover, the increasing militancy of the black movement left the whites with little assurance that, if they did work in their own communities, they might meet their former comrades farther on down the road. The black militant began to sound as though no matter what the "white boy" did, either in the black or in the white community, it was of no interest or help to the black man. He could not be saved by anything that came from the other side of the fence, but only by overthrowing the white system altogether and creating his own separate black society.

Black separatism, a concept with a long history in American Negro thought, although temporarily covered up by the Negro civil rights leaders, surfaced again as the ultimate symbol. The realization of this hope for a dissolution of the black man's relation to America remained as vague as ever. For some there was still the concept of a black homeland to be found in Africa. For others, the black homeland was the American South itself, and they demanded that this area be granted to them as a national homeland. For the more realistic, black separatism came to mean building up power and autonomy in separate black communities scattered across the United States as a kind of provisional solution in lieu of that ultimate solution whose shape had not yet appeared.[8] However vague the realization, the idea remained a potent one and was endorsed by virtually all the younger leaders of the black movement as an ultimate symbol of the black aspiration to full autonomy.

Black caucuses in political organizations and churches and black studies programs in colleges and universities became the new tactic of the black movement wherever it confronted white institutions. By withdrawal and consolidation, the black movement could then confront the white institution and wrest autonomous territory on which to conduct its own program. At the conference on New Politics held in the spring of 1967, the black caucus even forced the white majority to eat their former commitment to integration and endorse black power and even black nationalism and separatism. By so doing the whites made a kind of symbolic abdication to demonstrate their acceptance of the fact that they could in no way formulate the program for blacks, but would merely agree to and support whatever blacks thought best for themselves. In fact, even this white abdication itself was irrelevant to black aspirations, and to this assertion whites also were willing to agree. This strange psychological reversal of black and white roles that took place at this conference received scandalized or puzzled notice from the press. The best one can say is that it functioned as a kind of exorcism of the myth of white supremacy that would allow the black and white movements to move on to new business. It was doubtless because the white members of the New Left understood it as such a symbolic yet necessary exorcism of this myth that they were willing to take what appeared to be outrageous treatment at the hands of the black caucus.

After this watershed, a tentative new working arrangement emerged in the youth movements. In effect, strictly separate black and white organizations appeared on campuses, usually SDS for the whites and an Afro-American Student Union for the blacks. Blacks planned their own programs and their own demands and confrontations without asking for any advice or consulting with the whites. Whites, in turn, rallied their students around the blacks' issues, endorsing whatever the black students were doing without expecting any endorsement in return. The two movements were coordinated only in the sense of focusing on the same citadels of power and around the same issues of racism and imperialism, although from their own vantage points.

The pattern of separate but parallel movements emerged rather clearly at the Columbia University uprising in the spring of 1968. The two groups ran separate movements, occupied separate buildings (the blacks having expelled the whites from Hamilton Hall, the first building seized). Both were attacking the University's subsidy by the Department of Defense as an indication of the subservience of the university system to the governmental-military-industrial complex. Both were attacking the obliviousness of the University to the needs of the black community around them, as evidenced by the Columbia gym being built on Morningside Park, which detracted from the recreation area of Harlem. The issues of war and race coalesced in a general confrontation of the University as an intimate part of the interlocking power structure of a "racist and warmongering society." The white student movement, like the Black Power movement, now began to see itself more and more in an international perspective and to interact sympathetically with student rebellions in France, Germany, and Japan.

The rather vaguely formulated ideology of the white movement up to that point was stated in terms of an individualistic or
communalist anarchism, derived from gurus such as Paul Good-
man. Traditional Communist anarchism rejected the idea of a
vanguard party structure. It believed in direct power in the hands
of the people. Its instincts were for total grassroots participation,
a rejection of any authority in any way over or against the people. Concepts of participatory democracy and community control, as these had been emerging as themes of the movement over
the past few years, fell instinctively into this pattern of thought,
often without the formulators even being aware of its antece-
dents. More careful attention to the Marxist revolutionary tradition and more explicit adoption of its rhetoric had not yet clearly
emerged. Later we shall examine some new signs in this direction and the confrontation of a more Marxist line in the movement with the older native anarchism. But up to the time of the
Columbia uprising, it might be said that the general orientation
of the white student radical was in the direction of creating a
space for the freedom of the individual in an increasingly technologically efficient but dehumanizing society that, in the name
of technological logic, is threatening the whole human race with
atomic oblivion.

The hippie side of the student movement began to emerge
about a year after the Free Speech Movement on the Berkeley
campus. Its capital at Haight-Asbury in San Francisco was, in
part, created by an emigration of Berkeley Free Speech activists
to that area. It would be easy to describe the hippie movement
simply as a dropout movement of frustrated white activists,
created partly by the shock of rejection by the black movement,
and partly by the frustrations of political activity within a system that seemed to have become immune to meaningful change.
These experiences are indeed partial explanations, but they are
not comprehensive. Certain strains in the hippie movement are
much older than the civil rights movement, and link up with an
aesthetic, antibourgeois disaffiliation in Western society of long
standing. Secondly, themes in the hippie movement can be
traced with some mutations to an anarchist side of the implicit

ideology of the student movement of the early 1960s itself.

Finally, the hippie movement has never entirely disaffiliated itself from the student movement. It did not so much drop out of the political arena as it represented an edge where the perspective and tactics of the movement itself were being transformed. The movement, both black and white, went into costume! The black activist, by his dashiki, his Afro haircut and his tiger-tooth necklace, represented the positive celebration of his blackness and his African heritage. The hippie, with his long hair, flowers, and bells is a distinctively white phenomenon, and represents a display of freedom from the middle class mores of his society. This side of the white movement is where the movement's tactics were being transformed from conventional political methods to expressions of disaffiliation from the current society expressed through liturgy, celebration, and sociodrama. Under the influence of this mood, demonstrations and rallies ceased to aim at making new laws or changing the political system within the known political rules. Rather, the rally and demonstration became a leap of consciousness outside the present system (reality) altogether, and an effort to hold up an entirely different kind of possibility that cannot even be discussed within the present political rules. The demonstration became a form of ritual theater, acting out the ending of the old world and the birth of a new world in ecstatic confrontation.

The emergence of this style of hippie activism was evident in the youth that converged on the Pentagon in November 1967. Although blacks as a movement were conspicuously absent (holding their own rally elsewhere in the city), two distinct groups were evident among the marchers: the militants charging under the revolutionary banner and the flower children with their carefree mockery of the system. The tactics and style were different, but the enemy was the same. While the militants were girding themselves for a taste of blood (their own) on the Pentagon steps, the flower children danced up and down in front of the poised rifles, inserting daisies in the barrels, or gathered in solemn chorus to exorcise and levitate the accursed home of evil destructive spirits.

"What do you think you guys are doing?"

"Measuring the Pentagon. We have to see how many people we'll need to form a ring around it."

"You're what!"

"It's very simple. You see, the Pentagon is a symbol of evil in most religions. You're religious, aren't you?"[9]

In these words, Abbie Hoffman, chief stagemaster for the Yippies!, represented a modest exchange between himself and security officers as he and his comrades prepared the ground for the central Yippie! event of the day, the exorcism and levitation of the Pentagon. In other, less printable passages he describes plots of Yippie! guerrilla theater, such as throwing away free money in the New York Stock Exchange and "the festival of love meets the theater of cruelty in Chicago."

The essence of Yippie! tactics is the "revolution in consciousness" created through guerrilla theater, the living theater of the streets. The dissenters become a new community incarnating freedom, fellowship, and mutuality within a sphere created by the symbolic overturning of the rules of "straight" society. The action is created for the purpose of temporarily disrupting the workings of straight society in order to raise an image of a new kind of relationship between man and man. The "rapping," in which a consensus on action is reached, becomes the word, the confrontation is the deed, and the joint of marijuana passed from hand to hand is the sacrament of the community that comes together to celebrate its own existence. The community exists through its rescue from the demonic powers of society in the seizing of a building or a street, and comes to light in the sacred space taken over from the powers and principalities that are marshalling for the counterattack outside. In that brief space and time, the old world is suspended and the new world brought into being. In Abbie Hoffman's words, "When we put on a large celebration, the aim is to create a liberated area. People can do whatever they want. They can begin to live the revolution even if only within a confined area. We will learn to govern ourselves. This goes on in every revolution.[10] Hoffman revels in contempt

for the grim, ideological New Left. Their style will simply reproduce the technological prison in even drearier tones. Like
their forebears in the Old Left, they will create a society which
is "dull, bureaucratic-sterile-puritanical."[11] While the New Left
solemnly debates tactics, the Yippies!

laugh at them, not in a hostile way, sort of like Buddhas smiling in a
corner. While they argued back and forth we got stoned, made love to all
the pretty girls, offered resolutions, like demanding an end to pay toilets
and support of the Polish student rebellion (just to upset the Russian-
linked U.S. Communist party), refused to pay for our meals and in general carried on like bad, crazy niggers.[12]

The Yippies! could afford to laugh while the political arguments rolled on because they had already discovered that demonstrations are not political events, but antipolitical, media events.
It is the manipulation of the media for the purpose of revolution-
izing consciousness that is the real name of the game. They could
claim for their constituency the leaders of the white dropout
movement, Leary and Ginsberg, the bulk of the underground
press, the rock musicians, and the most avant-garde figures in
the new forms of theater (living theater).[13] In addition, they had
behind them the uncounted troops of young alienated America,
reaching down even to the high school set, and it was these people who turned up faithfully for the "battle of Chicago."

When Hoffman bothers to expose the more serious side of his
thought, one recognizes the traditional confrontation between
Marxism and anarchism: Marxism believes in separating the
revolutionary process from its goal in the classless society;
anarchism believes that the tactics of the revolution must itself
be the life of the new society.[14] One creates the revolution by
living it. The vision is one of abolition of all alienation and the
substitution of a community of direct self-government and creative play beyond the work principle. The work principle is to be
overcome by automation in the postindustrial society. The
means to create such a society are already at hand, but the old
ethic of property, authority, and work necessary to the primitive

industrial society prevents it from emerging.[15] This is why the way to the classless society is not through a new political party but through "the politics of ecstacy," the creation of a new consciousness through actions and modes of life that begin, here and now, to explode the old presuppositions. While distinguishing themselves from both the true hippies, the nonpolitical dropouts, and the New Left, the Yippie! nevertheless seeks a myth that will include both in its coalition.

The hippie end of our mythical coalition dropped out. They failed to trust the Yippie! myth. There was a lot of name-calling but in the end it didn't matter; almost all the original hippies could be found on the streets of Chicago and they were all fighting in the style of their choice, all stoned out of their heads and all having a ball. The reason for this is that the energy centers that gravitated to the center of the myth were tough as all hell. Also a myth has a tendency to always pick the right symbols and strategy.... The media in a real sense never lie when you relate to them in a non-linear mythical manner. ... Even though we (proponents of various points of view) fought, we were all together.

The first blood I saw in Chicago was the blood of Stu Albert, Jerry (Rubin)'s closest friend. It happened in the first Sunday afternoon police riot in Lincoln Park. I embraced Stu, crying and swearing—sharing his blood. I went up to the cops and shook my fist. I made a haranguing speech, standing between rows of pig cops and scared spectators of the music festival, which of course by now was over. That kind of unity that Stu and I have, even though he is a Marxist-Leninist and I am a fuck-off, is impossible to explain. We are united in our determination to smash this system by using any means at our disposal and to build a new world.[16]

The anarchistic style is by no means entirely foreign to the New Left. Indeed, its own implicit ideology from the time of the Port Huron statement, and even before that in integrated SNCC, had elements that readily moved in an anarchistic direction. The concepts of community organization and participatory democracy held an anti–institutional, even antipolitical concept of community and interpersonal relations. Systems, governments, the authority of one person over another, are by their very nature considered bad, dehumanizing, and enslaving. Consequently all objectification of human relationships into systems, organizations, and institutions, even the concept that one person can represent others politically, is regarded as suspect. All such systems are ways of turning persons into things, into objects, into statistical and numerical weights and measures that can be manipulated externally.

Early in the sixties the student movement began to diverge from the presuppositions of their elders in the civil rights movement and to lean toward an existential humanism, which sees all objectification as dehumanizing. The personalist, antiobjective ethos was illustrated for me by a simple poem scrawled on a wall by a young black worker in the summer of 1965 at the headquarters of the Mississippi Child Development Group (Head Start).

> So O.E.O. and directors
> and boards of directors
> and senate inspectors
> and just plain spies
> meet in small rooms to create
> the fate of the poor.
> Like huge Delta dozers
> they mould and they shove
> without love.
> scraping and bowing the earth
> contour plowing, it's called.
> It keeps down erosion,
> explosion.
> Blades out, dollars rape, lose your shape,
> fit the line we design.
>
>
> Say, child!
> did you see the truth anywhere this summer?
> Can you choose which way to go?
> Now that you know, how far can you see?
> Can you see that black freighter out there?
> Or Polaris beyond?
> Do you see those brown children
> burned with napalm?
> Where are their mothers and fathers?
> They're dead.

Shall we give them a head start too?
Hush, listen now!
That's for *Freedom!!*
Just like you sing
in that song that you sing
when you clap and you smile
You know the one.

You don't like your choices?
Well, this is the world.
Be realistic.
The self-contradictions,
the evident frictions,
the lies, the wars and the deaths,
are your primary choices,
'cause so few people say No!
Washington thinks the Movement is crazy,
people in SNCC are nuts!
Do they know the fright of driving at night
in the Delta three years ago?
Where were they then with their head start?
Well, thanks for your blood
but what this movement needs is stable,
responsible people,
that means viable, buy-able people,
not YOU!!

Nevertheless, little child
We'll bend, we'll bend.
But if in the end,
our shape doesn't fit
to the line they design,
we'll have to do without them.
You can sit on my lap
and play with my hair,
we'll look for a flower together
(maybe they'll join us).
and we'll be clean in the grime
without their dime
Even six thousand children
change one at a time.[17]

The impersonal economic and political system inevitably makes people have "it relationships" as the external manipulation of objects, and, as such, it is inherently inauthentic. Thus the youth movement even in the early days of SNCC began to reach for a concept of personhood and community that undercut what their elders would consider "realistic political tactics." Freedom came to mean more than just access to goods and services. It took on the color of a revolt against all forms of dehumanization and an insistence on exclusively I–Thou or direct personal relationships as the only authentic society. Thus, even in the early phase of civil rights, the student mood had in it an antipolitical, anarchistic ideology.

The hippie-Yippie! side of the movement, then, is not entirely without roots in the earlier movement, but follows out this side of the movement to an extreme conclusion. This is expressed in an insistence on being rather than on doing. The community gathers together, not to agitate for anything and thereby produce a new law or system, but simply to *be*, to celebrate life, to celebrate their own community, and to experience their communal existence through whatever happens in this coming together. The "be-in" becomes the rites of spring for the hippie community. The ritualistic and liturgical dimensions of the hippie style are evident, and this is doubtless why they have exercised a strong influence on the liturgical and underground community radicals in the churches. Revolting against established society, they seek out various primitivist traits. They exalt the tribal life style and communion with nature of the American Indian, who became a new culture hero with the hippie movement.[18] They rediscover ritualistic play, dancing, and the mythopoetic style of speaking and acting together that goes back to prerational, tribal man. They revolt against the goal orientation of bourgeois society with its sacrifice of present existence for future achievement. Jobs, preparing yourself for a career, making something of yourself, all these familiar values of the work culture are to be overthrown for a style of immediate experience and awareness.

The hippies quickly began to reach for a new kind of communalism. At first this was expressed by the crash pads, the communal living in the hippie districts. When these areas were destroyed by police surveillance, groups of hippies moved into country areas and began to experiment in renewed forms of agrarian utopianism.[19] Not surprisingly, a religious core and a simple form of discipline soon was found to be necessary to make such communities work. Often the use of drugs as the center of the community's ecstatic experience became less important, and a substitute in the form of meditation and the relation of the community to each other was found. Doubtless many of these hippie communes lacked the discipline or the depth of religious center to become viable alternatives for long, but it cannot be questioned that the utopian side of the hippie movement was indeed on the track of an ancient but ever revivable form of contemplative utopian community.

Although the original hippie areas in big cities fell on evil days and the flower children were driven out by a tougher, gangster-style youth, the commune as a style of living for revolutionary youth is still a reality in American cities. The essence of the communal style of life is brotherhood and voluntary poverty. The radical youth experiences his revolt against a society based on endless dependence on more and more goods by discovering how little he really needs to live on. Everything in the hippie community is free! This is the primary revolt against the commercial system. The commune is available to anyone who comes in. Enough food and clothes for survival are given to anyone who needs them. Only the simplest jobs that will not detract from this freedom are sought. The communes are fed by a steady stream of runaway children from the white suburbs of the American middle class:

Runaways are the backbone of the youth revolution. We are all runaways, age is irrelevant. A fifteen-year-old kid who takes off from middle-class American life is an escaped slave crossing the Mason-Dixon line. They are hunted down by professional bounty-hunters, fidgety relatives and the law, because it is against the law to leave home (bondage) until you have finished your servitude. . . . It seems America has lost her children. They come down here, (the West Village) or to Haight-Ashbury or to the stops in between. An underground railroad exists. The runaways are hidden in crash pads, communes, apartments, in country communities. They let their hair grow, change their style of dress and vanish. ... Are the runaways going back? I don't know. Ask them. I'll tell you one thing—I sure as hell ain't, they'll have to kill me first.[20]

The hippie is the child of the white middle class who is in conscious revolt against its values and groping for a new life style. Being rather than doing, celebration of the moment, rejection of goal orientation, voluntary poverty and sharing, and the free communal existence that ignores the traditional mores of the family, including the puritanical-puerile attitudes toward sex, are all systematic rejections of the society from which they have come. The hippie is also aware that technology itself is rapidly making the traditional Calvinistic work culture obsolete, and sees himself as the avant-garde of a new leisure society devoted to celebration and creativity rather than alienated work. His primitivism has a paradisiacal background. He is recovering the Garden of Eden before men had to earn their living by the sweat of their brow. His utopianism and cultivation of liberty and innocence in all matters that the society takes with utmost seriousness—such as sex and money—spring from the paradisiacal ethic. Not surprisingly, then, they exhibit traits very similar to Adamic, paradisiacal-libertine sects of the past.[21] The themes of community, poverty, and contemplation are part of a continually recurring utopian tradition. Traditional elements of religious culture—myth-making, ritual, and mystical contemplation —also found a revival in the hippie world. It is not surprising, therefore, that the churchmen found themselves eying with interest this revival of religiosity out beyond the secularist rejection of churches and Christian society.[22] In some places, such as the Free Church of Berkeley, California, the hippie movement has even become the basis of a new Christian congregation.

The quality and the authenticity of the mystical, contemplative dimension of the hippie movement has been much debated, and the students of traditional mystical discipline were quick to

dismiss any movement whose mystical experience was generated by artificial stimulants. There is no doubt that a mystical
experience reached through drugs lacks the backbone of personal integrity and discipline created by the traditional practice.
Communities built around artificially induced experience lack
the substance and stability of communities created through the
practices of personal *ascesis*. But the traditionalists have not
been entirely able to rebut the claims of the drug cultists that the
experience itself is indeed within the same framework, however
different the paths. There seems to be no reason to deny (unless
one makes a platonic dualism between body and soul) that the
chemical changes in the body created by ascetic discipline might
indeed be artificially created by drugs. The difference, obviously,
is that the second method will not flower out of a depth-clarifica-
tion of the self through discipline, for there can be no short cut
to that. Thus the more serious contemplatives in the hippie
movement have gone beyond drugs to traditional methods of
contemplation.[23]

The discovery and use of LSD has been essential to understanding the emergence of a new cultural style in the youth movement. LSD art, light shows, and hard rock music are not confined
to true hippies, but have quickly become the popular style expressing a deep longing of American youth in general. Within the
youth context LSD expresses a short cut to ecstatic experience,
a way of dissolving the bounds of objectivity of thought and objectivity of social structure. The conscious ego itself is dissolved
in order to make way for immediate intuitive contact with the
unitary being that underlies all subjects and objects. This non-
objective thinking was already a part of the ideology of the student movement, as we have seen, and LSD caught on perhaps
because it provided a direct instrument for doing what the
nonobjectivist ideology had been pointing to, namely, a dissolution of the objective world created by the detached consciousness.

The objective world was seen as rising through a separation of
consciousness from nature. It rested on a distinction between the

ego and the object. Existential philosophy,[24] and before that, the mystical traditions, often decried this separation of subject and object as the primordial Fall of man, the act through which a false world of external structures was raised up and became a trap into which man had fallen. The mystic called man back from this Fall into objectivity and to a return to communion with primordial being that preceded the subject-object dualism and where man could experience a direct communion with divine nature in which he was subsumed and reunited. This kind of thought, deeply embedded in Western existentialism and mysticism, has often looked to the philosophy of the ancient East as a place where the understanding of primordial awareness has been preserved in its most profound form. The high priests of the hippie movement, such as Timothy Leary and Alan Watts, uniformly describe the LSD experience in terms of the dissolution of the objective ego and the reestablishment of the primordial paradise of direct awareness. Drawing on the Eastern traditions of Zen Buddhism and the Tibetan manuals of mystical experience, they describe, interpret, and guide the LSD trip.[25]

The feeling of self is no longer confined to the inside of the skin. Instead my individual being seems to grow out from the rest of the universe like a hair from a head or a limb from a body, so that my center is also the center of the whole. I find that in ordinary consciousness I am habitually trying to ring myself off from this totality, that I am perpetually on the defensive. But what am I trying to protect? ... For the most part I am defending my defenses; rings around rings around rings around nothing. Guards inside a fortress inside entrenchments inside a radar curtain. The military war is an outward parody of the war of the ego versus the world....

I trace myself back through the labyrinth of my brain, through the innumerable turns by which I have ringed myself off, and by perpetual circling, obliterated the original trail whereby I entered this forest. Back through the tunnels, through the devious status-and-survival strategy of adult life, through all the interminable passages which we remember in dreams—all the streets we have ever traveled, the corridors of schools, the winding pathways between the legs of tables and chairs where one crawled as a child, the tight and bloody exit from the womb, the fountainous surge through the channel of the penis, the timeless wanderings through the ducts and spongy caverns. ... Relentlessly back and back through endless and whirling dances in the astronomically proportioned spaces which surround the original nuclei of the world, the centers of centers, ...

Down and at last out—out of the cosmic maze to recognize in and as myself, the bewildered traveler, the forgotten yet familiar sensation of the original impulse of all things, supreme identity, inmost light, ultimate center, self more self than myself—*atman* is *Brahman.*[26]

So does Alan Watts describe one of his own drug journeys.

With the drug movement, the exploration of human alienation turned inward, to a search for its deepest roots in the consciousness of man himself. But this search is much broader and more profound than the drug that temporarily became its vehicle. It is leading both to an exploration of inner space and a projection of utopian life styles. But, as though recognizing that there is no longer any "other world" to which one can withdraw in seclusion, the incipient utopian, contemplative movement quickly found reentry into the arena of street confrontations in the form of guerrilla theater, designed to "blow" the political and cultural mind of American society and open up a liberated zone where new alternatives might be envisioned.

Chapter 15

The New Left: Revolutionaries After the Fall of the Revolution

The term "New Left" commonly evokes the image of the long-haired campus radical of American and European universities. Such an image lends itself to little clear definition, since such students include such variegated positions: Marxists, anarchists, and those in inchoate rebellion against the existing order.[1] Hence I shall try to suggest a larger historical and analytical perspective on what constitutes a New Left as against the Old Left of the Communist and socialist parties. Three broad characteristics might be discerned that distinguish a New Left from this older tradition and that link the variegated impulses of the world in a pool of common sentiment.

The New Left is, first of all, a critical renewal movement within the Marxist socialist tradition vis-à-vis the discredited Communist states, especially the Soviet Union, which has proclaimed itself the magisterial center of that tradition. This New Left critique of party communism is, of course, decisively different from reactionary anticommunism, because it shares the fundamental outlook and hope of the Marxist tradition while standing in a new historical and theoretical position that recognizes established Communist states as betrayers of this tradition. In this sense one might see the New Left as "Marxist Protestantism." As Marxists, the New Left wishes to recover the essence of the original tradition and apply it to a new day. It thus has the double burden of renewing the revolutionary tradition and accounting for and combatting the effects of the revolution that has failed. The remarkable power of the Left today, however, indicates that the "Revolution" still continues to be the dominant salvation myth of modern times.

The second characteristic of the New Left is that it stands in relationship to a postindustrial society, a society in the midst of a new stage of technological revolution. This new stage is described in Erich Fromm's recent book as one in which the industrial revolution of technological replacement of human physical energy is surpassed in technological replacement of human intelligence.[2] The new technological revolution signaled by cybernation and automation renders many of the old productive practices, including the protective practices of the labor unions, obsolete and disfunctional. It releases a new utopian promise of conquest of necessity and also a new threat of domination and dehumanization of the human world by its own creations. The new technological revolution offers a striking opportunity to revitalize and update the Marxist projection of the future Communist society, which had, previously, seemed to have been discredited by the short-term evolution of the old industrial society in which Marx first made his analysis.

It is commonplace to say that Marx's analysis has proven obsolete because he took to be the death throes of capitalism what were, in fact, only its birth pangs. His prediction of the pauperization of the working class was negated by the actual development of the factory worker toward integration and affluence in mature industrial societies. His assumption that the socialist revolution would break out in the most advanced capitalist societies as a stage beyond capitalism has been negated by the actual appearance of socialist revolutions in preindustrial societies as a means of creating rapid and enforced industrialization. Far from surpassing capitalism, the Soviet Union has increasingly approximated the system of advanced Western capitalism as that system itself has exhibited more and more the features of amalgamation of business, government, and centralized planning.

However, the appearance of a new stage of technological revolution may suggest that the dismissal of Marx as a bad prophet may be premature. Perhaps the conditions for a postcapitalist revolution that would abolish drudge labor and permit a humanized society of free creativity have only now begun to come into existence. Orthodox party Marxist-Leninism, however, tends to act as a strait jacket, repelling a fresh analysis of the revolutionary potential of this recent stage of technological innovation. The rigidity and authoritarianism of the party that have made older social descriptions into dogmas make it difficult to effect a development of dogma within the party itself. For this reason, innovative spirits who are engaged in a fresh analysis of capitalism are counted as "revisionists" or "deviationalists" by the party magisterium. In this sense, then, we have a New Left because, in order to renew the Marxist analysis, it becomes necessary to break with the party line and stand in an independent relationship to the official succession of the tradition.

The third characteristic of the New Left is that it looks with sympathy and solidarity on the revolutionary nationalist movements in the Third World. The Russian revolutionary experiment ceases to be the model and is now regarded as a betrayer of the Marxist hope, and instead the Left looks to the practice of the younger revolutionary movements in China, Cuba, and North Vietnam. Guerrilla movements that have developed a new technique of warfare that undercuts and stalemates the advanced weaponry of the superpowers are the new heroes of the Left.[3]

These three characteristics: (1) disassociation from the original Communist state in Russia, (2) a new Marxian analysis of the revolutionary possibilities of postindustrial society and finally, and (3) a turning from European revolutionary practice to that of the younger revolutionaries in the Third World by no means add up to a ready synthesis. In particular, the second and third characteristics are in considerable latent conflict. The practice of the revolutionary nationalists in Cuba or Vietnam jar uneasily against the projection of a revolution at the highest stage of advanced technological capacities in the West. The adulation of a Che, a Ho, or a Mao among American or Western European leftists has about it the romantic flavor of personal heroism from a bygone culture.

Here I can hope to do no more than provide a few introductory notes to a topic that encompasses the whole field of social ferment in the world as it faces the eighth decade of the twentieth century. The New Left as a revolt against Soviet-dictated party ideology in the name of Marxist humanism began in Eastern Europe at the end of the Stalinist era.[4] The "new revisionism" in Poland, Hungary, and other Eastern European countries was a demand for a return to the liberal democratic institutions and traditions that had been suppressed by the Soviet-dominated regimes. Earlier socialist traditions were revived, such as Bernstein's democratic socialism, the democratic and internationalist tradition of Rosa Luxemburg and Leon Trotsky against the perversion of internationalism in Soviet centrism, and the anarcho-syndicalist tradition of worker's self-government. Revived nationalism insisted on pluralism and independent national routes to socialism. In the struggle against the party bureaucracy in the factories and in the political and intellectual arenas, the party is seen as the new ruling class rather than as the authentic vanguard of the proletariat.[5] The criticism of the party ideology and the call for a Marxist humanism spelled the return of Eastern European intellectuals to the mainstream of the Western cultural tradition.[6] In the Titoist critique of Soviet imperialism the USSR was denounced as the enemy of socialism, a state capitalist despotism ruled by a bureaucratic caste that had sold out the authentic socialist heritage of the Revolution. By contrast, Western capitalist countries were seen as evolving toward socialism.[7] This struggle for a critical Marxism in thought and practice was repeatedly repressed, by Soviet invasion if necessary, but this suppression only served to establish more firmly an attitude of dissent to the organs of the Old Left that are now viewed as having become a New Right, which must be overcome by a renewed struggle to reinstate the original values of the liberal and socialist traditions.

In Leszek Kolakowski's essay, "The Concept of the Left," this leading Polish Marxist humanist summarizes the intellectual stance of a critical leftism that endeavors both to retain its basic values and yet to refrain from succumbing to dogmatism and domination, even in the wake of the success of its own party. Kolakowski describes social revolutions as continual compromises between utopian aspiration and historical possibility. The Left, by definition, is both negative and utopian. It is negative in its critique of existing reality and utopian in its hope of creating a new and better world. Its negation of present reality is defined by the direction of its negation, i.e., toward utopia. By contrast, the right seeks not to change but to idealize the status quo. To that end it can readily appropriate the slogans of the Left—freedom, equality, the "vanguard of the proletariat"—but it uses these ideals not to signify their true dynamism but to legitimize its own power. The Left becomes a material force through its struggle on behalf of the oppressed; however it cannot simply be equated with class interest but must be defined in terms of total human values. The practice of the Left is relative to existing historical conditions. In that sense the Left must be ready to compromise historically, i.e., to adapt itself to what is possible.

But its historical compromise must never be confused with intellectual compromise. It must constantly maintain its sense of critical distance between existing achievements and the full realization of its values. This critical distance prevents it from idolizing the status quo derived from past revolutions. Intellectually, the Left must take a stand of permanent revisionism toward existing reality, while the Right expresses the inertia of historical reality. The New Left revisionists in the Polish Communist party must develop a critique of the Stalinist party Right that will not be confused with a reactionary anti-Communist Right, but will continue the struggle against the Old Right as well. The New Left emerges in the party as a consequence of the failure of the Old Left to maintain authentic leftist criticism and its establishment as a ruling class of postrevolutionary states, unscrupulously using the slogans of the Left to legitimize its entrenchment. The New Left in Poland must simultaneously define itself against the Old Right of the clergy and feudal and bourgeois ruling class and the New Right of the party *apparatchiks.* The Left must continually hold up the values of a fully humanized world in critical judgment upon the existing reality.[8]

Leszek Kolakowski, as a Marxist humanist in a country both Roman Catholic and Communist, is particularly sensitive to the analogies between the clerical and the Communist bureaucratic ideologies. Like the dogmatism of the church, party dogmatism strives to exclude the very basis of critical independence. The renegade from Stalinism is denied a priori the possibility of an autonomous Marxism. Socialist values are absorbed into an absolutistic relationship to the party magisterium, so there is no alternative to party-line acquiescence except counterrevolutionary fascism. So it becomes extremely difficult for the Left to define a "third way" independent of these alternatives. The anti-Stalinist is thus pushed into a sectarian logic of anticommunism to which he frequently succumbs. The purpose of this sectarian logic is to destroy the existence and even theoretical possibility of an independent Left. Only when the strait jacket of this single alternative is broken culturally can there be a renaissance of the long-compromised revolutionary tradition.

Marxism, as the established party dogma, has taken on sacral characteristics. Like church doctrine, its content is defined in an absolutistic relationship to the "mind of the party." So completely is "truth" absorbed into the party's mind that there ceases to be any content that can stand autonomously and critically against it. Its content is whatever the party authorities define it to be. What is infallible Marxist-Leninism one day is heresy the next, as soon as it is denounced by the infallible institution. Consequently, the Marxist ceases to be a man with a particular worldview, becoming a man with a mental attitude that is capable of continually adapting itself to institutionally defined truth. So the struggle for an independent Left is also a struggle for the resecularization of Marxism. It is a struggle against a pseudo-Marxist myth and cult upholding a sacralized party, and it is a rebuilding of respect for secular reason that stands on its independent ability to communicate and convince the mind. It is an effort to restore the truly scientific character of Marxism as an analysis of society open to continual revision based on experience as opposed to an unscientific dogmatizing of an older analysis in the name of science. Basically the attempt to reduce Marxism to a unitary, authoritarian synthesis is itself contrary to the Marxian understanding of theory and practice, because the living stream of history by its nature is composed of unresolved contradictions.[9]

In Western Europe the post-Stalinist period saw an increasing disaffiliation of the Communist parties from Soviet direction in favor of polycentrism, national roads to socialism, and rapprochement with parliamentary politics.[10] In addition, new leftist forces emerged, repudiating the old parties. In Britain, ex-Communist and left Labor party intellectuals rallied around antiestablishment, antiwar, and anti-colonial themes. Naive in international theory and hidebound by an orthodoxy that could not admit that the working class was not progressive on such issues as racism, the British New Left is its most incisive in philosophical and cultural areas. G. L. Arnold finds its most significant contribution in the criticism of the culture of capitalist, technological society.[11] In this period, both Germany and France saw the development of a tradition of Marxist scholarship independent of party control. Indeed, in Jean Duvignaud's opinion, there is virtually no "orthodox" Marxist thought in France.[12]

The mid-sixties was a period of sprouting New Left student movements in Europe that, in a reversal of the usual lines of influence, looked to the tactics of the American civil rights and student movements for inspiration. The most notable event among European student uprisings to date was doubtless the startling "May Revolution" of 1968, which appeared to come within an inch of toppling the Gaullist regime and revealed a general disenchantment with the General that expressed itself in the April 1969 referendum. As E. J. Hobshawn phrased it in his review sampling the literature on the revolution that burgeoned in the following year: "It seemed to demonstrate what practically no radical over the age of twenty-five, including Mao Tsetung and Fidel Castro, believed; namely that revolution in an advanced industrial country was possible in conditions of peace, prosperity and apparent political stability."[13] The significant characteristic of the May Revolution was that it was initiated and represented at the crucial stages by the students, without any help from those in the power structure or the Communists (who had previously dubbed the students an insignificant "groupuscle"), thus establishing the students as a real political force to be reckoned with. Moreover, this student movement was able to forge, however briefly, an alliance with a worker's rebellion at a grass-roots level, unaided by and even against union and party leadership.

The statement of the strategy and ideology of the student movement, as well as its own view of the experience, can be found in the volume by one of its leading spokesman, Daniel Cohn-Bendit, *Obsolete Communism: The Left-Wing Alternative*. Rejecting the Leninist concept of the party vanguard, the student leftists dipped back into the tradition of French libertarian socialism for guidelines. The abolition of all alienated authority, whether of the political or the economic bureaucracies, the unions, or the party, and direct workers' self-government constitute the main themes of the May revolutionaries.[14] The students restituted the earliest and most sweeping form of the socialist tradition, a socialism concerned with personal freedom and self-expression in contrast to one of state-controlled industrialization. The students also restored the Marxist faith that such a society can rise as a new stage beyond the technological revolution in an advanced industrial nation, whereas the revolutionary movements in preindustrial societies in the Third World were seen as state-directed industrial revolutions rather than as true socialism. They systematically combated the Old Left insistence on party direction and representation of the workers in favor of a conviction that the workers could represent themselves in direct, spontaneous revolutionary action. They also closed the gap between the revolutionary process and its goal by their belief that the radically democratic aim of the classless society can only be brought about by revolutionary processes that are themselves radically democratic. Party direction of the revolution will only install the party itself as the new bureaucracy and ruling class. Only if the revolution is carried out by the direct initiative of the working community can the authentically communist state arise.

Cohn-Bendit's book is designed not only to expose the Gaullist regime but also the bureaucratic nature of the French Communist party, its complete failure to relate to the authentic resurgence of the leftist tradition and, finally, the betrayal of socialism by the Bolshevik party leadership in Russia, resulting in a totalitarian, state-capitalist state there. The aim of the May revolutionaries was, in their words, "to smash the entire state apparatus, to show the people ... how the whole of society had to be reconstituted afresh on the basis of worker's control."[15] The students hoped to create a general strike that would bring all the bureaucratic and hierarchical forms of domination to a halt, and, in the space created by their temporary abeyance, to initiate a practice of direct, communal self-government that would be, at the least, a premonition of what the true socialist society should be like. Ultimately such a society waits not only for the overthrow of alienated orders and powers but for the creation of a new socialist man who is no longer passively dependent, but has recovered his own creative powers in face-to-face community with his fellow workers. Not state control, but the abolition of the state and all ruling powers that are alienated from the person in his local productive community is the authentic socialist tradition. The vision of what this socialist state should look like echoes the accents of Proudhon: "a federation of worker's councils, soviets, a classless society, a society where the social division of labor between manual and intellectual workers no longer exists."[16]

The betrayal of this revolutionary vision is laid at the door of the unions and the Communist party, which revealed its true colors by working with the Gaullist state to put down the alarming spectre of popular socialism. Somewhat more reluctantly Cohn-Bendit admits that the workers themselves faltered before the final leap into utopia and drew back, guarding their pensions and settling for a few labor union concessions. In any case, Cohn-Bendit's story is intended to establish firmly the counterrevolutionary nature of the party and the Communist-dominated unions. He rounds out his story by arguing that the authentic socialism of the Russian Revolution was also of the anarchist-communal tradition over against the Leninist party, which lagged behind the popular revolutionaries and ultimately betrayed their ideals. It was the initiative of popular socialism in peasant and worker's communes, in the Makhno movement in the Ukraine, and in the Kronstadt rebellion that created the true revolutionary possibility over against the party direction. Even Lenin himself had to temporarily turn anarchist in order to ride the coattails of the popular uprising. The Bolshevik party neither created nor led the authentic socialist revolution, but used and then destroyed it in order to install themselves in power.

Cohn-Bendit's book is then a bid to rewrite the history of the Russian Revolution in favor of the left-wing alternative.[17] However he offers no real analysis of how this would be possible, and his own fundamental orientation is less to economic possibilities than to the values of existential human freedom. He suggests that even if the authentic revolution lasts for only a few days, those few days are their own reward, for in the temporary overthrow of the rule of alien powers, men ecstatically experience the kingdom of freedom beyond the kingdom of necessity. Even if the ecstasy is doomed to disappear and life to relapse into finite orders of control and causality, that experience remains as a shining vision:

What matters is not working out a reform of capitalist society, but launching an experiment that completely breaks with that society, an experiment that will not last, but which allows a glimpse of a possibility;

something which is revealed for a moment and then vanishes. But that is enough to prove that something could exist.[18]

It is not simply the results but the joy, the ecstacy of the revolutionary process that is its raison d'être. The role of the leftist is not to construct another organization in behalf of the worker but to keep that memory and hope alive. *C'est pour toi que tu fais la révolution.*[19]

The American student Left has pioneered in the tactics of confrontation, but it is perhaps even less coherent in its ideology than the European students, who have a leftist tradition that is more developed, institutionally and intellectually, to serve as a point of reference and a point of departure. The original SDS ideology was that of a renewed expectation of the American faith in democracy and social justice for all citizens. The radicals posited a revived sense of utopian hope, of trust in human possibilities for remaking the earth, as against a jaded liberalism of "political reality." It was humanistic against a technological culture, personalist and vaguely communalist, but it entirely lacked a Marxist language of class struggle, even declaring Marxism obsolete.[20] Insofar as it fell into a socialist tradition, it was for the most part unconsciously that of individualistic and communistic anarchism that valued grass-roots democracy, community organization, and community control.

In the seven years that have elapsed between the Port Huron statement and the 1968–69 campus struggles, experience has altered the tone to one of increasing sectarianism, hostility, and revolutionary violence toward existing American society. At the same time a fanaticism and an urge for radical purity increasingly sets radical groups against one another. From about the time of the Columbia uprising (March 1968), official SDS rhetoric veered sharply toward Marxism. The categories of the "worker" and the "class struggle" and of revolutionary overthrow now dominate the rhetoric. There is an idealization of the Cuban and Chinese models of revolt. The Viet Cong and the Arab guerrillas are considered allies in a worldwide struggle. The Black Panthers are proclaimed the vanguard of the international working class.[21] The earlier forms of campus confrontation are now played down in favor of ideas of organizing the worker against both management and the established unions. The SDS summer programs in Detroit and elsewhere, in which members are expected to take jobs as laborers in the city, represent an effort to move away from the colleges of the affluent toward working class youth. The shift of focus to city colleges and high schools follows the same direction.[22] One of the early signs of the possibilities of such a change of focus has been provided by the wild-cat strike led by the United Black Brothers, an independent Negro union, against the Ford assembly plant in Mahwah, New Jersey, where support forces of SDS members and Black Panthers were called.

The new SDS rhetoric is ostensibly Maoist, even absurdly so, witness its solemn chanting of the official Chinese formula that the Chinese Communists are the "true Marxist-Leninists" against Soviet revisionist puppets of the United States.[23] SDS ideology is nevertheless a maverick from the point of view of Marxist orthodoxy. The more orthodox Progressive Labor Party (PLP), which rejects any cultural or national revolutionary movements for "pure" working class struggle, tried to swing SDS to their view at the Spring National Council meeting in Austin, Texas, but were rebuked by the majority. In June 1969, when PLP came on in the Chicago national meeting with an effort at organized takeover, the two groups feel into open schism and mutual anathemas.[24] Even so, SDS remains strangely ideocentric from the point of view of traditional party-line Marxism and is unlikely to yield to any direction from the American Communist party, which has remained the least autonomous and nationalist of all Western parties.[25]

If the Marxism of SDS is strident and lacks the "Protestant substance" of the Eastern Europeans, this may ironically be due to their lack of exposure to this whole chapter of history. The suppression of the Left in the United States has left the new leftist innocent enough chant the old slogans with a fresh, uncritical zeal. Marxist language in the hands of the young radicals

has a dogmatic bookish quality, as though lifted from revolutionary categories of Chinese or early Leninist pamphlet literature
and pressed superficially and often rather incongruously upon
the American scene. Yet SDS neo-Marxism should be viewed as
rather tentative and experimental, despite its apparently rigid
tone. New experience with the "white working class" could
transform it rapidly in a year's time. Moreover, it should be seen
as only one expression of a broad base of dissent among students,
blacks, young intellectuals, and concerned older liberals, who
would agree with most of SDS's concerns without finding its
current rhetoric very helpful. This pool of dissent has grown
more militant and radical in its assessment of the illness of the
American body politic through the 1960s, and this development
has markedly altered the American ethos from one of trium-
phant liberalism to one of deep polarization.[26]

The name most frequently mentioned as the ideologist of the
New Left in Europe and America is that of Herbert Marcuse, an
elderly, independent, Marxist philosopher, born and educated in
Germany, but an American university professor since 1934. The
New Left's association with Marcuse is perhaps one of convergence rather than initial discipleship. Although Marcuse's name
has been mentioned in the press for the past few years as the
guru of the New Left, many of the student leaders confessed to
having never read him or even heard of him. His name now
established, however, he has become "must" reading for young
radicals. He is also listed among the mandatory reading for
members of the Black Panther party, along with Mao Tse-tung,
Che Guevara, and Frantz Fanon. In *One Dimensional Man,* Marcuse deplores the emasculation of the Left under what he deems
the "repressive tolerance" of liberalism. In the more recent *Essay on Liberation,* however, he sees a new generation of radicals, both black and white, as creating that vital dissenting
culture for which he previously looked in vain. The alliance of
Marcuse and the young Left, then, is perhaps a case of an elderly
ideologist in search of revolutionaries meeting young revoluti-
naries in search of an ideology.

Marcuse's writings articulate the concerns of the young radicals while giving these a framework of analysis with an intellectual tradition and a perspective on the future. For Marcuse, "one-dimensional man" is technological man who has lost the dimension of transcendence given by philosophical and historical consciousness. Philosophical transcendence was the transcendence of the idea or essence over fact or existence. Classical thought identified reality with essence, and so judged existence by the standard of essence. Truth by its nature could not be value free, but was a value judgment upon present existence. Truth or essence was a demand laid upon existence that defined what the thing "really was" and so what it "should be." In Christian mythological language the same idea is present in the images of "Creation" and "the Kingdom." Creation is not the historical origin of present existence but stands for the true nature of things which is recovered or fulfilled only at the End. Both poles are necessary because without the creational pole the demand upon existence loses its foundation. Only with the doctrine of creation as the foundation is it clear that what the world "should be" is to become "what it really is," its true nature. Existence, by contrast, is in tension with what creation truly is. Classical thought in its Aristotelian form also translated the philosophical dialectic into a teleological one by asserting that the essence of the thing is also its goal or destiny. Classical man (and Christian man, although Marcuse does not take this tradition into account) lived in a two-dimensional universe of tension between the "is" and the "ought," between existence and essence. Dialectical or critical philosophy belongs to this classical heritage while revealing the historical, dynamic nature of the dialectic. "Being" or "true reality" is understood as a demand laid upon existence both in negation of its present failure and an exhortation to struggle toward self-transcendence. Truth or essence is subversive of the existing order. The search for truth is sociohistorical. It is the search for the new *polis.* Historical being is a dynamic continuum of tension and negation and élan toward the 'true world'.

One-dimensional man flattens and reduces this tension. The dreams and myths of the past fail before the technological wonders of modernity. The heroes and villains of antiquity become mere aberrations to be treated on the psychiatrist's couch. All the dissenting, utopian traditions of the past are emasculated and their rhetoric appropriated into praise of the present system. The higher culture of earlier times is vulgarized so that it loses its distance, power, and mystery. This ability to accommodate and appropriate while at the same time suppressing the radicality of this culture produces the one-dimensional man who has lost the dimension of transcendence, who has neither a past to judge him nor a future to which to aspire. He lives in a closed universe in which the "is" is reduced to value-free "facts" (the cloak for an ideological benediction upon the present system) and whose history is reduced to the all-enclosing "now." This one-dimensional man, for Marcuse, is a peculiar product of technological proficiency that has proven complex enough in its sociopolitical accommodation and fertile enough in its productive powers that the old dreams and dissenting culture have grown pale beside it. Visions of another world and room for dissent against present existence dies out before a reality that staggers the imagination.

Yet what is desperately needed is not this demise of dissent and aspiration but their updating in a renewed form that can stand out beyond and in critical judgment upon this technological civilization for all its wonder, for this wonder is, in fact, a dark and sinister wonder, fed on oppression and breeding war. The welfare state has for its underpinnings the warfare state and the oppression of aliens within and without its borders. This warfare state is now so entrenched in its logic of prosperity and security built on exploitation and destruction that it has closed off any interior space for a dissenting and critical logic. So encompassing is its logic that dissent to it appears insane and utopian. Yet if the present course of this system continues it will result in the ruin of the environment and the annihilation of the human race. Dissent, then, is urgent toward this very society that has closed off all the avenues for a dissenting and self-transcending culture.

Much of *One Dimensional Man* is devoted to an analysis of the culture of this "transcendence-less" society and the ways in which the two-dimensional culture of the past was overcome and absorbed to produce the present closed cultural universe. The liberal empirical culture of early industrial society was originally a dissenting tradition over against the earlier social status quo. With the success of the bourgeois, the liberal freedoms have lost their critical content. Society has progressed to the point where it can maintain the forms of earlier freedoms without their having an emancipating force. New expressions of freedom are needed to correspond to present capacities and forms of domination. For example, one of the most pervasive forms of domination is now expressed through what was once a critical freedom, the free press. Advertising in the "free press" virtually surrounds the consciousness of present society like a great octopus. With its all-encompassing blare it stimulates a thousand artificial needs as the technique for keeping aloft an economy of overproduction, waste, and planned obsolescence. "Free enterprise" and "free choice" are part of the seductive domination of the media that maintains the appearance of free decision among many brands or many candidates, which, however, all represent the same thing. Free economic choice, free political choice, and free press become emptied of critical content and incorporated into the system of domination. There are choices, but no really free choice because no choice available offers a real alternative to the given system, only an appearance of it within the status quo.

In a similar way the dissenting tradition of socialism has also been incorporated into the present system. Labor takes its place within the system rather than as its contradiction. Capitalist and so-called socialist countries approximate each other. The structure of productivity itself has altered to the point where there is no longer a sharp chasm between factory worker and owner. The factory worker has become a technician, a skilled supervisor of a complex mechanism that he manages through intelligence rather than through brute labor. The corporation itself has grown so large and impersonal that the "capitalist" has disappeared in favor of a hierarchy of "managers." The elimination of many of the old forms of brute labor and the incorporation of labor into the management system remove the dissenting force of the old working class. This possibility of increasing transcendence of brute labor through cybernation and automation itself points toward the possibility of a new society where work is surpassed by free creativity. But the present productive system, including the role of the labor unions, closes off the transcendent possibilities inherent in this new potential that, if actualized, would shatter the present economic and political power structure.

The possibility of the communist society, the society of free creativity beyond the work principle, is now within the grasp of mankind, whereas before the leisure society was the prerogative of a cultural elite. But this productive potential is diverted to a surfeit of wasteful consumer goods and war potential accompanied by unplanned destruction of the natural environment. Such wasteful production is designed to keep alive artificially an obsolete form of the struggle for existence and thus prevent the birth of that new order of society that is already gestating in the womb of present technological society. This is the basic contradiction of advanced technological society and provides both the handle for dissent against it and transcendence beyond it. However, with the absorption of the old working class, Marcuse despairs of finding an appropriate social vehicle for such dissent and transcendence. The outcasts within the society—the racial minorities, the unemployed, and the disadvantaged of the Third World—are potentially such a dissenting class but without the cohesion to mount an assault.

Not only is a social vehicle in the form of a new antithetical class lacking, but the culture of dissent is lacking as the basis for a revolutionary consciousness. This is the particularly sinister character of one-dimensional society. The very language of technological society is designed to reduce reality to the facts of the given world and so closing off that "excess of meaning" in substantive references that points beyond the given. The language of technological society is functional and operational. Things no longer have a "being." They are reduced to their functions, eliminating any tension between what a thing is and how it functions. The instinctual dimension of man was also once a powerful psychic force that could erupt against the established order, but this is now absorbed into the system of stimulation that keeps present consumer society moving. The constant use of eroticism in advertising, selling, and personnel is symptomatic of this harnessing of the instincts to consumer society, thereby eliminating their dissenting power. The philosophical analysis current in technological society likewise operates ideologically to confine the consciousness to the present system by systematically debunking the culture and language of transcendence. Logical positivism, linguistic analysis, and its behavioralist forms in the social sciences operate therapeutically to coordinate the mind with existing social reality. Positivism and behavioralism give intellectual justification for a defamation of alternate forms of thought and life.

The official language of technological society itself, whether it be that of government, the military, or business, is reduced to a peculiarly ritualistic, sloganistic jargon intended to inure the mind to accept all forms of outrageous contradictions as inevitable corollaries. This common sloganeering, manipulative language as it comes from many apparently different sources through the public media, is itself the ideological superstructure of the interlocking system of government, business, and the military. This manipulative language virtually surrounds the consciousness, molding it and closing off all other possibilities. Such phrases as "clean bombs," "luxury fallout shelters," or, more recently, "thin shields" are designed to reconcile the mind to outlandish antimonies. They conjure up images of an outrageously expensive and oppressive military system that is nevertheless to be accounted "too cheap", a destructive weapon that is to be believed "sanitary", and an incredible retreat to a new caveman barbarianism that is to be accounted "luxurious." Such antimonies themselves have their basis in an economy where affluence is built on war production, so that destruction and prosperity, military and industry mingle together. Upon this base a culture arises that is intended to artfully integrate and reconcile these contradictions. This same ritualistic and sloganeering language is to be found no less in the Soviet Union, although there it has the additional horror of being created through a ritualization of critical dialectical language. The party proclaims itself to be the incarnation of these critical principles by fiat, thereby closing off all space for true criticism. Its language of self-validating pronouncements abolishes the autonomy of facts. The critical past of this language as well as its future hope is dogmatically incorporated into the present in a way that blocks any mediation of the inner substance of that past and future hope to the present.

The productive basis for transcending this present society is already present, but its social and political structure contradicts and retards it and, diverting it into exploitive, destructive paths. Corresponding to this diversion of new possibilities is a culture designed to divert the mind from genuine alternatives to infinite amounts of the same thing. Marcuse ends *One Dimensional Man* with a note of defiant hope that does not yet see a social and cultural basis for a practical hopefulness. In *On Liberation,* however, Marcuse points to the new generation of radicals in Europe and America, as well as the black liberation movement, as the glimmerings of a new class that might be the bearer of such a social antithesis. With them has also appeared a new dissenting culture that is breaking across the monolithic culture of technological society to reveal its antimonies, and opening up alternative possibilities. A new dissenting class and a new dissenting culture are appearing as the practical basis for a new struggle for liberation.

In the new society that would be the goal of liberation, artificial production for false needs loses its social basis and the productive system can be geared to fulfilling the real needs of man. Today's existence must be pacified by breaking the power of an obsolete system of production that depends on war and waste. Nature itself can then be cultivated instead of exploited. The present exploitation is an obsolete expression of a struggle for the domination of nature that has become harmful to man. Having subdued nature, man must now becomes its cultivator, not its destroyer, so that the world may become a park and a garden, for now it is fast becoming a wasteland. Domination of nature and of one's fellow man are linked to the same obsolete relationship to man and the world that must now be replaced by a relationship of reciprocity and care. A new world of possibilities is opening up, but it cannot become a reality without a revolutionary struggle against economic and political systems that keep the old forms alive after they have become dysfunctional and destructive.

The young militants know or sense that what is at stake is simply their life, the life of human beings which has become a plaything in the hands of politicians and managers and generals. The rebels want to take it out of these hands and make it worth living. They realize that this is still possible today and that the attainment of this goal necessitates a struggle which can no longer be contained by the rules and regulations of a pseudo-democracy in a "Free Orwellian world."[27]

If a neo-Marxian language has captured the imagination of new radicals, it is doubtless because this tradition respects the radical antithesis, the need for negation and a projection of an alternative that cannot yet be known except by way of negation of the present because it goes beyond what is possible within the existing world. The puzzle of revolutionaries is ever that of reconciling apparent contradictions not only against the present but between alternative goals. On the one hand there is the conquest of external necessity, the rationalization of life that will end physical need. On the other hand lies the inner liberation of the self. The nightmare utopia of modern man is rooted in the apparent incompatibility of these two goals, so that the final conquest of the first results in the final enslavement of the second. Perhaps the continuous attraction of Marxism lies in its insistence that the two must ultimately go together, and that the authentic conquest of necessity must also be the inner liberation of the self.

CONCLUSION

Chapter 16

Man as Revolution

This study has tried to reveal the theological motifs operating in an overt or concealed form in movements of radical social change. Although in conventional interpretation revolution is classed as a subject of political study, and its theological implications would seem to be a doubtful area of inquiry, I would suggest that the more one studies the language of radical social change, especially in the West, the more one concludes that it is easier to analyze the theology of revolution as a salvation drama than it is to determine the practical possibility of realizing the longings inherent in its mythos. To say that revolutionary mythology reveals a longing not only for practical amelioration but, in and through this, for an ultimate salvation; to say that it stands for an ecstatic rebirth of hope, a judgment upon a fallen past-present, a vision of promise of a future paradise, an explosion of new life against a dying world, a willingness for self-sacrifice for the sake of this salvation; all this moral and religious substance, in language very little altered from the Biblical can be taken as the given of movements for radical social change. As such it is relatively easy to see how this longing has been translated from the religious language of a vertical universe to the language of society-in-history of a time-oriented worldview.

"The Revolution" represents a collective social ecstacy. Partly a direct experience, partly a culturally mediated creation, it represents a leaping out beyond the present state of existence, both in rejection of a disappointing reality and a transcending of it in hope and imaginative projection toward a new possibility that cannot even be described because it is not yet existent. Yet, although it can only be projected in emotive, mythic language, the twin elements of external pacification and glorification of the universe and the internal harmony of man with himself in community with his fellow man are always linked together in its hopes. Technological thinking tends to turn toward the mastery of nature at the expense of the subjective, personalist dimension of salvation, while the religious congregation works on the inner dimension at the expense of the transformation of the outer world. But the rebirth of the full sense of revolutionary hope ever brings the two sides back together in their dynamic unity.

When we ask the question of what good revolutions have done, what have been their practical effects and their capacities for constructive change, we find ourselves in a far more ambiguous area where one is almost forced to fall silent before the welter of contradictory evidence. Here Revolutionary Man is indeed man himself writ large, in all his paradox and contradictory elements of demon and angel. When I first thought of researching this topic, it was out of a very practical desire for historical perspective, so that the symbols of revolution and their practice could be seen in their roots and vicissitudes. Yet it became increasingly clear that nothing could be more unwelcome to the contemporary radical than precisely this historical perspective on himself. Radicalism is always new-born, without history, the final generation that will bring the old world to an end, the first and only generation of the world to come. Its ecstacy, by definition, is history-defying. It is an explosion beyond what has been confidently charted in the past as the limits of the possible. It has little real use for the laws of history, fixed concepts of the limits of nature, or the configurations of being such as underlie the presumption that "history teaches," for radicalism is out to dissolve the confines of a fixed nature to create a "new nature" beyond that which has hitherto prevailed. To know its own history is to waver in this self-transcending faith and to find itself reenclosed in a system of inevitablity and limit that it desires to leave behind. History, therefore, is faith-destroying knowledge for the revolutionary unless he, like Marx, conceives a historical science whereby the revolutionary can see himself as the exception to the laws of historical relativity and finitude.

The revolutionary élan naturally resists any effort to chart its path or guide its means and ends in a rational way, for to acquiesce is to be limited to the fundamental presuppositions of presently existing reality. Consequently, the revolutionary élan is like an explosion with random and unpredictable results. Its historical results depend very much on the counteracting forces that it encounters which may resist or subsume it. It may meet determined reaction amounting to a destructive sweep against it so violent and destructive that, indeed, the last state of that house may be worse than the first. Chiliastic peasant revolutions in the late medieval and Reformation periods generally met with this kind of counteraction. But on the other hand, its energy and idealism may be swept up by carrier forces that, at first, appear to be its realization, but sooner or later reveal demonic qualities that carry it to terrible excesses. In such a way were the youth movements of the 1920s subsumed by Nazism and fascism.

In some periods of history there seems to be a balance and meshing of the élan of hope and the availability of new productive forces ready to turn it to practical effect, and in such periods men feel themselves at the steering wheel of a boundlessly progressive history. But this sense of boundlessness, in fact, belongs rather to the mythos of revolution than to the actual possibilities of its context. The boundless revolutionary vision provides the energy and motive force for creative change, but the potential of the carrier context sets the direction and limit to the actual kind and degree of change that takes place. When this direction and limit become apparent, those caught by the vision experience a sense of betrayal. The vision promised a radically transfigured man and universe, not merely a modified system.

Yet, in longer retrospection, such moments of coalesion of boundless vision and practical possibility are probably the best moments of revolutionary history, when hope and possibility come
together to create some limited yet concrete and real change for
the better, either in terms of freer communication, extended
political rights for minority groups, greater protection of life and
health for larger numbers of persons, and so on. Nor could these
modest but real changes have happened without the far more
radical hopes that carried them into being, for these hopes sup-
plied the motivation to burst apart the bonds of what was previously seen as unchangeable, and such energy inspired by radical
hopes was essential to extend the bounds of the possible by even
such a little bit. When men tailor their hopes to the presently
possible, their accomplishments will surely fall far behind, yet
the vision of radical and sweeping renewal spins off into empty
frustration unless it does mesh in a practical way with matter
and in their interaction, the word to some extent becomes flesh.

The revolutionary poet depends for his practical effect on being heard by the practical mediator who perhaps could not have
formulated such a vision himself, but takes it from the poet and
meshes it with real possibility. This mediator between already-
and not-yet-created existence is the indispensible facilitator of
the historical dialectic, yet inevitably he is resisted by the revolutionary poet because, in giving the revolution flesh, he limits it,
confining it to a new but specific kind of possibility. He thus
foregoes the full radicality of the vision, while still living on and
justifying himself by its mythology. In this way the revolution
swallows its own prophets. The Left keeps its integrity both by
being willing to lend itself to concrete change, but also by continuing to stand out beyond what has been accomplished as the
ongoing gadfly and critic of the still unfulfilled existence.

The two sides of the dialectic must meet in active mutuality,
but without either completely merging or completely disengag-
ing with each other. When they fall completely out of contact,
then the Left spins off in bitter frustration and nihilism. But
when they identify completely, the revolutionary mythology is
installed in the seats of power as the source of a new absolutism

of the established regime. This absolutism of the "infallible magisterium," far from being alien to the messianic Left, is, as can be seen from both church history and revolutionary history, latent within it and actualized when it merges the transcendent vision completely with the newly established system. One must strive, therefore, chastened by this knowledge, to keep the dialectic ever moving and open-ended. One would wish each generation to take up anew the critical and utopian task upon the basis established by the past, without that past itself having been established with too much rigidity.

Yet the mystery is deeper than simply one of succeeding generations. Man by his nature is a paradoxical fusion of infinite aspiration and finite possibility. To confine him to finite possibility, bowed before the vision of the infinite as a nature alien to himself, is to deny him one of his essential dimensions and to consign him to death. This is why Niebuhrian realism moves so quickly to conservative complacency. Revolution, breaking the bonds of the possible, is essential to man's affirmation of his life against every stasis, including the stasis of liberal affluence. Man's nature abhors stasis, and this burdens him with the cruel dilemma of finding his vital élan as much threatened by the stasis of success as by the struggle against difficult foes. Man's life being constituted in and through the struggle for new being, it becomes unimaginable to project a final goal to this struggle that would not itself suggest stasis and so the sated form of death. Yet endless struggle without goal or meaning also denies an essential demand of man's nature and saps his life. Consequently every conceptualizing of the goal of salvation is caught in a contradictory dilemma. The struggle for salvation must have an ultimate goal, but it is impossible because it contradicts man's historical nature. So pictures of the final Kingdom of God either tend to look suspiciously like glorified death or else one must postulate the acquisition of an entirely new kind of nature, radically different from man's historical nature, that allows fulfillment without stultification. Yet such a new nature would itself be the end of historical man, so in yet another sense man finds his goal only through his own death. This is doubtless why descriptions of the final state of paradise at the conclusion of the apocalypse are so empty and dull in comparison ith the apocalyptic struggle itself. As every child in Sunday school recognizes in guilty secret, Heaven sounds so boring.

Yet within the bounds of present life, the struggle itself is its own reward. It is in the process of struggle against debased existence, with the attendant demands for moral sensitizing, self-discipline, and constant resetting of one's sights upon the vision of salvation, that one is closest to the secret of human life. Such a struggle, even in its failure and disappointment, is recollected as a time of fellowship, commitment, and ecstatic hopefulness as the highest point of living. The time of revolutionary expectation is the time when men come closest to experiencing the spirit dwelling in the community of man. In such a time of struggle one feels closest to one's brother. One glimpses what true fraternity and community might mean. The messianic brotherhood is then the root of the true church, and in its life one finds the present "foretaste of the Kingdom of God" and the "first fruits" of the resurrection. It is in this form that men experience the concrete presence of salvation, recollected in memory as the lost paradise and in hope as the ever-reborn revolutionary vision. One lays hold of this vision as the deepest moral certitude of one's life, notwithstanding that its practical possibility remains shrouded in the deepest uncertainty.

In St. Paul's words:

I consider that the sufferings of this present time are not worth comparing with the glory that is to be revealed to us. For the creation waits with eager longing for the revealing of the sons of God; for the creation was subjected to futility, not of its own will but by the will of him who subjected it in hope; because the creation itself will be set free from its bondage to decay and obtain the glorious liberty of the children of God. We know that the whole creation has been groaning in travail together until now, and not only the creation, but we ourselves who have the first fruits of the Spirit, groan inwardly as we await for adoption as sons, the redemption of our bodies. For in this hope we were saved.

Roman 8:18–24 (RSV).

Notes

CHAPTER 1. The Theology of Revolution and Social Change:
The Basic Motifs

1. Hannah Arendt, *On Revolution* (New York: Viking Press, 1963), p. 19.

2. George Huntston Williams, *Wilderness and Paradise in Christian Thought* (New York: Harper & Brothers, 1962), *passim.*

3. For example, in the *Vita* of St. Anthony by St. Athanasius. Also see Helen Waddell, *The Desert Fathers* (Ann Arbor: Univ. of Michigan Press, 1957).

CHAPTER 2. The Radicals of the Reformation and the
Puritan Revolution

1. Norman Cohn, *The Pursuit of the Millennium* (New York: Harper & Brothers, 1961), pp. 307 ff.

2. Eduard Bernstein, *Cromwell and Communism: Socialism and Democracy in the English Revolution* (New York: Schocken Books, 1963). See also chapter 11 in this volume.

3. George Huntston Williams, *The Radical Reformation* (Philadelphia: Westminster Press, 1962).

4. The standard summary of Anabaptist theology still remains Frank Littell, *The Anabaptist View of the Church* (Hartford, Conn.: Amer. Society of Church History, 1952).

5. Representative of Anabaptist voluntarism are such essays as John Denck's "Whether God is the Cause of Evil" (1526) and Balthasar Hubmaier's "On Free Will" (1527), in G. H. Williams and A. M. Mergal, eds., *Spiritual and Anabaptist Writers* (Philadelphia: Westminster Press, Library of Christian Classics, no. 25, 1957).

6. For example, Sebastian Castellio's famous response to the burning of Michael Servetus, "Concerning Heretics and Whether They Should Be Punished by the Sword of the Magistrate," in *ibid.*

7. Menno Simons, "On the Ban: Questions and Answers," (1550) in *ibid.*

8. For example, Dietrich Philips, "The Church of God," in *ibid.*, pp. 228 ff.

9. Melchior Hofmann, "The Ordinance of God," in *ibid.*, p. 188.

10. Thus the *Acta Martyrum* of Michael Sattler ends with these words: "After this had been done in the manner prescribed (his tongue torn out; his body 12 times torn with red-hot tongs), he was burned to ashes as a heretic. His fellow brethren were executed with a sword and the sisters drowned. His wife, also after being subjected to many entreaties, admonitions, and threats, under which she remained steadfast, was drowned a few days afterwards. Done the 21st day of May, A.D. 1527." *Ibid.*, pp. 144–45.

11. Cohn, *op. cit.*, chaps. 10–12.

12. *Ibid.*, p. 226.

13. Christopher Hill, *Puritanism and Revolution* (New York: Schocken Books, 1958), pp. 50 ff.

14. P. G. Rogers, *The Fifth Monarchy Men* (London: Oxford Univ. Press, 1966).

15. *Ibid.*, p. 145.

16. Williams, *Wilderness and Paradise in Christian Thought* (New York: Harper & Brothers, 1962), *passim.*

17. Cohn, *op. cit.*, chaps. 7–8 and appendix.

CHAPTER 3. The Enlightenment, Liberalism, and the French Revolution

1. John Calvin, *Institutes of the Christian Religion*, 6.1.

2. Matthew Tindal, in E. Graham Waring, ed., *Deism and Natural Religion* (New York: F. Ungar, 1967), pp. 107 ff.

3. John Locke's *Essay Concerning Civil Government* was originally written as an apologia for the Glorious Revolution. It was published in 1690 but written in Holland between 1684–89.

4. See especially Peter Gay, *The Enlightenment: The Rise of Modern Paganism* (New York: Alfred A. Knopf, 1966), *passim.*

5. "Project of Henry IV for Perpetual Peace" (1713); also "Project to Perfect the Governments of States" (1773). Plans for perpetual peace were common in the 18th century, ranging from Emerie Cruce's plan for a universal league of arbitration between states (1623) to Kant's "On Perpetual Peace" (1795). They are, in fact, the ancestors of the modern League of Nations and the United Nations.

6. Alfred Cobban, *In Search of Humanity: The Role of the Enlightenment in Modern History* (New York: George Braziller, 1960), p. 95 and no. 4.

7. Cobban, *Aspects of the French Revolution* (New York: George Braziller, 1968), pp. 136 ff.

8. Cobban, *In Search of Humanity, op. cit.,* pp. 181 ff.

9. Immanuel Kant, *Religion Within the Bounds of Reason Alone* (1793) (New York: Harper & Brothers, 1960).

10. Gottheld Ephraim Lessing, *The Education of the Human Race* (1780), Johann Gottfried von Herder, *The Idea as the Philosophy of the History of Mankind* (1784-91), and Johann Christoph Friedrich von Schiller, *Letters on the Aesthetic Education of Mankind* (1795).

11. T. H. Huxley in J. B. Bury, *The Idea of Progress* (New York: Macmillan Co., 1932), p. 345.

CHAPTER 4. Utopianism: Christian and Socialist

1. Mark Holloway, *Heavens on Earth: Utopian Communities in America 1680–1880* (New York: Dover Books, 1966), p. 40.

2. Shaker songs can be found in Edward Deming Andrews, *The Gift to be Simple: Songs, Dances and Rituals of the American Shakers* (New York: J. J. Augustin, 1940).

3. P. K. Conkin, *Two Paths in Utopia: The Hutterites and the Llano Colony* (Lincoln: Univ. of Nebraska Press, 1964), p. 28.

4. See George Huntston Williams, *Wilderness and Paradise in Christian Thought* (Harper & Brothers, 1962), pp. 141 ff., for a discussion of the utopian heritage of the American college.

5. Holloway, *op. cit.,* pp. 194–95.

6. Arthur Eugene Bestor, *Backwoods Utopias: The Sectarian and Owenite Phases of Communitarian Socialism in America, 1663–1829* (Philadelphia: Univ. of Pennsylvania Press, 1950), pp. 160 ff.

7. In Conkin, *op. cit.,* pp. 148 ff., he notes the same combination of economic disaster and spiritual success in one of the latest socialist communities, the Llano community of California and Louisiana, which lasted from 1914 to 1938.

8. Friedrich Engels, *Socialism: Utopian and Ssientific* (1882) (New York: International Publishers, 1935).

9. In examining the identity of the "revolutionary bourgeois," Cobban finds them bureaucrats and professionals and the new propertied classes who acquired land in the rural areas without necessarily living there. They were not "capitalists," since such an industrial class was scarcely developed. Alfred Cobban, *The Social Interpretation of the French Revolution* (Cambridge: Cambridge Univ. Press, 1964), *passim.*

10. G. D. H. Cole, *A History of Socialist Thought,* vol. 1, *The Forerunners 1789–1850* (London: Macmillan & Co., 1955), p. 1.

11. Robert Owen, "An Address to the Inhabitants of New Lanark" (1816), in G. D. H. Cole, ed., *A New View of Society and Other Writings* (New York: E. P. Dutton, 1927).

12. George Lichtheim, *The Origins of Socialism* (New York: Praeger Books, 1968), pp. 35–37.

13. Karl Marx, in Emile Burns, ed., *A Handbook of Marxism* (New York: Random House, 1959), p. 858.

14. See article and bibliography on "Anarchism" by Peter Kropotkin, *Encyclopaedia Brittanica,* 11th edition.

15. This double aspect of Marxism is especially stressed in Adam Ulam, *The Unfinished Revolution* (New York: Random House, 1960).

CHAPTER 5. Christian Socialism and the Social Gospel

1. Immanuel Kant, *Religion Within the Limits of Reason Alone* (1793) (New York: Harper & Brothers, 1960), pp. 113–14.
2. Peter Gay, *The Dilemma of Democratic Socialism: Eduard Bernstein's Challenge to Marx* (New York: Columbia Univ. Press, 1952).
3. Alexander Vidler, *A Century of Social Catholicism, 1820–1920* (London: S.P.C.K., 1964).
4. These motifs were already established by 1838 in the volume of F. D. Maurice, *The Kingdom of Christ* (London, SCM Press, 1958).
5. T. L. Smith, *Revivalism and Social Reform* (New York: Harper & Row, 1965), p. 20.
6. *Ibid.,* p. 205.
7. *Ibid.,* p. 225.
8. Walter Rauschenbusch, *The Theology for the Social Gospel* (New York: Macmillan Co., 1918), p. 227.
9. *Ibid.,* pp. 142–43.
10. *Ibid.,* p. 141.
11. C. H. Hopkins, *The Rise of the Social Gospel in American Protestantism, 1865–1915* (New Haven; Yale Univ. Press, 1940), pp. 140–48.
12. *Ibid.,* pp. 167–69.
13. *Ibid.,* p. 291.

CHAPTER 6. Marx: The Secular Apocalypse

1. The famous phrase, "So far the philosophers have only interpreted the world; the point is to change it," occurs at the end of the eleven theses on Feuerbach, which were published by Engels.
2. See Sidney Hook, *From Hegel to Marx: Studies in the Intellectual Development of Karl Marx* (Ann Arbor: Univ. of Michigan Press, 1962).
3. Robert C. Tucker, *Philosophy and Myth in Karl Marx* (Cambridge: Cambridge Univ. Press, 1961), p. 55.
4. For the movement from Hegel to Feuerbach to Moses Hess in the development of Marx's view, see *ibid.,* pp. 73–120. Marx's analysis of money as the final reification of alienated labor is found in the third Manuscript. See Erich Fromm, *Marx's Concept of Man,* with a translation of Marx's *Economic and Philosophical Manuscripts* by T. B. Bottomore (New York: F. Ungar, 1961), pp. 163–68.
5. Karl Marx, *Capital: A Critical Analysis of Capitalist Production,* vol. I, trans. from the 3d Ger. edition, F. Engels, S. Moore, and E. Aveling, eds. (Moscow: Progress Publishers, 1965–67), pt. 1, chap. 1, sect. 4, pp. 71 ff.
6. V. I. Lenin, *What Is to be Done? Burning Questions of Our Movement* (1902) (New York: International Publishers, 1929).
7. Fromm, *op. cit.,* p. 95.
8. *Ibid.,* p. 119.
9. Tucker, *op. cit.,* p. 176. Also Fromm, *op. cit.,* pp. 67–77.

10. Karl Marx, Preface to he Critique of Political Economy, in Fromm, *op. cit.,* p. 219.

11. *Ibid.,* p. 125.

12. "Private Property and Communism," in *ibid.,* p. 127.

13. Friedrich Engels, *Socialism: Utopian and Scientific* (1882) (New York: International Publishers, 1935), pp. 70, 72–73.

14. Fromm, *op. cit.,* p. 108.

15. See especially Adam Ulam, *The Unfinished Revolution* (New York: Random House, 1960), pp. 209 ff.

16. Fromm, *op. cit.,* p. 108.

CHAPTER 7. Crisis Theology and the Attack on Liberalism

1. Friedrich E. D. Schleiermacher, *On Religion: Speeches to Its Cultured Despisers* (1799) (New York: Harper & Brothers, 1958), and *The Christian Faith* (1821–22) (New York: Harper & Row, 1963).

2. The radicalism of the political Left, especially the Communist party in this period, which consistently lumped liberals and social democrats with fascists and saw the reformers of the middle as the chief enemy to be combatted, declaring their preference for the "unmasked" dictatorship of the fascists, were undoubtedly instrumental in paving the way for the victory of fascism. As late as 1934 the Communists still harbored the illusion that an unmasked dictatorship of the fascists would be preferable to the "veiled" fascism of the liberals and would produce a crisis that would lead to a proletariat revolution. See Theodore Draper, "The Ghost of Social Fascism," *Commentary* (February 1969), pp. 29–42.

3. Karl Barth, *Letters to East German Christians,* published in English as Karl Barth and Johannes Hamel, *How to Serve God in a Marxist Land* (New York: Association Press, 1959).

4. G. C. Berkouwer, *The Triumph of Grace in the Theology of Karl Barth* (Grand Rapids, Mich.: Wm. B. Eerdmans, 1956), p. 49 and *passim.*

5. On the relation of Barth's Christology to the doctrine of Creation, see Rosemary Ruether, "The Left Hand of God in the Theology of Karl Barth," *The Journal of Religious Thought* 25 (1968–69):3–26.

6. See especially the book by Niebuhr's brother, H. Richard Niebuhr, *The Kingdom of God in America* (New York: Harper & Brothers, 1959).

7. Reinhold Niebuhr, *An Interpretation of Christian Ethics* (New York: Harper & Bros., 1935) was originally delivered as the Rauschenbusch Memorial Lectures at Colgate-Rochester Divinity School in 1934.

8. Ibid., pp. 23–28.

9. R. Niebuhr, *Moral Man and Immoral Society* (New York: Scribner's, 1932), pp. 169–230.

10. Ibid., pp. 251–54.

11. Donald B. Meyer, *The Protestant Search for Political Realism, 1917–1941* (Berkeley: Univ. of California Press, 1960), pp. 256 ff.

12. See chapter 9 in this volume.

13. R. Niebuhr, *The Nature and Destiny of Man,* vol. II (New York: Scribner's, 1941), p. 320.

CHAPTER 8. The Mood of the Resistance: Rebel Against God

1. Albert Camus, *The Myth of Sisyphus and Other Essays* (New York: Random House, 1955), p. 91.
2. Camus, *The Rebel* (New York: Random House, 1959), p. 138.
3. *Ibid.*, p. 251.
4. *Ibid.*, p. 22.
5. Camus's assumption of the irreversibility of this movement might be questioned. Historically we find a similar "modern man" that emerges in classical times in the age of Euripides until the Silver Age of Latin literature, and then a retreat of man thereafter back into the religious and mythological stage.
6. *Ibid.*, p. 22.
7. *Ibid.*, pp. 120, 133.
8. *Ibid.*, pp. 114, 117–21.
9. *Ibid.*, pp. 302, 305–6.

CHAPTER 9. Secular Theology: Man, History, and the Church

1. See Leslie Dewart, *The Future of Belief* (New York: Herder & Herder, 1966).
2. Dietrich Bonhoeffer, *Letters and Papers from Prison* (New York: Macmillan Co., 1962). Written between April 1943 and January 1945.
3. Friedrich Gogarten, *Der Mensch zwischen Gott und Welt* (Stuttgart: Friedrich Vorwerk Verlag, 1956) and *Verhängnis und Hoffnung der Neuzeit: Die Säkularisierung als Theologische Problem* (Stuttgart: Friedrich Vorwerk Verlag, 1958). Two recent English interpretations are Larry Shiner, *The Secularization of History: An Introduction to the Theology of Friedrich Gogarten* (Nashville: Abingdon Press, 1966), and Ronald Gregor Smith, *Secular Christianity* (London: Collins, 1966).
4. For example, see Gibson Winter, *The New Creation as Metropolis* (New York: Macmillan Co., 1963); J. C. Hoekendijk, *The Church Inside Out,* I. C. Rottenberg, trans., (Philadelphia: Westminster Press, 1966); Robert Adolfs, *The Grave of God: Has the Church a Future* (New York: Harper & Row, 1967); and Rosemary Ruether, *The Church Against Itself* (New York: Herder & Herder, 1967).
5. Bonhoeffer, *op. cit.,* pp. 164–5, 168.
6. For example, see Bonhoeffer, *Creation and Fall* (1937) (London: SCM Press, 1959).
7. This modality of church life is particularly well described in the chapter on "The Church as God's Avant-Garde," in Harvey Cox, *The Secular City* (New York: Macmillan Co., 1965), pp. 125 ff.

CHAPTER 10. Post-Christendom and the Death of God

1. The best of these is probably John Macquarrie, *God-Talk: An Examination of the Language and Logic of Theology* (London: SCM Press, 1967).
2. See chapter 8 in this volume.
3. Fritz Buri, "Entmythologisierung oder Entkerygmatisierung der

Theologie," in Hans Werner Bartsch, ed., *Kerygma and Mythos* (Hamburg, 1952), band II, pp. 85 ff.; and "Theologie der Existenz, in Bartsch, ed., *op. cit.,* band III, pp. 81 ff. See also Macquarrie, *The Scope of Demythologizing* (1960).

4. Helmut Gollwitzer, *The Existence of God as Confessed by Faith,* J. M. Leitch, trans. (London: SCM Press, 1964).

5. Lewis Carroll, *Alice in Wonderland* (New York: World Pub. Co., 1946), pp. 82–83.

6. Thomas J. J. Altizer and William Hamilton, *Radical Theology and the Death of God* (Indianapolis: Bobbs-Merrill, 1966), p. 6 and *passim.*

7. Wallace Stevens, in C. W. Christian and Glenn Wittig, eds., *Radical Theology: Phase Two* (Philadelphia: Lippincott, 1967), pp. 49–50.

8. Altizer and Hamilton, *op. cit.,* p. 6.

9. Paul Van Buren, *The Secular Meaning of the Gospel* (New York: Macmillan Co., 1963).

10. Altizer and Hamilton, *op. cit.,* p. xiii.

11. The fullest statement of Altizer's thought is found in his *The Gospel of Christian Atheism* (Philadelphia: Westminster Press, 1966).

12. Gabriel Vahanian, *The Death of God* (New York: George Braziller, 1961), and *Wait Without Idols* (New York: George Braziller, 1964).

13. Christian and Wittig, eds., *op. cit.,* p. 51.

14. This thought was expressed iconoclastically by Harvey Cox at the recent (March 1969) conference on atheism sponsored by the Vatican Secretariat for Non-Believers in Rome. Cox said that there should be a secretariat for hypocrisy rather than for disbelief, for that is the real religious problem of our time.

15. Vahanian, *No Other God* (New York: George Braziller, 1966), pp. xi-xii.

16. Dean Peerman and Martin Marty, *New Theology,* nos. 1–6 (New York: Macmillan Co., 1964–69).

CHAPTER II. Christian-Marxist Dialogue

1. Peter d'A. Jones, *The Christian Socialist Revival, 1877–1914* (Princeton: Princeton Univ. Press, 1968).

2. Leopold Labedz, *Revisionism: Essays on the History of Marxist Ideas* (London: George Allen & Unwin, 1962).

3. See the collected essays of Engels in *Marx and Engels on Religion* (1964).

4. Ernst Bloch, *Thomas Münzer als Theologie der Revolution* (Frankfurt: Suhrkamp Verlag, 1921); *Der Prinzip Hoffnung* (Berlin: Aufbau-Verlag, 1954–59). Karl Klausky, *The Foundations of Christianity,* Henry F. Mins, trans. (New York: S. A. Russell, 1958); *Communism in Central Europe in the Time of the Reformation* (New York: Russell & Russell, 1959); *Thomas More and His Utopia* (New York: Russell & Russell, 1959). Eduard Bernstein, *Cromwell and Communism: Socialism and Democracy in the English Revolution* (New York: Schocken Books, 1963).

5. Labedz, *op. cit.,* pp. 215–96.

6. Leszek Kolakowski, "The Escapist Conspiracy," in *Towards a*

Marxist Humanism: Essays on the Left Today, Jane Zielenka Peel, trans. (New York: Grove Press, 1968).

7. Irving Fletcher, "Germany: Marxismus-Studien," in Labedz, *op. cit.,* pp. 337–50.

8. This tradition was summed up in Charles West, *Communism and the Theologians* (New York: Macmillan Co., 1958).

9. Josef L. Hromadka, *Evangelium für Atheisten* (Berlin: K. Vogt, 1958).

10. Hromadka, "The Meaning of the Present Era," in *Theology between Yesterday and Tomorrow* (Philadelphia: Westminster Press, 1957), pp. 54–55.

11. *Ibid.,* p. 57.

12. *Ibid.,* p. 64.

13. *Ibid.,* pp. 70–78.

14. *Ibid.,* pp. 70–85.

15. Jürgen Moltmann responded to this Marxist distinction between a Constantinian Christianity identified with the ruling powers and a chiliastic wing united with the oppressed in a revolutionary way by noting the same distinction in Marxism between a Stalinist Marxism acting as a Byzantine state ideology and a humanist Marxism that is self-critical and allied with those also humiliated and disappointed in socialist countries. The distinction thus boomerangs on Marxism and demands a like repentance from Marxists. In Thomas W. Ogletree, *Openings for Christian-Marxist Dialogue* (Nashville: Abingdon Press, 1968), p. 56.

16. Roger Garaudy, *From Anathema to Dialogue: A Marxist Challenge to the Christian Churches,* Luke O'Neill, trans. (New York: Herder & Herder, 1966), p. 58.

17. *Ibid.,* p. 60.

18. *Ibid.,* pp. 60–61.

19. *Ibid.,* p. 86.

20. *Ibid.,* pp. 90–91.

21. *Ibid.,* pp. 94–95.

22. Moltmann, "The Revolution of Freedom," in Ogletree, *op. cit.,* pp. 47–48.

23. Ogletree, *op. cit.,* pp. 37, 43–44. Also Paul Lehmann, "Christian Theology in a World of Revolution," in *ibid.,* pp. 129 ff.

24. See, for example, Harvey Cox, "Christian-Marxist Dialogue," *Dialog VII* (Winter 1968), pp. 18–26. Also see Cox, ed., *Christianity Amid Revolution* (New York: Association Press, 1967), a selection of essays prepared for the World Council of Churches Geneva Conference on Church and Society.

CHAPTER 13. The American Apocalypse

1. For example, Vittorio Lanternari, *The Religion of the Oppressed* (New York: Alfred A. Knopf, 1963).

2. Eldridge Cleaver, *Post-Prison Speeches and Writings,* Robert Sheer, ed. (New York: Random House, 1969), p. 61.

3. Cleaver quotes Lincoln as saying, "I will say, then, that I am not, nor ever have been in favor of bringing about in any way the social and political equality of the white and black races (applause); that I am not nor ever have been in favor of making voters or jurors of Negroes, nor of qualifying them to hold office, not to intermarry with white people . . . while they remain together, there must be a position of superior and inferior, and I as much as any other man am in favor of having the superior position assigned to the white race." Quoted from Richard Hofstadter, *The American Political Tradition,* in Cleaver, *ibid.,* p. 58.

4. The Mormons did some evangelistic work among the Indians, partly due to their belief that they were the lost tribes of Israel, and some believe that messianism and the ghost shirt came by way of Indian adaptation of Mormon teaching. James Mooney, *The Ghost Dance Religion and the Sioux Outbreak of 1890* (Chicago: Univ. of Chicago Press, 1965), p. 5.

5. *Ibid.,* p. 23.

6. *Ibid.,* p. 25.

7. Mooney details this counsel of passivity, expectation, and the reformed life as the normal content of the ghost-dance preachers. *Ibid.,* p. 26.

8. Peter Nabokov, "The Peyote Road," *The New York Times Magazine* (March 9, 1969), pp. 30–34.

9. "Nat Turner's Confessions, 1831," in Floyd B. Barbour, ed., *The Black Power Revolt* (Boston: Porter Sargent Pubs., 1968), pp. 30, 31.

10. See the chapter "Tuskegee, Alabama: The Politics of Deference," in Stokely Carmichael and Charles V. Hamilton, *Black Power: The Politics of Liberation in America* (New York: Random House, 1967), pp. 122–145.

11. E. U. Essien-Udon, *Black Nationalism* (New York: Dell, 1962), pp. 39–59.

12. *Ibid.,* pp. 76 ff.

13. The main source for Malcolm's life is his *Autobiography* (New York: Grove Press, 1964). See also George Breitman, ed., *Malcolm X Speaks* (New York: Grove Press, 1965).

14. Malcolm X, *Autobiography, op. cit.,* pp. 376–82.

15. Cleaver, "The Courage to Kill: Meeting the Black Panthers," in *Post-Prison Speeches and Writings, op. cit.,* p. 29.

16. *Ibid.,* pp. 171–72.

17. *Ibid.,* p. 173.

18. *Ibid.,* pp. 68–69.

19. In July 1969, Stokely Carmichael resigned from the Black Panthers because of their rejection of black cultural nationalism in favor of revolutionary solidarity with the oppressed of all races. In their reply the Panthers chided him, loftily: "We tried to bring him around, but he just did not come to understand that you can't fight racism with racism. The world is our neighborhood. All oppressed people are a part of it." See *The Washington Post,* July 4, 1969, pp. 1 ff., and July 5, 1969, pp. 1 ff.

20. Cleaver, *op. cit.,* pp. 206–9.

CHAPTER 14. The American Youth Movement from Sit-in to Be-in

1. Lewis S. Feuer, *The Conflict of Generations* (New York: Basic Books, 1969).

2. Kenneth Keniston, *Young Radicals: Notes on Committed Youth* (New York: Harcourt, Brace, 1968).

3. Keniston, *The Uncommitted: Alienated Youth in American Society* (New York: Harcourt, Brace, 1965).

4. Frantz Fanon, *The Wretched of the Earth* (New York: Grove Press, 1966).

5. See William H. Grier and Price M. Cobbs, *Black Rage* (New York: Basic Books, 1968), for a study of the problem of "cultural paranoia" in the black American.

6. See Julius Lester, *Look Out Whitey! Black Power's Gon' Get Your Mama!* (New York: Grove Press, 1968), chap. 1.

7. Mitchell Cohen and Dennis Hale, eds., *The New Student Left* (Boston: Beacon Press, 1967), pp. 97–100.

8. See Eldridge Cleaver, Post-Prison Speeches and Writings (New York: Random House, 1969), pp. 68–69.

9. Abbie Hoffman, *Revolution for the Hell of It* (New York: Dial Press, 1968), p. 43.

10. *Ibid.,* p. 69.

11. *Ibid.,* p. 58.

12. *Ibid.,* p. 90.

13. *Ibid.*

14. See Irving L. Horowitz, ed., *The Anarchists* (New York: Dell, 1964).

15. Hoffman, *op. cit.,* p. 57.

16. *Ibid.,* pp. 92, 94.

17. This poem was found tacked on a door at the headquarters of the Mississippi Child Development Group at Beulah, Edwards, Mississippi. I was never able to learn the poet's name, but was told that it was written by a black youth in the movement.

18. For a representative collection of hippie thought from the underground press, see Jerry Hopkins, ed., *The Hippy Papers: Notes from the Underground Press* (New York: New American Library, 1968).

19. Robert Houriet, "The Life and Death of a Commune Called Oz," *The New York Times Magazine* (Feb. 16, 1969), pp. 28 ff. See also Vivian Gornick, "The Hippie as Survivor: Mecca on the Mesa," *The Village Voice* (May 29, 1969), pp. 5 ff.

20. Hoffman, *op. cit.,* p. 74.

21. See chapter 2 in this volume. Also see Delbert L. Earisman, *Hippies in our Midst* (Philadelphia: Fortress Press, 1968), pp. 99–132.

22. Andrew Greeley, "The Sacred and the Psychedelic," *The Critic* (April-May 1969), pp. 24 ff.

23. William Braden, *The Private Sea: LSD and the Search for God* (Chicago: Quadrangle Books, 1967).

24. See, for example, the writings of N. Berdyaev or Erich Fromm.

25. Timothy Leary, *The Psychedelic Experience: A Manual Based on the Tibetan Book of the Dead* (New York: University Books, 1964).

26. Alan W. Watts, *The Joyous Cosmology* (New York: Random House, 1962), pp. 65, 67, 63.

CHAPTER 15. The New Left: Revolutionaries After the
Fall of the Revolution

1. For a popular treatment of student rebellion in 1968, see Stephen Spender, *The Year of the Young Rebels* (New York: Random House, 1969).

2. Erich Fromm, *The Revolution of Hope: Towards a Humanized Technology* (New York: Harper & Row, 1968), p. 25.

3. Guerilla warfare theory is spelled out in such works as Che Guevara's *Guerilla Warfare* (1961) and Regis Debray, *Revolution in a Revolution: Armed Struggle and Political Struggle in Latin America* (New York: Grove Press, 1967), both bestsellers among student radicals.

4. See Fromm, ed., *Socialist Humanism: An International Symposium* (New York: Doubleday, 1965).

5. See Milovan Djilas, *The New Class: An Analysis of the Communist System* (New York: Praeger Books, 1957).

6. Karl Reyman and Herman Singer, "The Origins and Significance of Eastern European Revisionism," in Leopold Labedz, *Revisionism: Essays on the History of Marxist Ideas* (London: George Allen & Unwin, 1962), pp. 215 ff.

7. Alfred Sherman, "Tito—The Reluctant Revisionist," in *ibid.*

8. Leszek Kolakowski, "The Concept of the Left," in *Essays in Marxist Humanism* (1968), pp. 67 ff.

9. See "Responsibility and History," "Intellectuals and the Communist Movement," "Permanent and Transitory Aspects of Marxism," and "In Praise of Inconsistency," in *Essays in Marxist Humanism*.

10. Giorgio Galli, "Italy: The Choice of the Left," in Labedz, *op. cit.*, pp. 324 ff.

11. G. L. Arnold, "The New Reasoners," in *ibid.*, pp. 299 ff.

12. Jean Duvignaud, "France: The Neo-Marxists," in *ibid.*, pp. 313 ff. Also see Irving Fletcher, "Germany: Marxismus-Studien," in *ibid.*, pp. 337 ff.

13. E. J. Hobshawn, in *The New York Review of Books* (May 22, 1969), pp. 4 ff.

14. See the interview with Jacques Sauvageot of the National Student Union in *The French Student Revolt: The Leaders Speak*, Hervé Bourges, ed. (New York: Hill & Wang, 1968), p. 23.

15. Daniel and Gabriel Cohn-Bendit, *Obsolete Communism: The Left-Wing Alternative*, Arnold Pomerans, trans. (New York: McGraw-Hill, 1968), p. 70.

16. Bourges, ed., *op. cit.*, p. 55.

17. See V. I. Lenin, *Left Wing Communism: An Infantile Disorder* (New York: International Publishers, 1943).

18. Bourges, ed., *op. cit.*, p. 81.

19. Cohn-Bendit and Cohn-Bendit, *op. cit.*, p. 256.

20. See Thomas Hayden's "Letter to the New Young Left," in Cohen and Hale, eds., *op. cit.*, p. 3.

21. See the SDS National Council resolution in support of the Black

Panther party that proclaimed, among other things, that the Black Panthers were "uniting and leading the whole working class" and were the "vanguard in our common struggle against capitalism and imperialism." *New Left Notes* (April 4, 1969), p. 3.

22. See the SDS National Council resolution on "Summer in the City," in *ibid.*, pp. 8–9.

23. See the SDS National Council resolution of "U.S.–Soviet Collusion Against China," in *ibid.*, p. 7.

24. See the report on the March 1969 National Council meeting in Austin, Texas, in *ibid.*, pp. 1–2. Reports on the schism between SDS and PLP appeared in *New Left Notes* (June 25, 1969), *passim.*

25. Lewis Coser, "USA: Marxists at Bay," in Labedz, *op. cit.*, pp. 351 ff.

26. For example, the largely white middle class peace movement, which has moved from legal agitation to draft resistance, antiwar organizing in the military and open sabotage of draft offices and industrial representatives of the war effort. See Catonsville Nine-Milwaukee Fourteen Defense Committee, *Delivered to Resistance* (New Haven: Advocate Press, 1969); Alice Lynd, ed., *We Won't Go* (Boston: Beacon Press, 1968); Philip Berrigan, *Punishment for Peace* (London: Macmillan & Co., 1969); and Daniel Berrigan, *Night Flight to Hanoi* (New York: Macmillan Co., 1968).

27. Herbert Marcuse, *An Essay on Liberation* (Boston: Beacon Press, 1969), p. x.

Index